THIS IS NOT A BOOK ABOUT GAVIN TURK

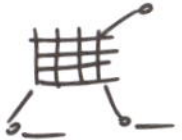

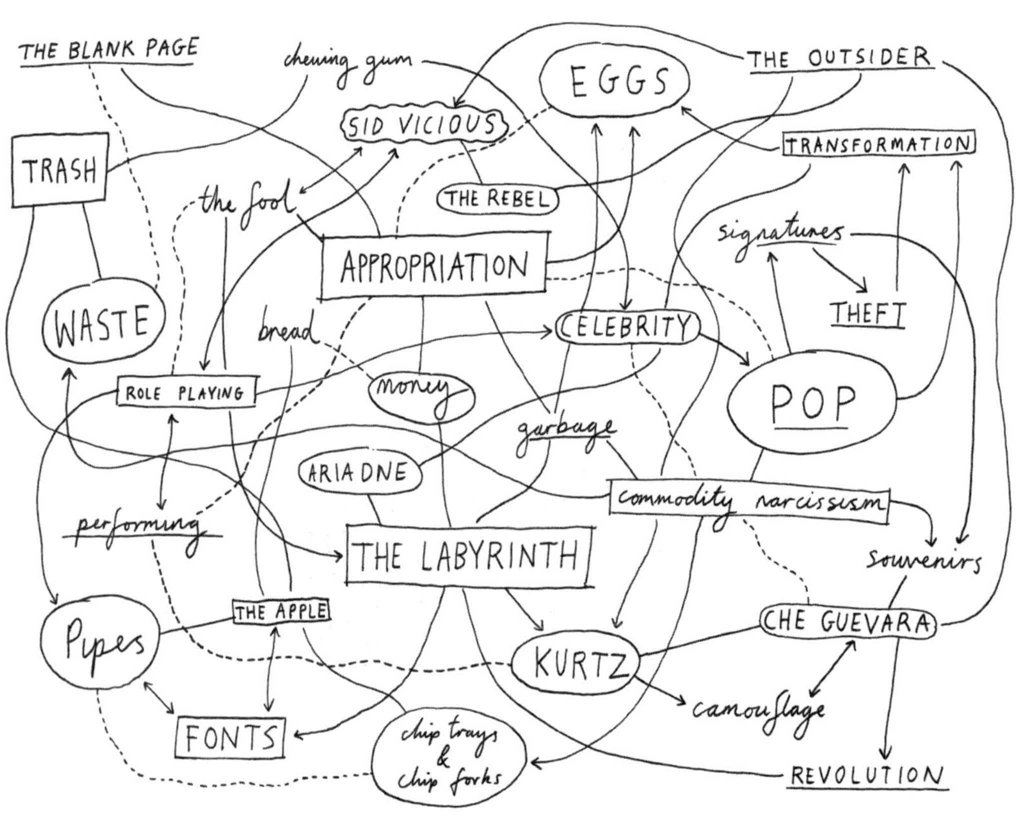

THE BLANK PAGE
chewing gum
EGGS
THE OUTSIDER
SID VICIOUS
TRANSFORMATION
TRASH
the fool
THE REBEL
signatures
APPROPRIATION
THEFT
WASTE
bread
CELEBRITY
ROLE PLAYING
money
POP
garbage
ARIADNE
commodity narcissism
performing
THE LABYRINTH
souvenirs
Pipes
THE APPLE
CHE GUEVARA
KURTZ
FONTS
camouflage
chip trays & chip forks
REVOLUTION

CONTENTS

PREFACE

Deborah Curtis

In the ten long, distracted, economically compromised years that this book has taken to publish, the world around us has changed transformatively and dramatically. We are arguably in the last decadent phase of the most self-destructive global civilisation ever. We are also in an era of almost transparent access to information — all definitions, histories and creative arts are available at the click of a search button on algorithmic engines with numbers beyond our imagination.

¶ In the light of these transformations this little handbook is an auspicious guide to the state of existence. If this is *not* a book about "the artist", then it is also not a book about our perception of the artist. Instead the concerns, preoccupations, observations and forms that catch the artist's thoughts and eyes are unpacked, transposed, explored and investigated by a cacophonic jamboree of perspectives.

¶ The voices in this book range from the factual and encyclopaedic to the unpalatable and strange and so, with humour, whimsy and surreal references, allow the reader to find their own final perspective. Inevitably the meaning arrives at the moment of un-focus when we don't try to understand, but let the references, associations and triggers play with our memories — when we "read between the lines".

¶ Powerful artworks and culture experiences can help the mind to comprehend complex ideas as effectively as the most eloquent science if they are embraced not resisted. At the same time, whilst shocking or unpleasant references and dissonance are allowed to irritate us, we are more open to the beauty and melancholic profundity of the human condition.

¶ When it was first mooted, this open-source-editorial-methodology augured the future invention and the democracy of the internet, back then still only a vague doctrine, early adopted by the geek world. Now this practice is becoming more common, with endless "miscellanies" attracting our increasingly short attention spans away from the magazine rack. From crowd-funding and social media to Wikipedia and the gift economy, we are realising we are stronger and quicker if we work together. This is at the ironic heart of a publication perversely called *This Is Not A Book About Gavin Turk.*

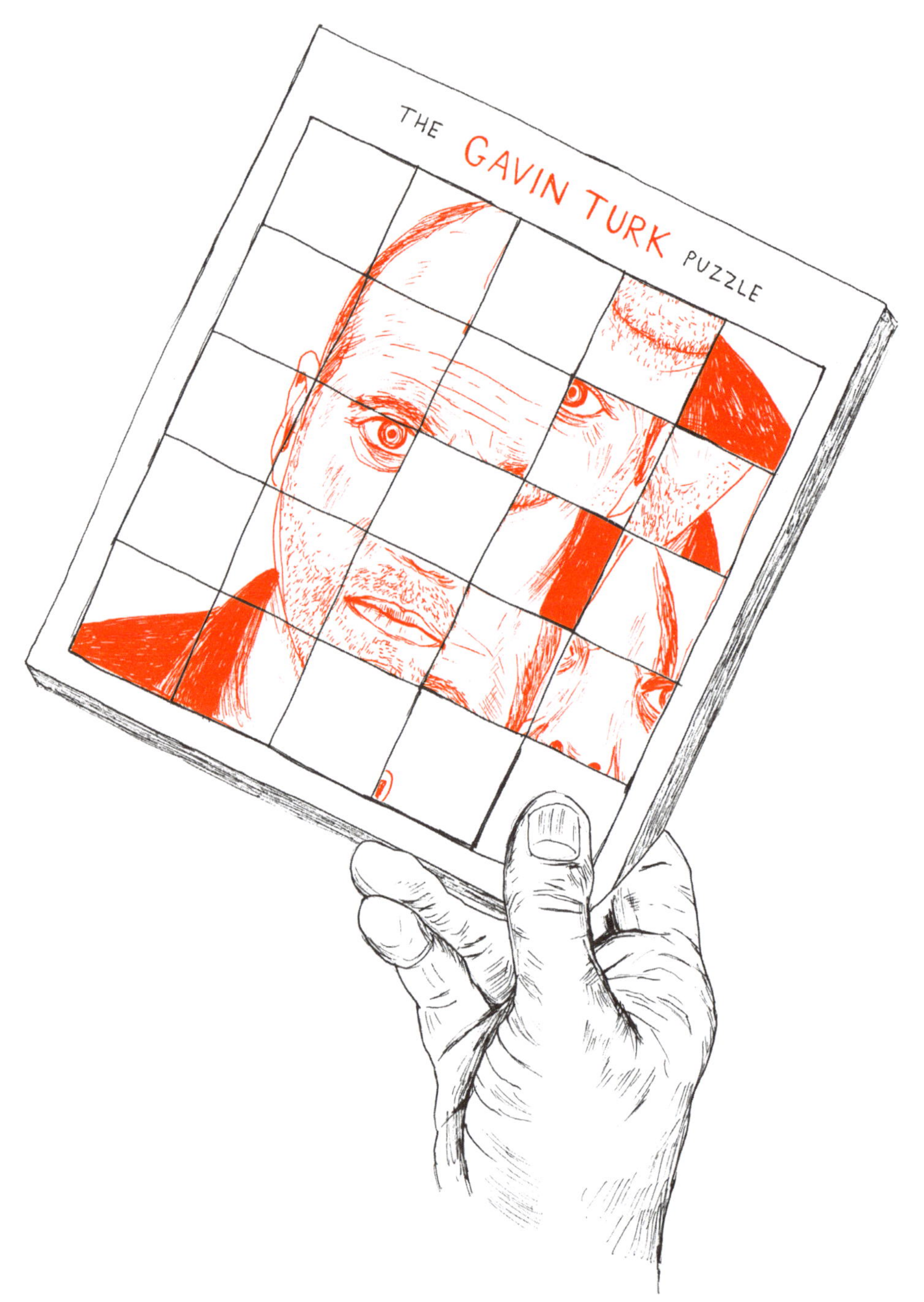

THE GAVIN TURK PUZZLE

INTRODUCTION

Rachel Newsome

A joker, hoaxer, trash-collector, punk, seer and unholy fool, British artist Gavin Turk makes art about art from the debris and decay of modern civilisation. A modern day Fisher King on his riverbank, as behind the city crumbles in a turmoil of economic meltdown, unreal spectacle and fame for fame's sake, Turk rummages through the remains of Minimalism, Modernism, Surrealism and Pop, alongside the trash of the street in search of clues as to what art may or may not be.

¶ Operating under the fictional persona of "Gavin Turk: The Artist", his work explores the angst between the mythical and the modern, the outcast and the institution, the rebel and the consumer, the artist and the advertiser, and between the acquisition of knowledge and the admission of confusion. Who are we? What is real? What does it mean to be an artist? Can we ever know the real value of things? Never mind the end of art, where does it begin?

¶ The title *This Is Not A Book About Gavin Turk* is a pun on Magritte's famous visual puzzle, *The Treachery of Images*, which shows a drawing of a pipe accompanied by the text; "this is not a pipe". The book itself is a collection of essays that consider big philosophical questions relating to art and life by way of small forensic details relating to apple cores, union jacks, Che Guevara t-shirts, doors and more.

¶ Inspired by the themes explored in Turk's work, *This Is Not A Book About Gavin Turk* features thought-provoking and playful reflections on everything from advertising to Ariadne, chewing gum to celebrity, eggs to endgames and Sid Vicious to signatures, written by an illustrious collection of art critics, novelists, cultural commentators, artists and psychoanalysts. Some of these essays refer directly to Turk's art; many do not.

If this is not a book about Gavin Turk but a book about art, it is also a book about money, value, status, tradition, modernity, identity and what it means to live through the advanced stages of consumer capitalism in the early part of the 21st century.

The section **WHAT IS REAL?** is an exploration of representation, originality, identity and the notion of the artist as an outsider. Pitting the modernist idea of purity against that of a fluid, eccentric self defined by uncertainty, this section wants to know, who is the artist Gavin Turk, anyway? Answer: it all depends on how he is framed.

In **THE MACHINE**, the artist is no longer an outsider but a celebrity brand, whose life and work is merged into a single on-going performance. Adrift in a postmodern maze of relativism, commodification and appropriation in which nothing is pure and the true value and meaning of things is no longer clear — here today and gone tomorrow — the real Gavin Turk is nowhere to be seen.

ZERO wonders whether all art is an illusion and all products trash waiting to happen. Whether what's left is the decaying remains of an ancient form of expression long past its shelf life or the ashes from which a new, equally radical, form might phoenix-like arise. As for the artist, it is the very uncertainty of his existence that might also be his one saving grace.

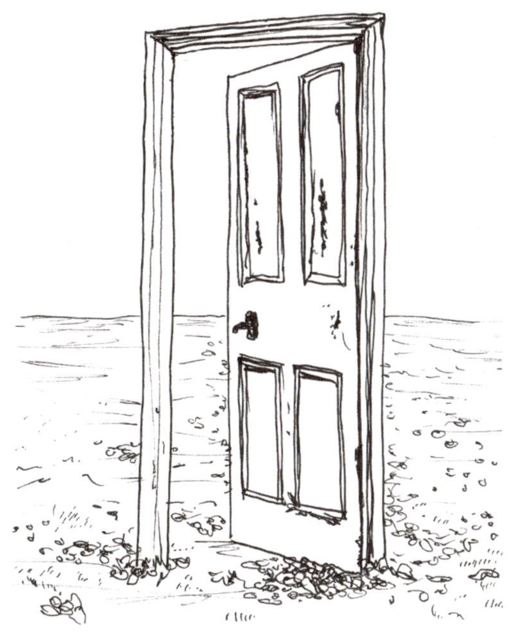

Gavin Turk Ajar 2011
Painted bronze, 216 × 91 × 68 cm
Outdoor sculpture of an old door attached to door frame

WHAT IS REAL?

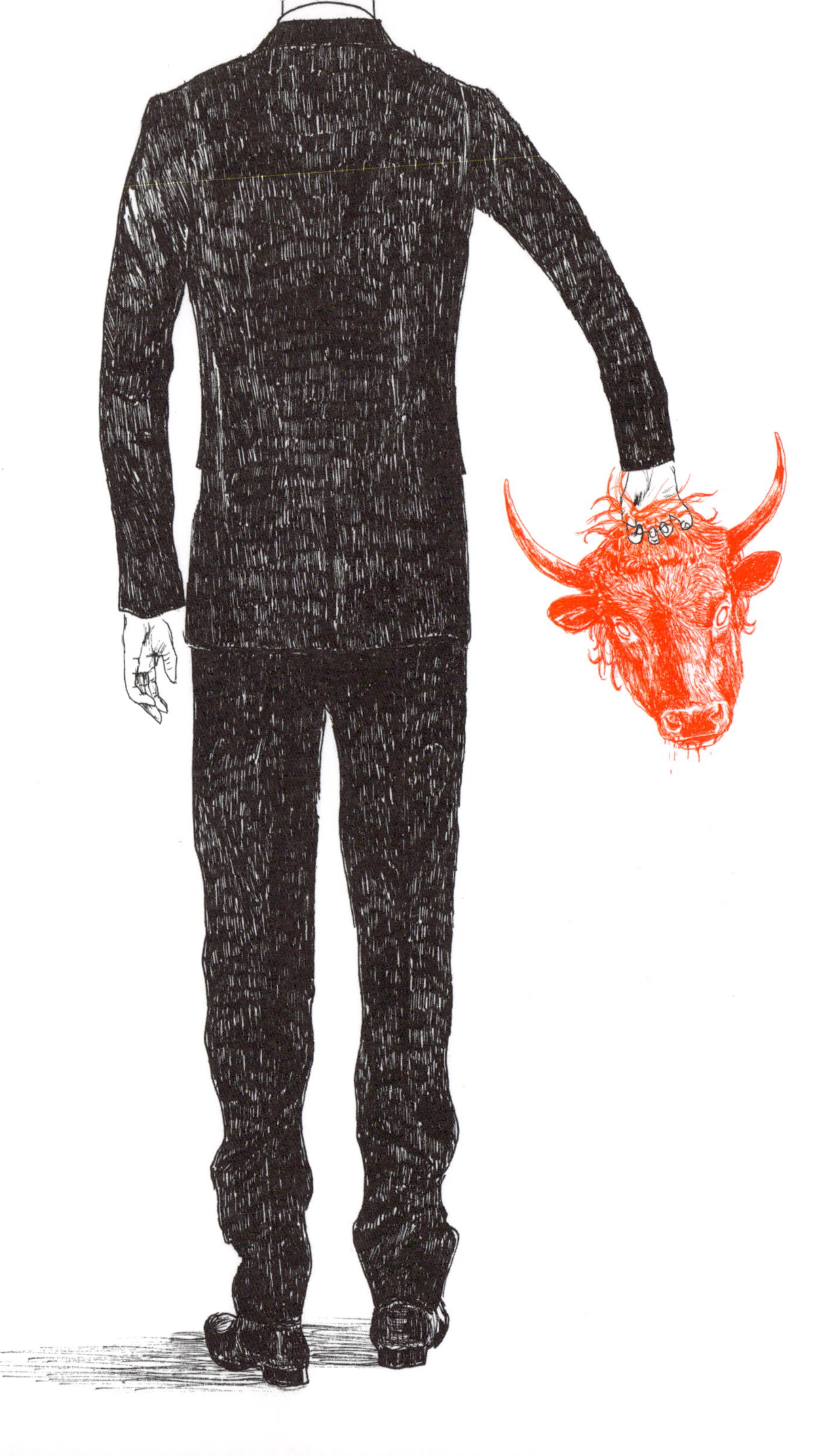

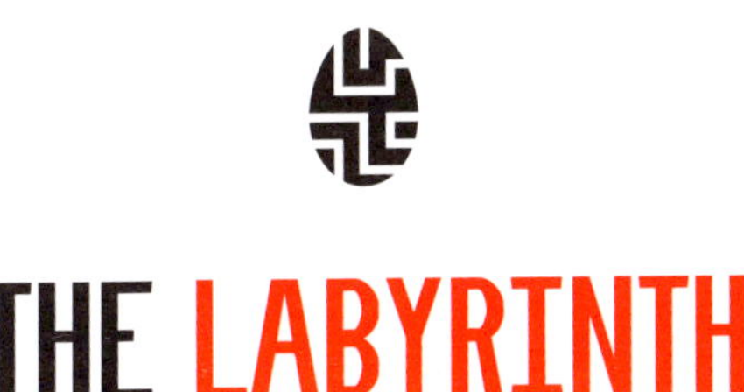

THE LABYRINTH

Damien Hirst

You shouldn't really be starting from here

There are an infinite number of ways to get to the same point, to get from any starting point to anywhere else.

¶ At some point in the recent past, between the end of the Greek empire and today, the Minotaur disappeared and the myth dissolved into the labyrinth. The fearsome creature stopped being an avoidable thing — a real monster — and became something deep within the labyrinth itself: a psychological monster, the state of being lost, the fear of being lost, lost forever. At this point, loss of memory became worse than death. It was Daedalus who built the fiendishly complex labyrinth to house the Minotaur, and the Minotaur was a motherfucker — or was that Oedipus? *Hey, Greek food is better than no food.*

¶ With a leap of faith and a twist of the imagination and looking through the kaleido-scope backwards, Theseus (the man in the labyrinth) can be seen as the artist on his way to work. Here's the scenario: if you are an artist, then you are an artist to your very core. It's not 9 to 5. It's most certainly 24/7. You eat it. You put mustard on it and eat the shit. Art, Art, Art, Art, Art. You eat Art, you breathe Art, you shit Art. But it is also a job, like any other job. You can write it under "occupation" on your passport. *What do you do?" "Oh, me? I'm an artist."*

¶ So, if it's a job, and it's 24/7, then when you're at work, you're definitely an artist. And when you're at home, then you must be an artist too. But when you go to work, when you are on the way to work, what are you on the journey? "I'm in between things at the moment, waiting for something better to come along" — the artist on his way to work, lost in the labyrinth of life. *A-maze-ing, huh?*

¶ You lost yet? If you get lost, then you have to look for something you know. Feeling sick? Keep your eye on the horizon, don't go below deck, take deep breaths. Lost the plot? The artist lost his way. He's found a new direction, built something concrete, something that obscures your view of the horizon, something that takes what you know, and throws it back in your face.

¶ Who built the labyrinth again? Was it Gavin Turk? I don't know. Was it my artist's assistants? I don't know. Maybe I'm losing my mind. Losing my business. Lost my wife and kids. Lost my kids somewhere between back then, when it was good, and now. I somehow lost my way. You stole the sixties from me. Was it you who stole my tent at Glastonbury?

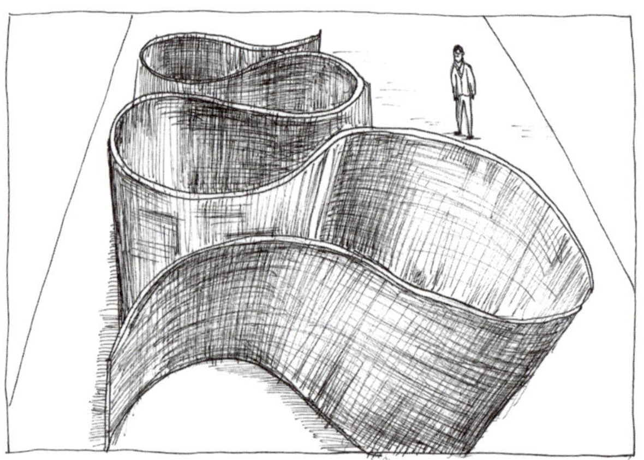

Richard Serra Junction **2011**
Weatherproof steel, 4 × 22.87 × 15.19 m

Where were the air hostesses when I needed them to point out the exits? No Hansel and Gretel to lay the sweetie trails. Adam and Eve shat on me long ago, hung me up, left me high and dry. Where's the treasure buried? Show me a map. I want to make a life-size map of everything that exists. *Don't we all, sweetie?*

¶ Max Beckmann used to paint his canvases black to represent the void so that spiritually he saw everything he painted as objects or marks placed between himself and the void, something to slow the inevitable rush of all things into the void. (Maybe death is black holes.) Every journey is littered with dead ends, wrong turns, stop-offs and stations. All we are really interested in today is mathematically how to get from A to B. But there are so many points on a line, so many other possible trajectories, that it is becoming more and more impossible to look at things mathematically. Emotion is screwing up science. The fact of getting from A to B is no longer about transport, but about transportation.

¶ Everything in art is, always has been, and always will be, a throwback, from way back, trying to make a comeback. In the beginning was a maze. Then came the people. The people born into the maze began putting objects into the maze, and the weather inhabited the maze, and time laid down blankets in the maze until the maze was lost beneath the clatter of tiny feet, and man inhabited life above the maze. But still the feeling was there, a feeling of isolation, of lost-ness, of feeling alone and trying not to be lonely, separated from every other living thing by flesh and bone. Searching, but searching for what? Searching for a way out that is not death. Searching for truth. Now with the maze long gone, lost, buried in time, there is no way to find a way out. We must find the maze before we can even begin to contemplate a way out. And quickly, because night is falling fast.

¶ In the Tommy Cooper sketch, when the man asks a stranger for directions, his reply is: "You shouldn't really be starting from here."

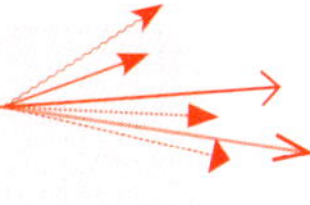

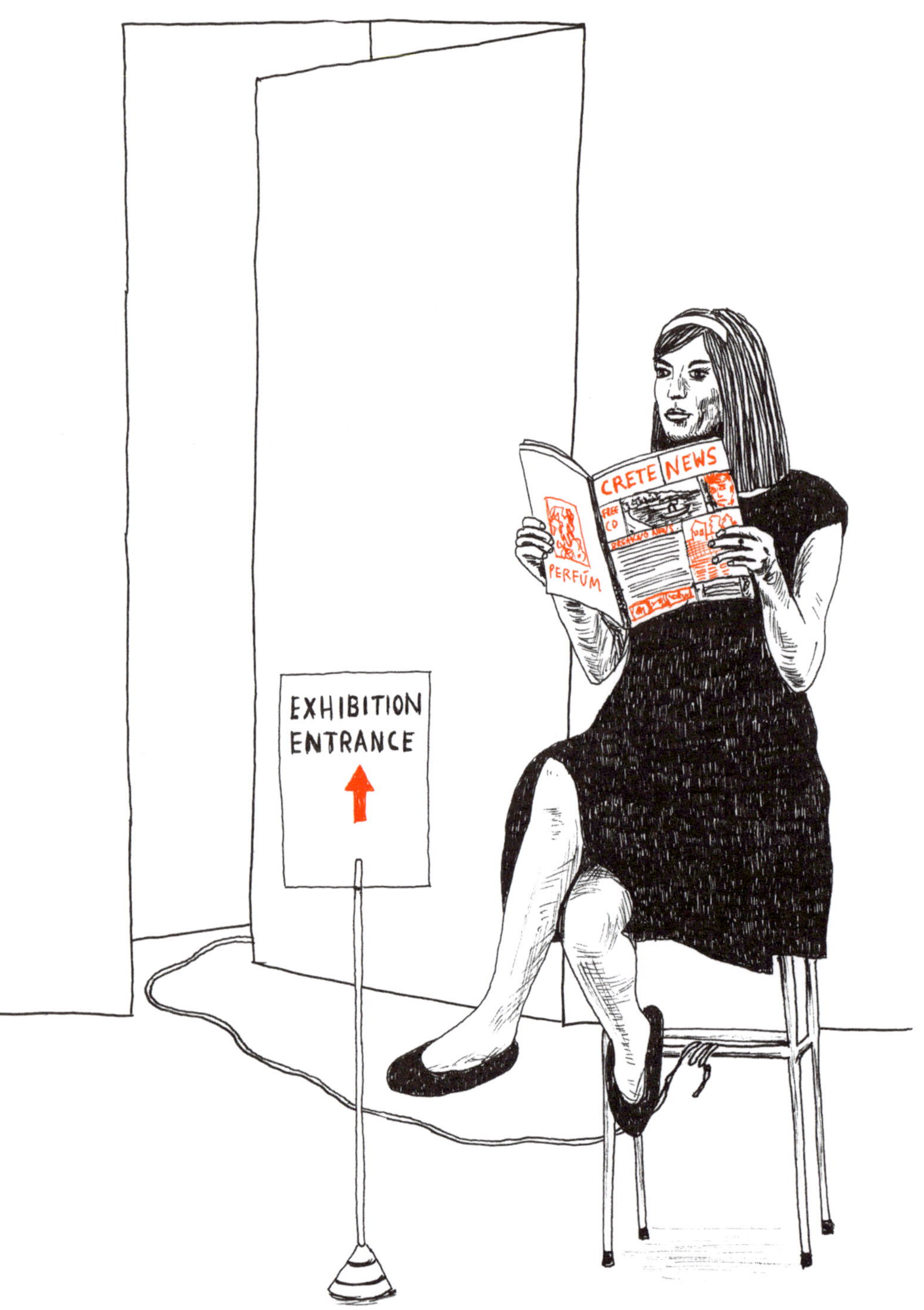

CRETE NEWS
FREE CD
PERFUM
EXHIBITION
ENTRANCE

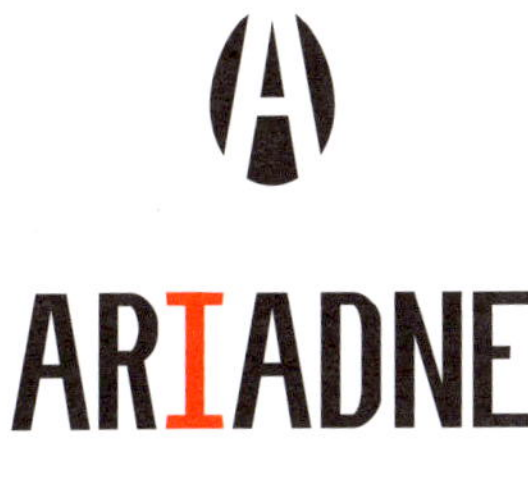

ARIADNE

Betsy de Lotbinière

Bull lust, catharsis and second chances

Ariadne's life is awash with bull lust. Her paternal grandmother, **Europa**, was seduced by the god **Zeus** who assumed the form of a white bull. Europa was made Queen of Crete and went on to marry the mortal **Asterion** who adopted her demi-god son, **Minos**. When Minos wanted to ascend to his step-father's throne, **Poseidon** pulled a bull "from the depths" and told the new King of Crete to slay it. Minos couldn't bring himself to kill the beautiful white bull and instead sacrificed a lesser double. An enraged Poseidon recruited **Aphrodite** to cast a curse on Minos' wife, **Queen Pasiphae**, to fall in love with the white bull. The queen would not rest until she had mated with her horned beloved. She ordered **Daedalus** to construct a cow and he carved a decoy of hollowed wood, covering it in cow skin. The queen climbed inside and lured the white beast successfully; her half-bull half-human son Asterion was named after his grandfather.

¶   As a princess of ancient Crete, Ariadne was ordered by her father King Minos to serve as gate-keeper of the Labyrinth. Every year she stood watch as seven Athenian maids and seven youths walked into the puzzle palace built by Daedalus to confound and contain the sacrificed and the monstrous **Minotaur**. Fourteen walked in, no one came out; the half-man half-bull had feasted on their flesh.

¶   When **Theseus**, son of King **Aegeus**, hero of Athens, disembarked on the island of Crete, intent upon killing the monster that snacked on his countrymen, Ariadne fell in love at first sight and set to helping the young warrior. Before he entered the Labyrinth, she slipped him a sword and a ball of thread, telling him to attach one end to the front entrance so that he could find his way both in and out.

¶ Theseus did vanquish the Minotaur with Ariadne's sword; he found his way out of the maze and carried Ariadne away as his wife. Later, after bedding her in a cave on the island of Naxos, Theseus set sail and deserted his saviour while she slept. In **Richard Strauss**' musical depiction of her abandonment, *Ariadne auf Naxos*, Ariadne is so bereaved she sings a love song to death. This scene, a woman prostrate with grief, left in utter isolation, has over centuries become a favourite subject of artists. It has also been a good excuse to show bare flesh; in more censorious times, the viewer could in all innocence glimpse Ariadne's nakedness as a metaphor for her catharsis.

¶ In becoming an archetype, her immortality is affirmed. God of madness and ecstasy, ruler of the irrational, lord of intoxication as a way of encountering the divine, Dionysius descended upon Naxos and instantly fell in love with Ariadne. In modern terms, he embodies that moment when you've cried so much that you laugh at the absurdity of your predicament and get drunk with your friends. Dionysius married Ariadne and transformed her princess's crown into a constellation of stars, elevating her to eternal life as a goddess.

¶ In **Titian**'s version of this moment, the brightly virile young god is depicted surrounded by his extraordinary, clamorous entourage of merry satyrs dressed in vine leaves, tambourine-banging ladies, a fat drunk man on a donkey, several chickens, a pack of hunting dogs and a horned bearded man arrayed amongst slithering snakes as he travels on a flying chariot pulled by cheetahs. Here, the story's re-branding is readily apparent. Titian's title is *Ariadne and Bacchus* because that's what the Romans re-named Dionysus. While educated Greeks still correct you when you call her one of their goddesses — "she is not Greek, she is Minoan" — yet Ariadne has retained her name all these millennia.

¶ The characters and the story were plucked apart and re-used as touchstones by

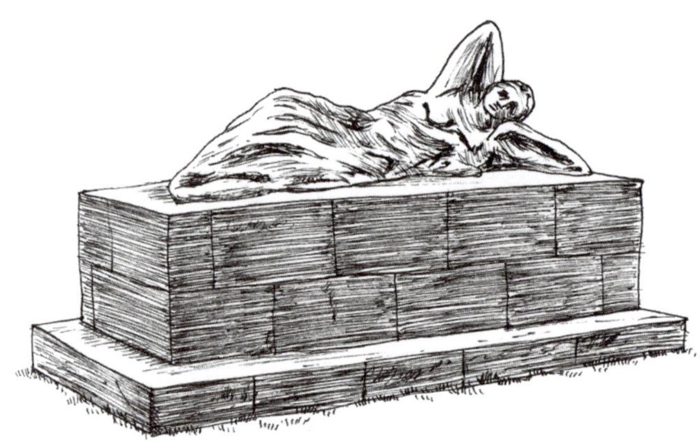

Gavin Turk Her **2003**
Stainless steel, marble dust and painted cement, 140 × 152 × 292 cm
A loosely worked sculpture of a reclining woman after Giorgio De Chirico's *Ariadne*

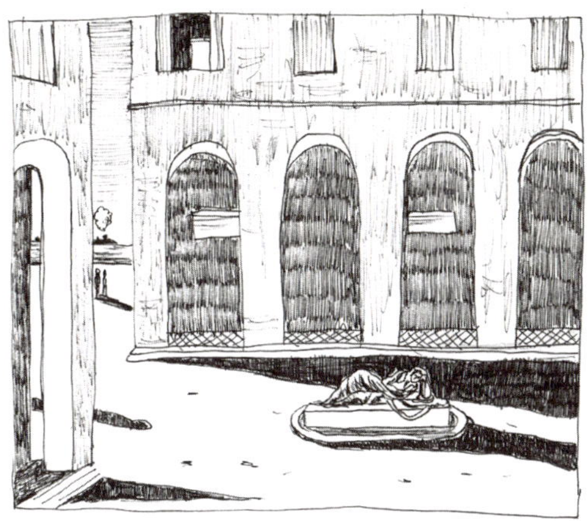

Giorgio de Chirico Place d'Italie 1913
Oil on canvas, 25 × 35.2 cm

everyone from **Hesiod** to **Homer**, kicking off a whole industry of vase and plate depictions of the tale. Ariadne survives on the walls of Pompeii. In Rome (where the story was retold by the exiled Ovid), she was chiselled into countless chunks of marble, a Hellenic version of which made its way to the Louvre in Paris, where it was admired and copied by countless French academicians. In England, Ariadne's tale was picked up by **Chaucer**, her famed golden thread woven into tales by **Spenser**, **Longfellow** and all the attendant image-makers of their coteries. Even **Turner** had a go at wrapping eroticism in myth.

¶   In the last century, the vogue for personal interpretation of forms becomes more radical and abstract. Give a challenging new image an ancient name and the viewer can be lulled into accepting even the outrageous. **Picasso** favoured posing as the Minotaur as a way of encapsulating the ownership of his shadow side. **James Joyce** named Stephen Daedalus as the great hero of his epic *Ulysses* — timeless classical information straddling a modern setting. **Giorgio de Chirico** painted Ariadne as a lifeless sculpture in a geometric dystopia. **Cy Twombly**'s *Bacchus* series includes a wild red scribbling of exuberance, an expressionistic vision of passion. On screen, director **Christopher Nolan** turns this trick in his dreamscape *Inception* — what other name for a female architect hired to create mazes through the subconscious but Ariadne?

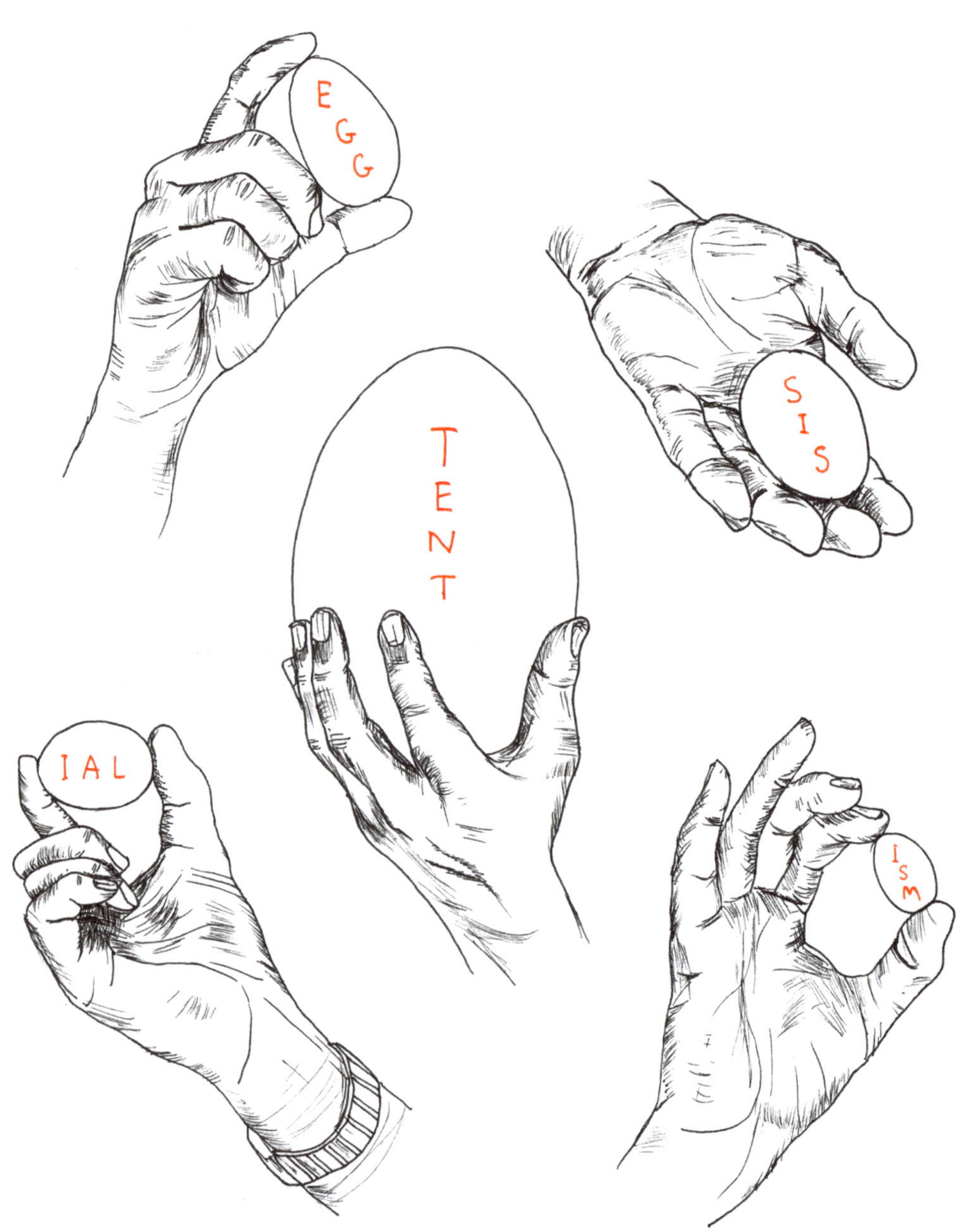

EGG
SIS
TENT
IAL
ISM

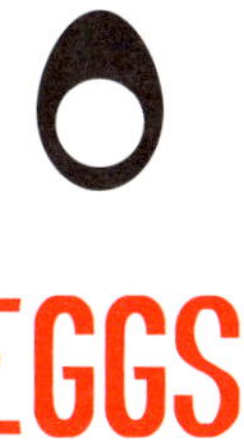

EGGS

Martine Rouleau

Conceived in a whirlwind, symbols of life

Eggs incarnate pure balance. The harmonious simplicity of their form is rendered more poignant by their function: they hold and protect life. The strength of the shell that harbours the makings of a living creature is all the more impressive because although it can withstand surprising levels of pressure — an ostrich egg can reputedly support up to 20 stone in weight — it cannot resist the impact of a drop or a knock. When this ovoid shape is cracked by an *external* force, the life it was meant to protect can no longer develop; once it is broken from the *inside*, this life begins.

¶ The powers of the egg have carried over to many cultural beliefs. Although most often perceived as tokens of affection with nurturing virtues, exchanged as expressions of love (by the Alsatians) and used to announce the forthcoming birth of a child (by the Chinese), eggs are sometimes destroyed as a form of protection. The Romans crushed egg shells on their plate to ward off evil and other cultures later adopted the tradition in the belief that witches could use shells as boats on which to navigate the seas to sink other vessels.

¶ It is no coincidence that a number of mythical characters originated from eggs.

Legend has it that twin brothers Castor and Pollux were born from eggs alongside their twin sisters Helen of Troy and Clytemnestra. Fittingly, the birth of Eros, Greek god of love, is sometimes described as a hatching:

> *Of Darkness an egg,*
> *From the whirlwind conceived,*
> *Was laid by the sable plumed Night.*
> *And out of that egg, as the seasons revolved,*
> *Sprang Love, the entrancing, the bright,*
> *Love brilliant and bold, with his pinions of gold,*
> *Like a whirlwind, refulgent and sparkling.*
>
> Aristophanes, *The Birds*

¶ Art appropriates the egg both as a material (tempera) and a form that conveys ideas of femininity, maternity and protection. When I was a child, my father was given a bronze sculpture of a giant egg, a self-portrait by Salvador Dali. The egg is cracked and through this fissure sprouts a twisted lock of hair, the infamous moustache and an eye of the artist, forever struggling to hatch. Symbolising birth and inspiration, the egg becomes an emblematic origin for the artist and his genius.

¶ This unassuming and familiar object at times aspires to the status of a work of art. Easter eggs decorated with wax and vegetable dyes are perhaps the most familiar version but the obscenely precious jewelled eggs that Carl Fabergé fabricated held a wealth of surprises: from clocks and jewellery to miniature replicas of palaces. Such decoration highlights their wondrous side: out of such a modest and simple thing can spring the most precious and mysterious gift whether a jewel, inspiration or life itself.

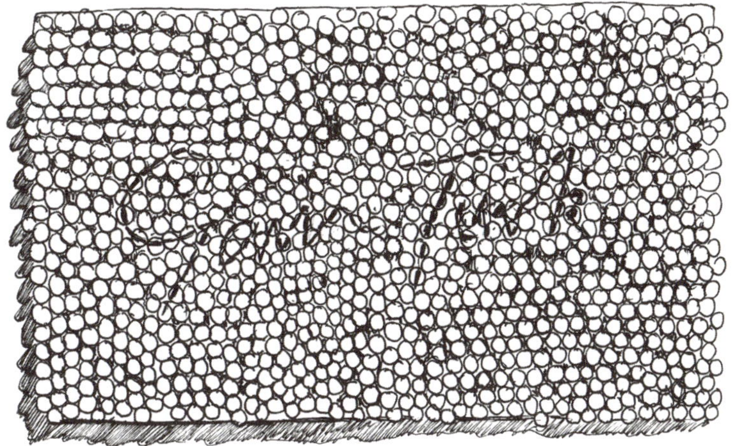

Gavin Turk   One Thousand, Two Hundred and Thirty-Four Eggs   1997
Egg shells on canvas, 132 × 221 cm
The artist's signature nibbled out of a field of white eggshells stuck to a canvas

SEE ALSO:

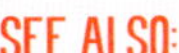 | 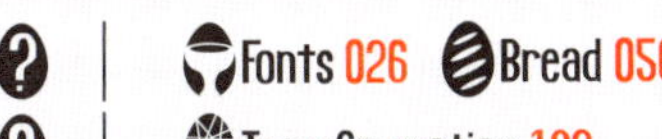Fonts 026   Bread 056

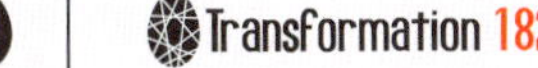Transformation 182

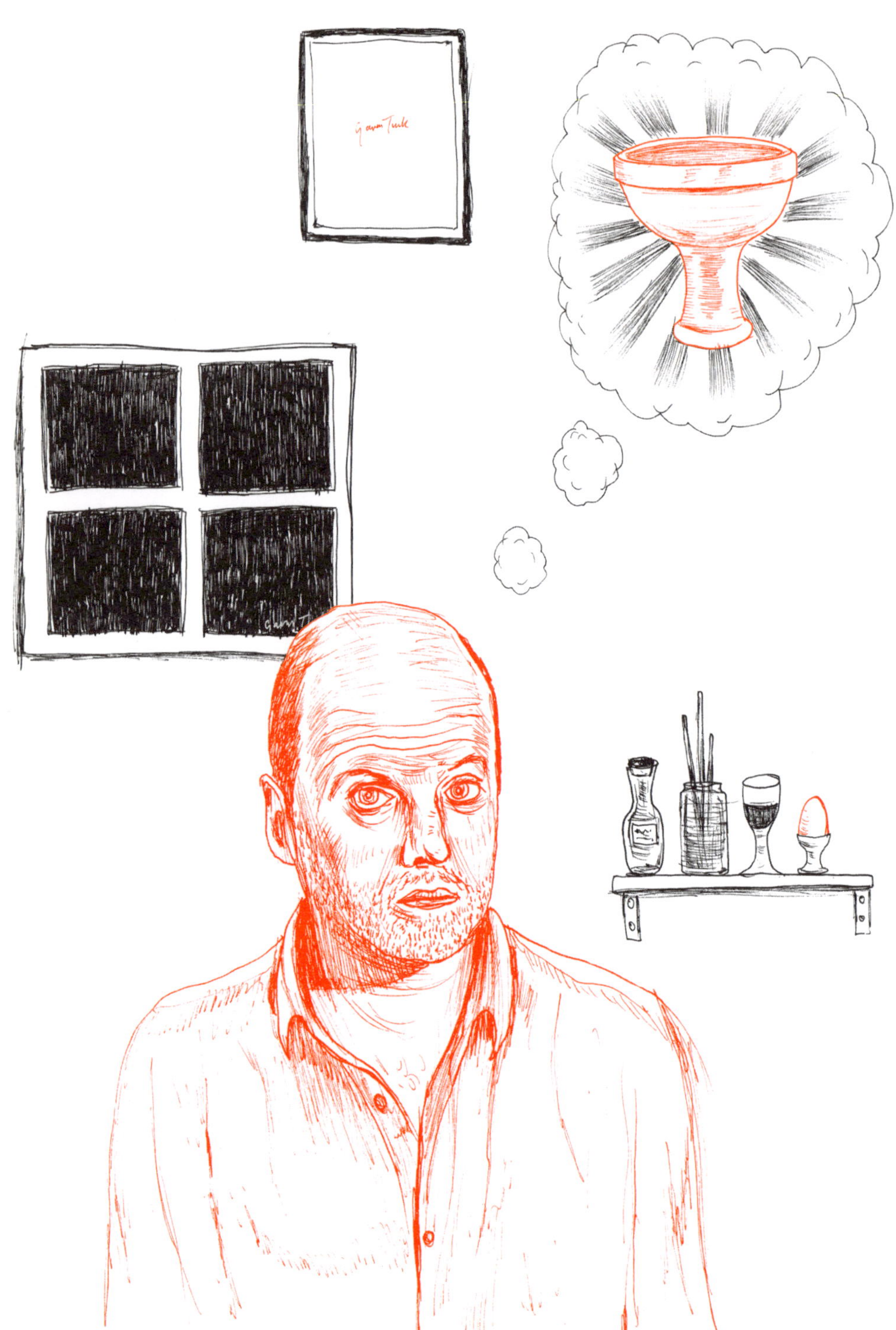
Gavin Turk

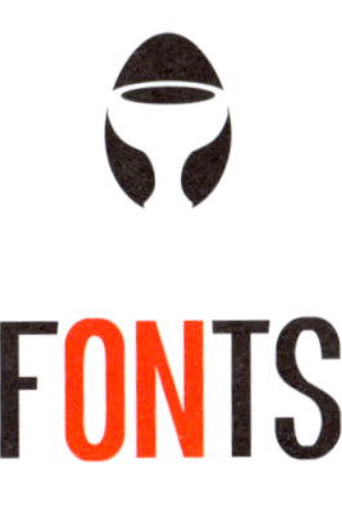

FONTS

Deborah Curtis

The artist was daydreaming in his studio

At some point during this musing, a vision appears like a dream. A totemic monad, whose gleaming white glaze offers itself up to the world of art as a challenge: a chess piece that looks like a pawn but can move like the queen.

The daydream moves on and other doors of perception open to reveal: a spiral jetty, curling like a fossil into the water. In the next room on its solid plinth sits a laughing Buddha. The dried-up fountain is a pivotal moment and sets the pace. Cups and vases appear on shelves like little mocking trophies.

Another door reveals the cold, incense-choked chamber of a cathedral with a holy font on the wall. Dip your fingers in the water — it's only London Tap. All around echoes the mysteries of religion, a species trying to understand itself. Move along. Next door there's a shock of scale change: from cavernous cathedral to water closet. Two feet away, a Victorian toilet with flushing cistern is decorated with floral patterns — a statement of affluence during a civilising period of effluence. A history of civilisation and our relationship with shame: the history of shit. The flushing toilet is a comical symbol of the state of the institution. From spotlessly clean squat toilets in India to shit-splattered portaloos in British festivals via the hole-in-the-ground in the Kalahari bush, the story, organisation and style of society is portrayed.

This door closes with a slam. Further down the maze, the artist takes a wrong turn and opens the door at the end to find a table with a display of historical egg cups lined up like miniature chalices carrying the blood of Christ turned egg-yolk yellow. Hang on, some of these are from Turkey, dated 3AD, and seem to represent a life's collecting by a lady in York. The surreal egg: an exquisite form created by nature expressing the journey down the birth channel. Sexual, optimistic, nutritious. The beginning of life. A symbol as potent as a light bulb for the expression of an idea.

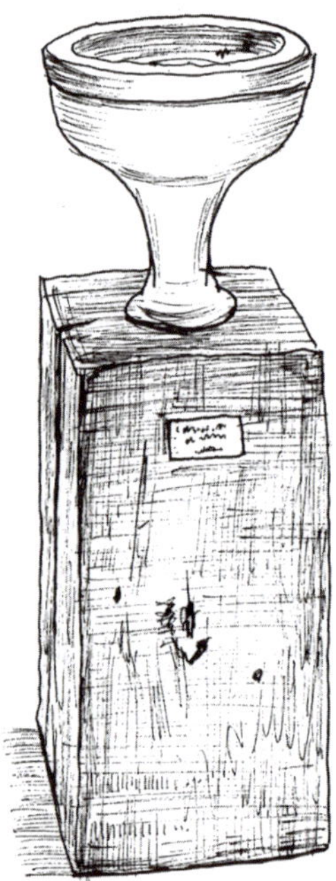

Gavin Turk Font (Museum Ludwig, Köln) **2009**
Ceramic, oak plinth and bronze plaque, 110 × 40 × 40 cm
A ceramic vase with a toilet bowl profile on a plinth with a plaque reading "Museum Ludwig, Köln"

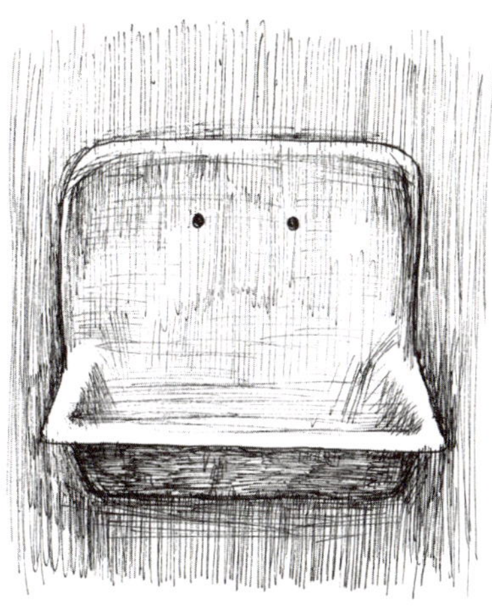

Robert Gober Sink 1988
Enamel, plaster, wire, lath and wood, 55.3 × 39.4 × 38.1 cm

❧ Leaving the egg room behind, the wandering minstrel moves past dozens more characters displayed in the Modern Art mausoleum, punctuated with trophies proclaiming unknown awards to unknown heroes. In the panic-free space of the daydream, an uneasy excitement motivates the artist's journey. The labyrinth forms a Möbius strip with one continuous edge, the universe bending elliptically in on itself. The final hall is at the centre of the dream. The door opens and the Minotaur is wearing a white coat, pouring slip into moulds; its lair is a sanitary ware factory producing row upon row of giant ceramic pots, balancing balletically on solid hardwood blocks hewn from ancient trees.

❧ Technicians are meticulously researching museums from countries across the globe. They award each ceramic its own plinth already embossed with a nameplate of its destination museum. Packing the artworks into crates ready for their journeys out into the world.

SEE ALSO:

 | 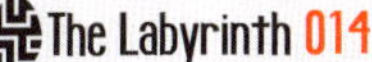The Labyrinth 014 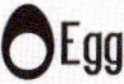Eggs 022

 | 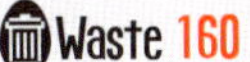Waste 160 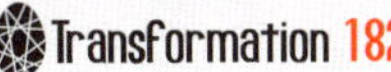Transformation 182

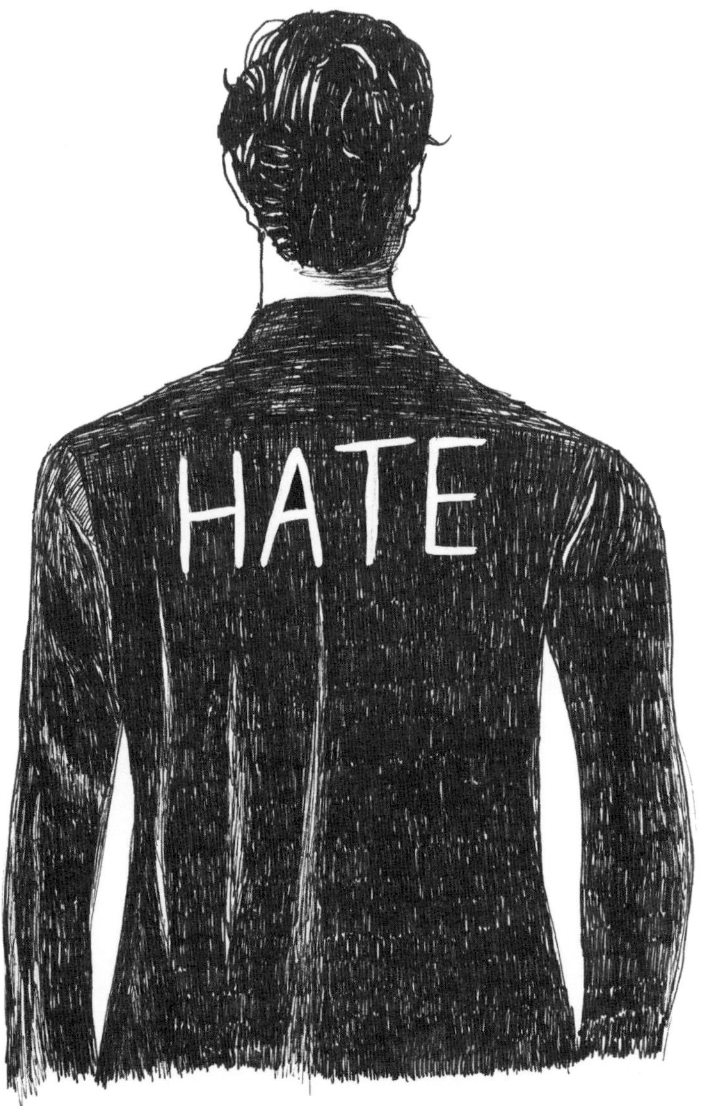
HATE

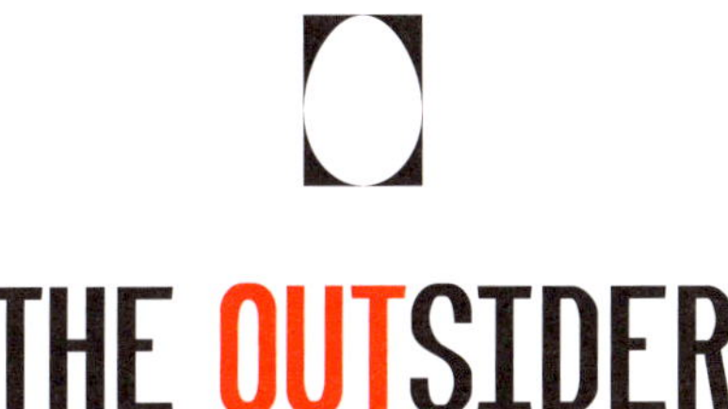

THE OUTSIDER

Amber Trentham

We need them more than we love them

On the whole, outsiders don't survive well. Take the revolutionaries, for example: poor old Prometheus was bound to a rock for eternity, Lucifer was consigned to hell, Oedipus gouged his own eyes out with a brooch pin, Jesus was crucified, John the Baptist decapitated, Che Guevara assassinated, Marat too, Bobby Sands starved himself dead, Socrates drank hemlock and who knows what happened to Hitler, but it didn't end well. The half-mad visionaries — Van Gogh, Sylvia Plath, Sid Vicious, Virginia Woolf, Kurt Cobain, Ian Curtis *et al.* — the brooding souls whose depressive talent sets them so apart from their community they die of loneliness. Those beyond the institutional radar who make art not from fancy but out of a strange, obsessive compulsion to heal some deep psychic wound. The reviled, the drop-outs, the misfits, the junkies, the street urchins, the bums, all those who just can't swim in the mainstream. *Ad infinitum.* Find yourself an outsider , someone who lives on the periphery of social norms, and more often than not some kind of grisly extinction follows.

¶   There's something about being outside the inside that's unsustainable, impossible, un-survivable. The community needs these raging individuals to drive it forwards, to push through evolution — the system itself creates outsiders — but ultimately it always brings them to a sticky end. Having served their function in various extremes, satisfied the community's vampiric hunger for saints and martyrs, then it's "Goodbye, Charlie" and curtains all round. Chewed up, spat out. Outsiders must be sacrificed.

¶ This relationship between "outsider" and the community of "insiders" has a strange alchemy to it, at one moment graspable, at another vague and mercurial; it's a quandary. The relationship is symbiotic, co-dependent; each defines the other, like black and white, light and dark, knowledge and Eden, good and bad.

¶ Long ago, in small communities, there were goats instead: scapegoats. Upon these goats depended the wellbeing of the community. Once a year, people would daub the goat with symbols of all the ills of the community and then they would banish it. The sacrifice of the painted goat restored order, calm and unity by purging the community's defilement. The Greeks transformed the scapegoat into human form. Rather than a goat, they would exile a *pharmakos* (a cripple, slave or criminal) who would perform the purifying function. The *pharmakos* was led outside the city and sacrificed in order to "purify" the city's interior.

¶ Greek tragedy both civilised and formalised this ritual on stage, the domain of fictional outsiders; the Greek work for tragedy translates literally as "song of the he-goat". *Catharsis*, coined by Aristotle in his *Poetics*, was a purification that happened through the experience of watching tragedy on stage; the emotions evoked — pity for undeserved suffering and fear for the man like yourself — are the essence of this purging, cleansing experience.

¶ The outsider is both a ritual embodiment of all that is wrong inside the community, while at the same time being the very means of healing it. He is both sacred and profane, remedy and poison. We watch extraordinary tragic heroes taking their stand outside the norm, becoming "other" through a profound, extreme and often noble character flaw that they are unable to abate. The chorus stands by, watching and reporting events; passive,

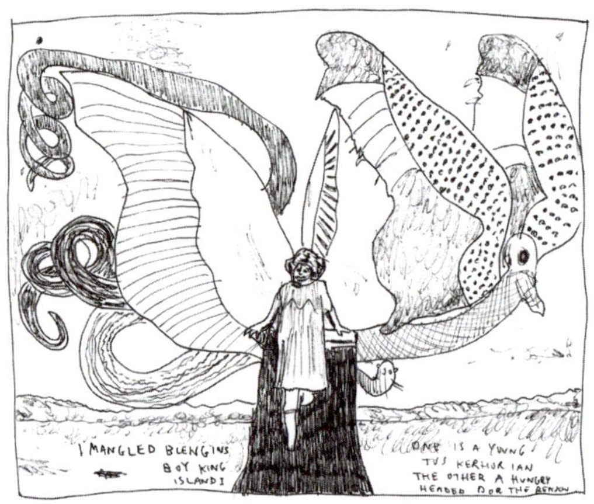

Henry Darger from The Story of the Vivian Girls 1892-1973
watercolour, pencil carbon tracing and collage on pieced paper

observant. When the tragic hero is undone, the chorus laments and says they told him so, before returning to their ordinary lives, now reinforced and vindicated.

¶ Even today, this sophisticated socio-political, community-based theatre performs a similar function. Onto the outsider we project our ills, our hopes, our fears; he acts them out. A living archetype, he exudes extraordinariness, excellence, loneliness, exclusion, rebellion, anarchy. Going against the grain, he is punished for it, sacrificed. He is exiled. Banished. Rejected. And as such he assumes responsibility for the collective salvation of the group.

¶ As history relates, outsiders are extraordinary, either as exceptionally talented human beings or as sub-human, Hogarthian quasi-monsters like the *pharmakos* — junkies covered in lesions and beggars on the street. Even the extraordinarily talented, those who are too gifted or successful, ultimately inspire a mixture of envy and distrust, and won't be tolerated by the community. Solon, one of the Seven Sages of Greece, observed, "A city perishes from its too great men." They have to be culled, as if someone's exaggerated good luck or excellence might call down the wrath of the gods. Aristotle noted that if a man over-steps the common level of virtue, he cannot be accepted on equal footing with other citizens; so the democratic state introduces a policy of ostracism. In terms of the wretched, the community pushes them out for fear of contagion. We cross to the other side of the street; we don't want to be infected or sullied. Displaying an animal mentality, we exclude the diseased among us in order to protect the survival of the group.

¶ Outsiders are living out something that is buried deep in all of us, that asocial, anarchic, monstrous part of ourselves. Theirs is an important and painful job for the community; they both sacrifice themselves and are sacrificed. The outsider's destruction allows us to commune with the part of ourselves that is isolated, separate, outside — but safely. We, like the chorus of old, purge the outsider inside us by ritually observing their downfall so that we can return indoors to the ironing and the soaps on TV, gratefully. Because it's cold outside.

¶ We should give more thanks to all those oddballs, for whether they know it or not, whether they want to or not, they realign the natural balance of our lives and restore the ever-so-fragile eco-system of our community. They allow us our normality.

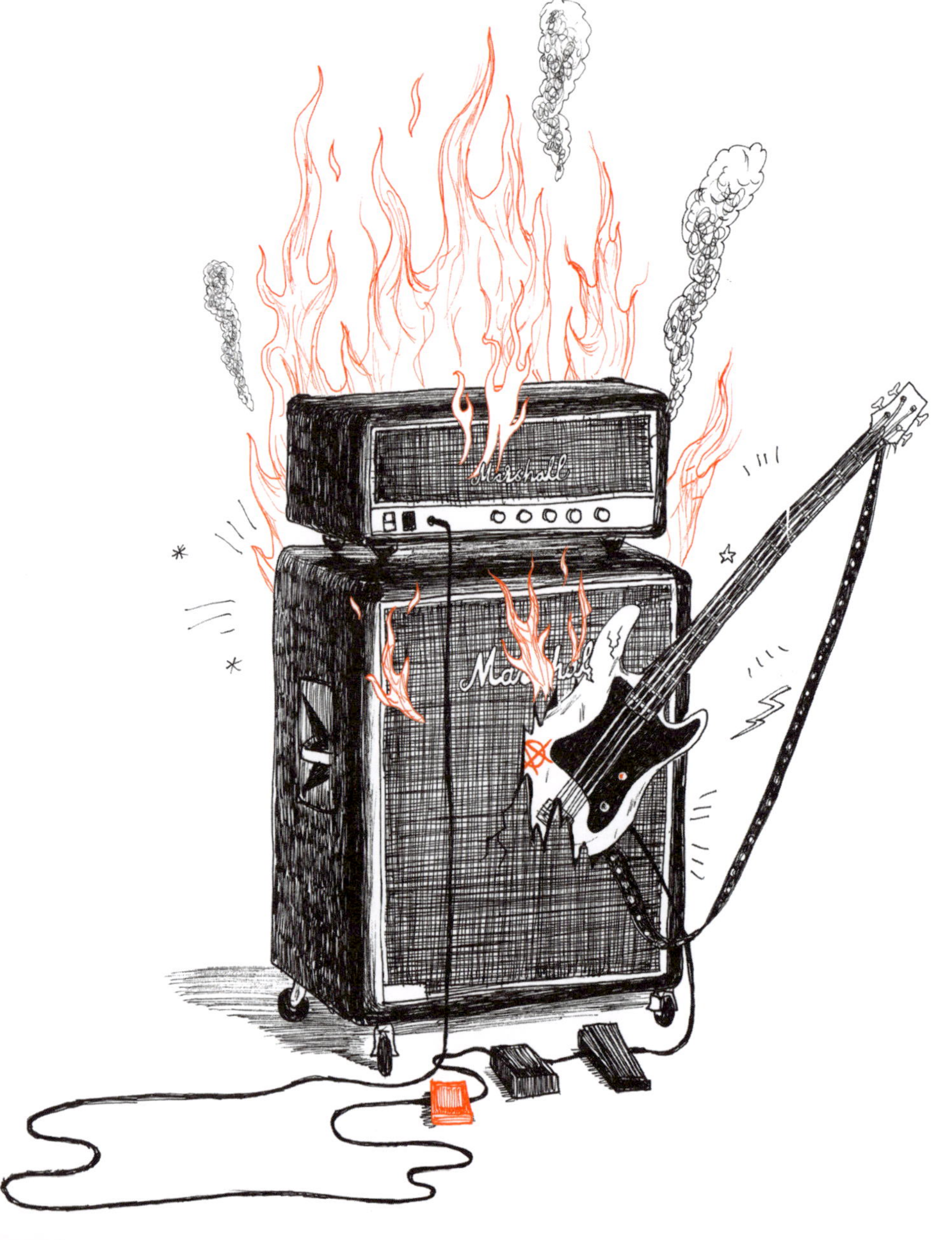
Marshall
Marshall

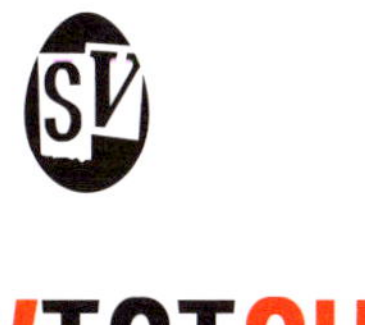

SID VICIOUS

Jon Savage

A truth this country never wants to hear

EVERY GENERATION has its brave ones — the artists, stylists, intellectuals, street kids, who heedlessly launch themselves into the future, refusing to be trapped by convention. Within this small group, there is always a figure who doesn't necessarily produce very much, if anything at all, but whose presence defines his or her time and place, whose every gesture sums up the spirit of their age. In the late 1920s, era of the Bright Young Things, it was androgynous socialite Stephen Tennant. In Andy Warhol's Factory it was the elfin, amphetamined Edie Sedgwick who danced the high wire with consummate grace. In British punk, it was Sid Vicious.

SID COULD HAVE BEEN the front man of the Sex Pistols, and eventually was. He was one of the four Johns — Lydon, Wardle, Beverley and Grey — herberts all from North and East London, who crashed down the King's Road during 1975, sneering at everything in sight. When Malcolm McLaren decided to hold an audition for the fledgling Sex group, Sid was absent. His friend John Lydon got the call.

UNHAPPY ABOUT THIS turn of events, Sid became the Sex Pistols *ur*-fan and began to get attention for his violent behaviour. He was, after all, called Vicious. Sid was known under a couple of names — John Beverley and Simon Ritchie — but sometime in 1974 or '75, in the spirit of pop re/creation, Lydon gave him a new pseudonym: Sid, after his hamster, and Vicious, after the song by Lou Reed. It was a joke, a laugh and, in later years, Lydon would downplay his involvement in what turned out to be the creation of a monster.

BUT RE/CREATION is an unpredictable undertaking. In the Warholian ambience of early London punk, Vicious was a leading character: his name offered him a fast track to fame, if not notoriety. By the time the music press began to run features about punk as something more than a couple of rock groups, Sid was an avatar of this new, troubled age. In John Ingham's seminal article for *Sounds* in October 1976, *Welcome to the "?" Rock Special*, Sid dominated the pull-quotes:

> "I didn't even know the Summer of Love was happening. I was too busy playing with my Action Man."

> "I don't understand why people think it's so difficult to learn to play guitar. I found it incredibly easy. You just pick a chord, go twang, and you've got music."

`AND` there was more:

> "I don't believe in sexuality at all. People are very unsexy. I don't enjoy that side of life. Being sexy is just a fat arse and tits that will do anything you want. I personally look upon myself as one of the most sexless monsters ever."

`IN THE END`, it was a kind of manifesto:

> "I've only been in love with a beer bottle and a mirror."

`SID'S COMMENTS` were a mixture of posturing and candid revelation. They introduced a character unafraid to take the limelight, with a catchy, if slightly ludicrous, pseudonym ("Sid" after all was redolent of the 1920's) that seemed to match the half-serious, half-joking brutality of early punk. Violence was both theatre and tool: to clear space, to reproduce the ambience of England in 1976.

`UNLIKE THE MORONIC MONSTER` of legend, Sid was sharp, as his friend Viv Albertine remembered:

> "I always felt very comfortable with him. He was so strict and so idealistic and so clever, which people don't seem to realise. The reason he went scooting downhill — he was so idealistic, and he really couldn't stand the world and its pettiness."

`I FIRST ENCOUNTERED` Sid in November 1976, at a Clash gig at the Royal College of Art. Standing at the front, I became aware of the person next to me swaying and strutting. I kept watch and wasn't surprised when he got up on stage, sharing Joe Strummer's mike and threatening the students who were busy showering the band with beer glasses. His threat was blunt and to the point:

> "C'mon cunt and I'll do ya."

`IT WAS THIS BRUTAL EARTHINESS` that characterised Sid's verbal pronouncements before the persona and drugs took him over. In the summer of 1977, he gave an excoriating interview to Fred and Judy Vermorel:

> "I think largely they're scum and they make me physically sick, the general public. They are scum."

`BY THEN HE HAD BECOME A SEX PISTOL`. The selection wasn't made on

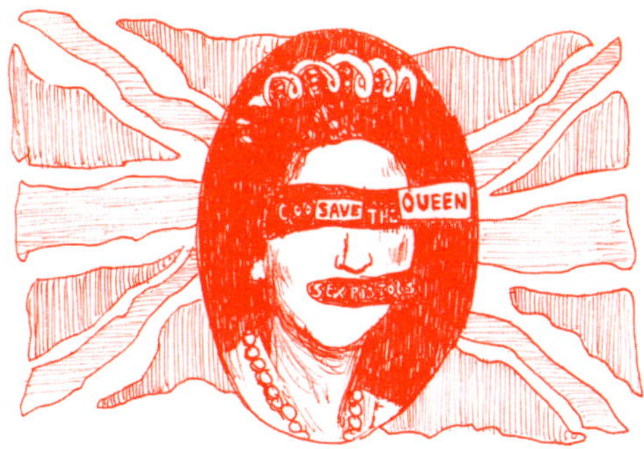

Jamie Reid God Save The Queen 2007
Screem print on canvas
Cut-up image of the Queen from the cover of the Sex Pistols' single *God Save The Queen* superimposed on a union jack

musical ability (although Sid could play Ramonic bass lines well enough) but on his persona and friendship with John Lydon. He looked like a Sex Pistol and, as the other three members of the group began to withdraw from the media attention, he began to take centre stage. His slow and wracked downfall was conducted in public. Part of Sid's problem was also the reason for his iconic status: he followed a bad idea all the way. He was in love with the New York punk ethos that ran from the Velvets to Lou Reed to the New York Dolls and then to Richard Hell and the Ramones. That's where Nancy Spungen and the hard drugs came from.

PHOTOGRAPHER ROBERTA BAYLEY befriended him during the Sex Pistols' January 1978 tour of the US, when Sid was going cold turkey. The climactic show of the tour occurred at San Antonio in Texas when the band played under a hail of material thrown by the local rednecks. Sid took up the challenge and clubbed a sample member of the audience with his bass. As far as Sid was concerned, he was the only one of the band who had stood up to the cowboys. He was the true Sex Pistol.

"I was sitting with him at the sound check," Bayley remembers.

"He said, 'I wanna be like Iggy and die before I'm thirty', and I said 'Sid, Iggy is over thirty and he's still alive. You got the story wrong.'"

A WEEK LATER, the Sex Pistols broke up and Sid was in Jamaica Hospital after an overdose on his flight from LA. He was alone and reflective when Bayley called him up:

"I've got six months to live," he told her.

"Oh well, don't drink you asshole."

"I'll end up burning myself out."

"But what will you do if you go back to London? The same thing?"

"Yeah. I probably will die in six months, actually."

`SID'S SELF-DESTRUCTION` cast him as an archetypal Romantic figurehead, the embodiment of London punk's headlong, heedless momentum that in 1978 was on the point of burnout just as it was becoming mainstream. After John Lydon abdicated, Sid fronted on *My Way* and the group's two bestsellers of the 1970s, *Somethin' Else* and *C'mon Everybody*. These Eddie Cochran covers recast Sid as the archetypal Too Fast to Live Too Young to Die rock hero.

`AS FILMED IN` *My Way*, Sid was the young gunslinger, the fanatical assassin out to murder a world; the human being underneath all this didn't have much of a chance. The most disturbing moment in *My Way* comes when Sid shoots a middle-aged woman. The idea was for this to represent not just the hated hippy generation but specifically Sid's mother, Anne Beverley; she was the one who bought the heroin that would kill him in February 1979.

`IN THE VERMORELS' INTERVIEW`, Sid locked into one of his characteristic rants: "Grown-ups have just got no intelligence at all. As soon as somebody stops being a kid, they stop being aware. And it doesn't matter how old you are — you can be 99 and still be a kid. As long as you're a kid, you're aware and you know what's happening. But as soon as you 'grow up'…"

`SID NEVER GREW UP`, throughout all his spectacular crash and burn. This focus on child-like awareness had, ironically, been one of the hallmarks of the hippies and had, in the hands of leading exponents John Lennon (*Strawberry Fields Forever*) and

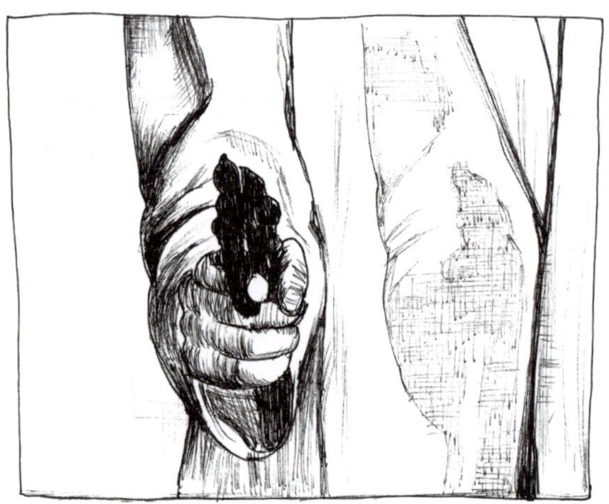

Gavin Turk **Blue Pop Gun** **2011**
Silkscreen ink on canvas, 38 × 48 cm
Hand gun section taken from *Pop* image of the artist as Sid Vicious in the pose of Andy Warhol's *Elvis Presley*

Syd Barrett (*Matilda Mother*), been just as redolent of emotional damage. But Sid also did it to himself. He bought the script, much of which was already a cliché by the time he was living it. How wearing was that New York junkie style, that blind sense of rock'n'roll entitlement with the black clothes, leather trousers and sunglasses after dark. You'd avoid those people on the street, not because they were dangerous, but because they were boring.

EVEN SO, there was something in Sid that made the script all his own, that transcended his self-destruction. In his thuggish poses and rebarbative discourse, Sid announced himself as a particular kind of English archetype — the intelligent hooligan whose stylised sarcasm flays the established, the bourgeois and the boring, telling a truth this country never wants to hear.

SEE ALSO:

 | 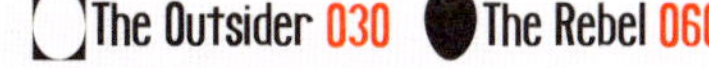 The Outsider 030 The Rebel 060

 | 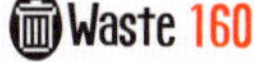 Waste 160 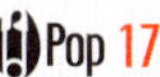 Pop 174

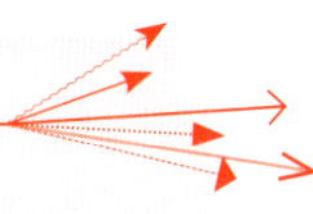

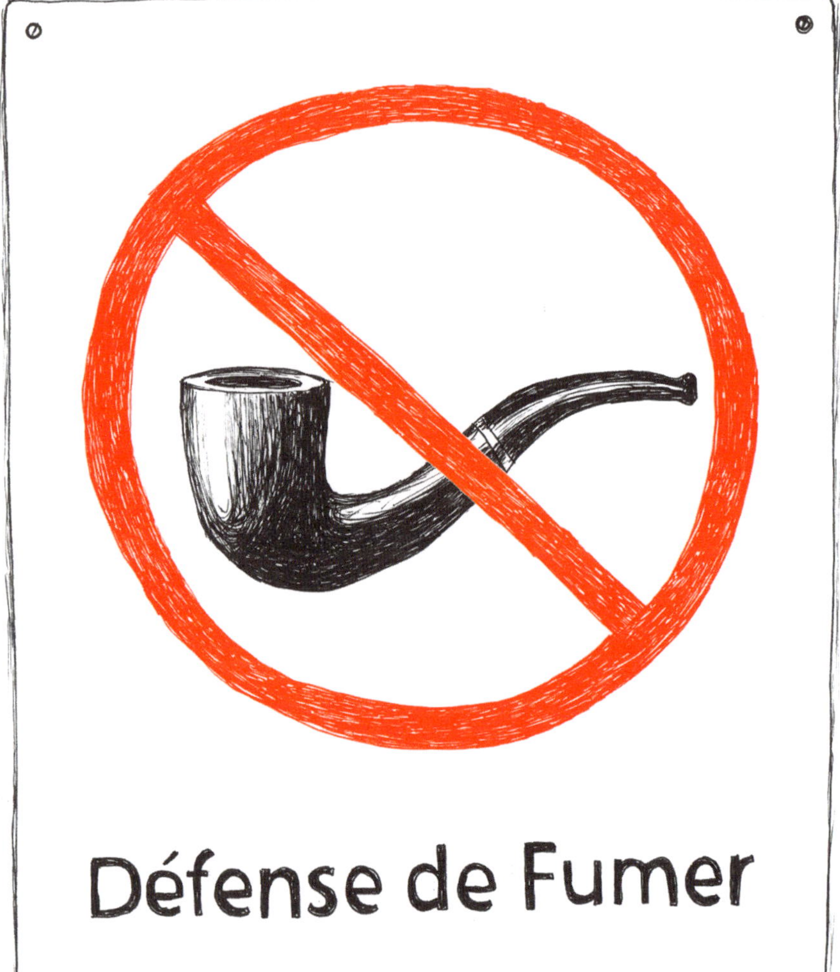

Défense de Fumer

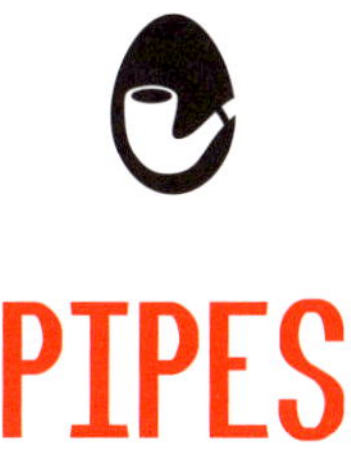

PIPES

Charlie Porter

When a pipe is just a pipe

Of its moment, an object such as a pipe can seem so symbolic that to possess it becomes a powerful act of self-definition. But once that item becomes obsolete, its symbolism vanishes. Indeed the absence of relevancy can have a negative mirroring effect on its symbolism, as if to cancel out its previous power with impotency.

¶ All this symbolism has an inbuilt nostalgia, especially as Western culture speeds up. For much of the 20h century, items had a purpose and longevity that allowed symbolism to gather round them. Now it seems the mission of the 21st century is to shed the unnecessary. That may sound weird in such materialistic times, but it also seems true — we may buy more stuff but the sheer volume of what we buy makes us care less about what we own. If we don't care about something enough to associate ourselves with it, symbolism cannot build up.

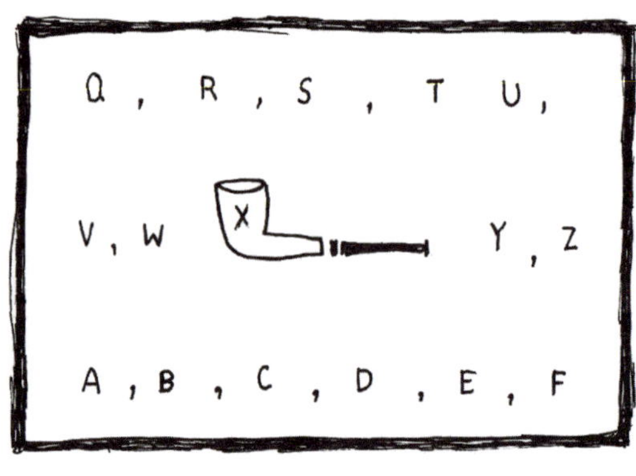

Marcel Broodthaers Pipe 1969
Embossed relief on plastic, 85 × 210 cm

¶ This is particularly true of a man and his possessions. The male wardrobe was once both an outfit and a symbol of stature, intelligence and physical endowment. Accessories such as a pipe, cane or bowler hat were loaded with symbolism about a man's wealth and prowess, certainly overt enough for René Magritte to parody in *Ceci N'est Pas Une Pipe* as part of his series *The Treachery of Images* (1928-9).

¶ Magritte was a young man when he made this painting of a pipe. It came at a time when cigarettes began to be marketed through movies, intentionally or not, as the modern way to smoke; the pipe was losing its symbolism of virility and contemplation, to be replaced by an evocation of fustiness, even thought-avoidance. To sit with a pipe in modern-day life is to pretend that everything is how it once was, to avoid having to deal with life as it is.

¶ I have a strange relationship with pipes, which makes the distinction between the pipe itself and its use important. Until the late 80s, my father smoked a pipe — something I loaded with no symbolism, I just wished he didn't do it. I was never attracted to smoking as a child, and have only ever tried a cigarette once, in my late twenties, when a friend asked me to hold hers while she tied her shoelace; I figured I might as well see what it tasted like. It was like a McDonald's: ineffective on every level.

¶ At the time, I never considered my father's use of a pipe as odd, outlandish or self-indulgent. He didn't use a pipe as some sort of urban fashion statement; we lived in the country, our family life was fairly isolated and it was simply his preferred way of taking in tobacco. His father had smoked a pipe and I remember a photograph of them both, with pipes proudly in their mouths, my father a young man.

¶ I didn't like my father smoking at all, and probably would have liked him smoking cigarettes even less. He gave up after he suffered a heart attack in the mid-80s, the pipe soon

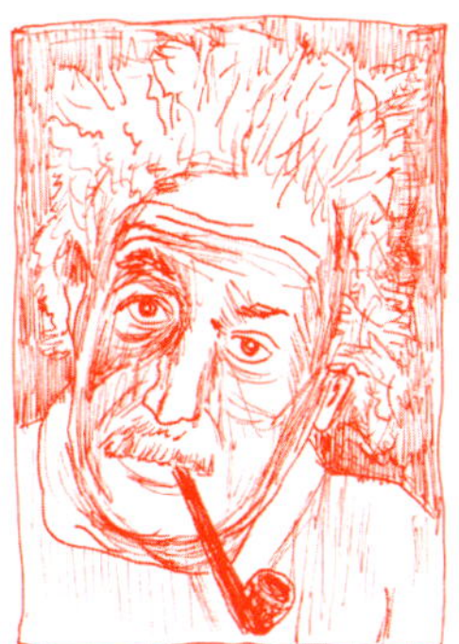

forgotten, by me at least, as part of his daily make-up. My father is a painter and is alone for prolonged periods while he's working. He has managed to do so just as well without his pipe. Smoking as an aid to contemplation being probably just an excuse conjured up by smokers to justify their habit. The mind focuses very well on its own.

¶ I cannot think of the last time I saw a man with a pipe. The modern male wardrobe has become a thing of functionality and comfort; few men wear a suit but they tend to look as if they wish they could be wearing something else. Modern dress is now a middle ground between the two genders, indeed the stuff we carry around has lost its symbolism in the race to become more useful, more efficient, less burdensome. If symbolism is one of the great casualties of modern life, it is not one we should mourn.

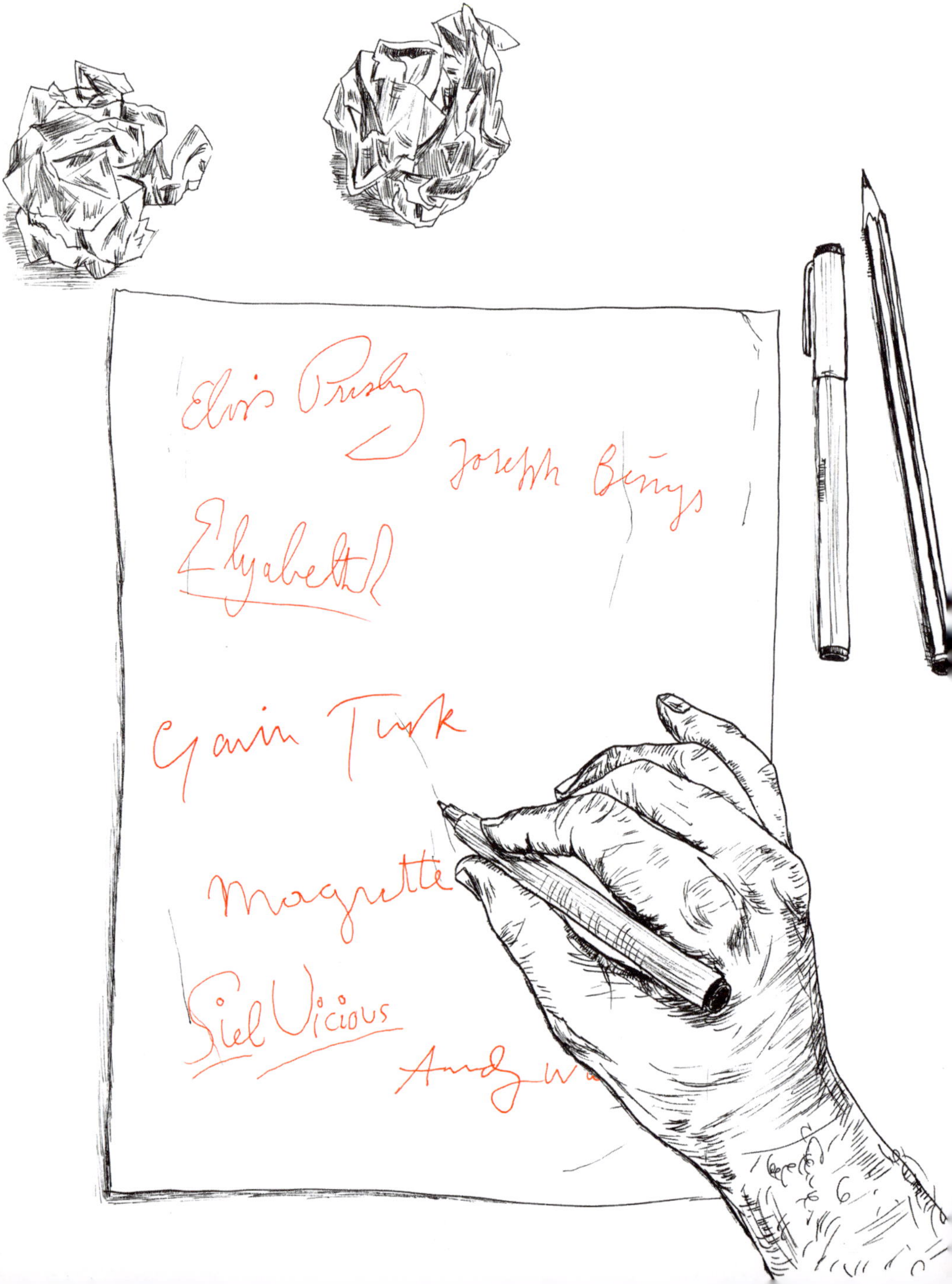

Elvis Presley   Joseph Beuys

Elyabeth

Gavin Turk

Magritte

Siel Vicious

Andy Wa

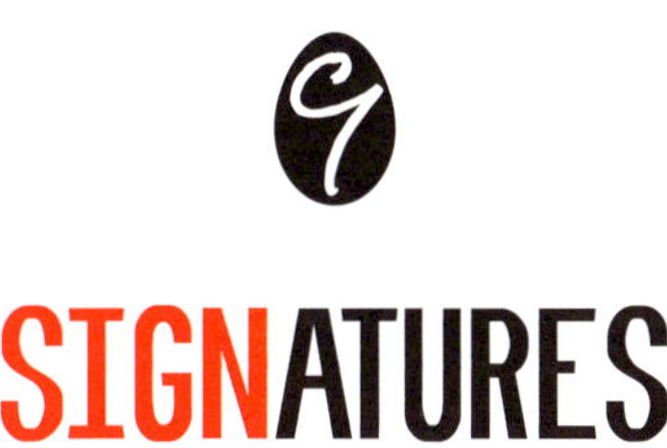

SIGNATURES

Josie Barnard

A dying art

When a child reaches the age of nine or so, he or she begins to understand that in adulthood a "signature" is necessary. At this point, the idea of a signature as a means of authentication and identification is hazy. For a pre-teen, it's a chance to take control of who they are. They often start practicing. I know I did. My signature became a project, an opportunity to start moulding my identity. The perfected signature was to be a condensed version of the future me — except I was a child of my time. The 1970s was an era of Holly Hobby cartoons and Love Is posters. Along with most of the other girls in my class, I tried a whole host of decorative possibilities. I dotted the "i" with a smiley; I turned the "o" into a heart; I experimented with a looser, freer "J", at one stage looping it right round my whole name and concluding with a perky flower.

¶ Kids today seem rather more sophisticated. The day my daughter and her class-mates set to developing their signatures, she came home with selected examples. Not one featured childish flourishes. These 21st century nine-year-olds' signatures were all about encrypting. Manic tangles of ink, they were pretty good approximations of adult signatures. And adult signatures do tend to become illegible. After any initial excitement about a signature as a way of expressing oneself, it tends to get rushed — scrawled on cheques, invoices, letters, postcards, credit cards; scribbled on legal documents, prescriptions, report cards. Signatures are high-speed marks; it's not always possible to read them, because writing them has become a chore.

¶ Some signatures are collected and hunted. When I was in my early 20s, I got a job in a publishing house as a blurb writer and fancied becoming "a writer" myself one day. I'd just discovered the Australian novelist Patrick White and found his lyrical, tough treatment of the outsider deeply inspiring. Having had no prior interest in collecting signatures, suddenly I wanted his.

¶ White lived in Australia. It was the days of snail mail. He was notoriously reclusive and cantankerous to boot. The book I wanted him to sign was *Three Uneasy Pieces*, a collection that starts with a story called *The Screaming Potato* and goes on to explore whether we should gouge out "warts of the soul" or wait for the "evil in us" to die naturally. The photo in the front of the book showed the author standing at his kitchen table — mouth down-turned, one brow raised slightly — implacable, apparently humourless. He was a Nobel Prize winner. He received piles of fan mail. The chance that my request for a signature would even make it past his agent was, I thought, low to nil. I had nothing to lose. I popped it in the post.

¶ To my real surprise, perhaps two months later, the package came back. The note from his agent says, "Patrick was happy to sign your book". Happy. The signature is a bit shaky (he was in his late 70s) — the "P" looks like an "O", the crosses of the "t"s float a little way from the main text. But it is a clear, open, friendly signature. It still gives me goose bumps to see it. The book remains one of my most treasured objects. Why? Because Patrick White, a writer I admire enormously, had it in front of him, perhaps on the very kitchen table that is in the photo. With his hand, he signed his name, for me. He gave me something of himself.

¶ One of the precious things about a hero's signature is that it's personal. I was surprised to hear that Canadian writer Margaret Atwood had invented a machine that enables her to sign fans' books while she is in a different country altogether. In 2006, when LongPen was launched, Atwood told the *Independent* newspaper what had inspired her. "As I was whizzing around the United States on yet another demented book tour, getting up at four in the morning to catch planes... I thought, 'There must be a better way of doing this'."

¶   LongPen is an ingenious concept; I had a toy that used the same principle when I was a child. With my toy, the author's pen had a robotic arm attached so that marks made were replicated by another quite separate pen. It meant I could write simultaneously on bits of paper that were several inches apart. Technology may allow the gap between pens to be thousands of miles, but getting a signature is about touch and physical presence, surely, not gizmos and gadgets. If someone wants a signature, don't they want to feel they've gained a one-to-one exchange with the author? I gather that if you go to a LongPen signing, you'll find a pen attached to a computer as well as a monitor and speakers. You'll be able to look at the author, close up, and have a chat, too, before they sign. In a virtual way, you can feel as if you are alone with the author — even in their home. You might glimpse their personal effects, perhaps a pepper pot in the kitchen, a calendar on the wall. ....

¶   Autograph hunters may want to sell their bounty on. If Atwood, and now a whole bunch of other authors, can sign books anywhere in the world without stepping outside their front doors, that affects the market. Online sellers are very careful to make distinctions. One clarifies, "This signature was obtained in person, not through the author's 'high-tech' invention called the LongPen. Copies 'signed' in the latter manner must be identified as such because they have no collectible value. The point of a signed copy is that it unmistakably indicates that the author held the copy of the book and left his or her trace on it."

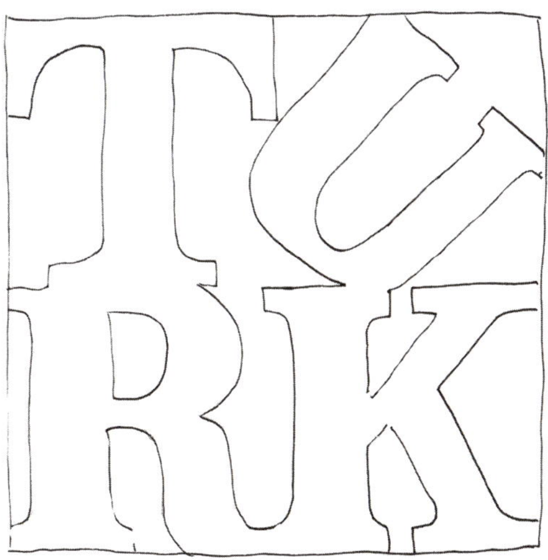

Gavin Turk *Turk Love Black on White* **2010**
Silkscreen ink on canvas, 120 × 120 cm
After Robert Indiana's iconic *LOVE* image

¶   If a signature is not unique, does it count? LongPen puts signatures centre frame and draws attention to the idea that they might become outmoded. Purchases and bank transactions are made remotely using pin numbers and codes. At more and more schools, children queuing for dinner have to present their fingerprint for verification in order to get their pasta.

¶   Signatures are often beautiful. There is something archaic about them, and they have been taken for granted. Their alluring illegibility may become a thing of the past if we don't have to sign our names on a day-to-day basis; signatures won't evolve in the same way. For anyone who worked on them as a child, as I did, or hunts signatures of others, that could feel tragic.

¶   However, as I think that, I smile. Signatures are only a convention. In the short story *Amy Foster* by Joseph Conrad, the main character, Yanko Goorall, is an exile from central Europe who has been shipwrecked on the English coast. A sign of just how excluded he is from Eastbay society comes when the rector has to write Yanko's name for him in the marriage registry. The castaway can only make a "crooked cross" himself; he is disenfranchised by his inability to effect a signature. Yet, Conrad notes, the other people in the Eastbay community look "heavy". The soles of Yanko's feet do not seem to "touch the dust of the road," he "vaults" over stiles and "pace[s] these slopes with a long elastic stride". Throughout the story, Conrad emphasises it is not the rector nor the doctor nor the landowner, but rather Yanko, the man who can't even sign his name, who is bursting with life. He is a "soft and passionate adventurer... lithe, supple and strong-limbed, straight like a pine, with something striving upwards in his appearance as though the heart within him had been buoyant."

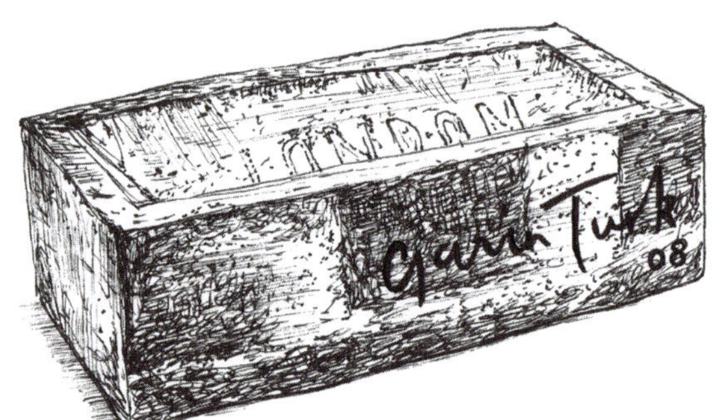

Gavin Turk Revolting Brick 2008
Marker pen on brick, 6 × 7 × 22 cm
Edition of 10
A brick signed by the artist

 | 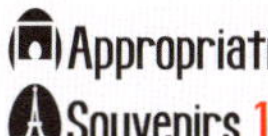Appropriation **066** 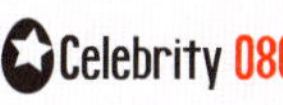Celebrity **086** 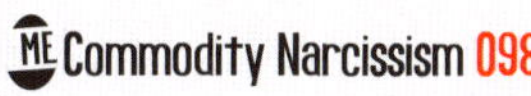Commodity Narcissism **098**
Souvenirs **122**

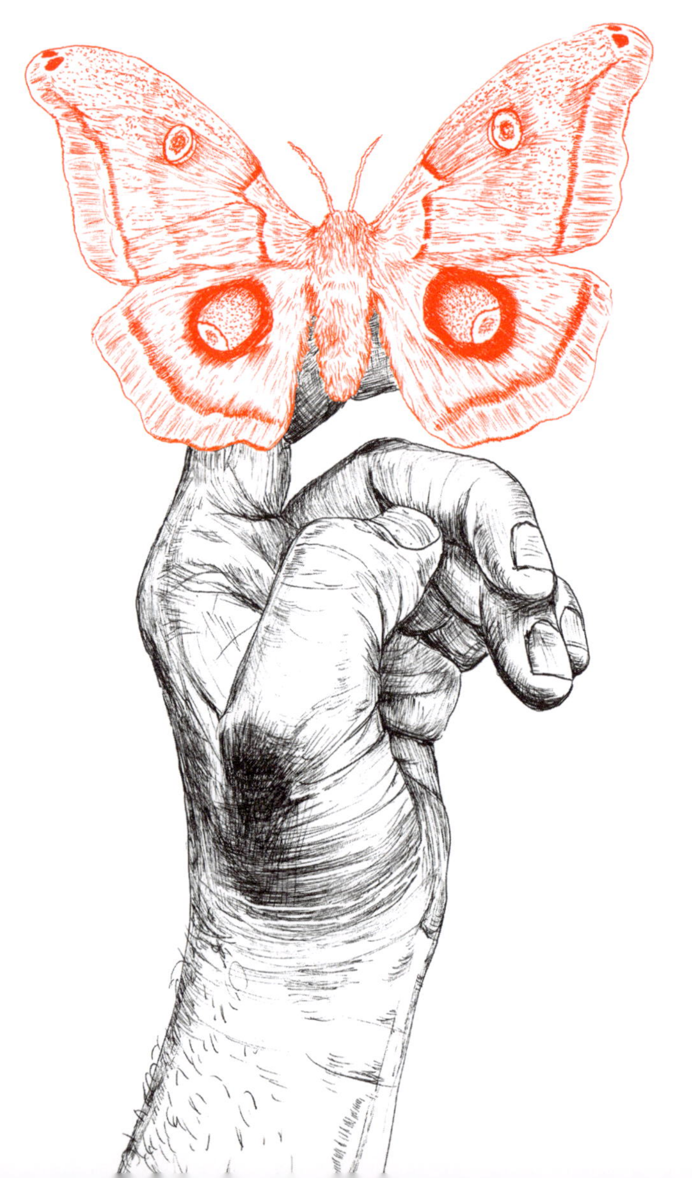

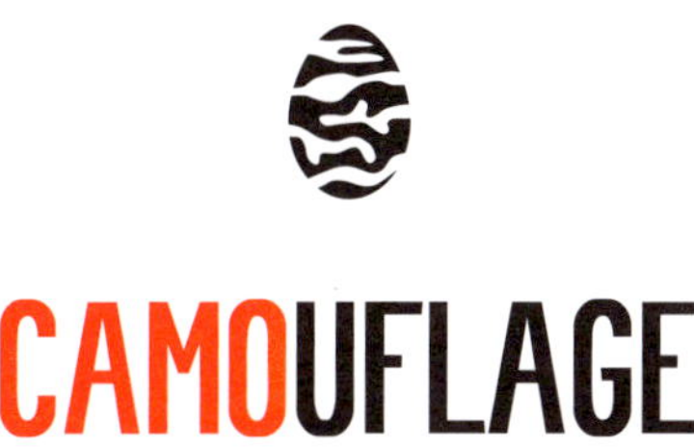

CAMOUFLAGE

Hardy Blechman

The art of concealment

In 1909, when Victorian naturalist and painter Abbott H. Thayer published his observations about concealment in nature it's fairly certain he had no idea what he was starting.

¶ *Concealing Coloration in the Animal Kingdom* was the first comprehensive catalogue of the many camouflage techniques employed in the natural world and Thayer argued that nature was acting as an artist, creating optical effects with colour and light. On this basis, he proposed his study belonged in the realm of art as well as nature. His thesis coincided with the birth of Cubism and, interestingly, with the emergence of Gestalt psychology.

¶ The many significant changes of the early 20th century included a seismic shift in techniques employed by military forces worldwide. Primarily a result of the development of longer range and more accurate weaponry, new technological developments negated the traditional use of the military uniform. The famous red coat of the nineteenth century British army had long been a symbol of military pride, intended to visibly intimidate the

enemy on the battlefield. But the trench warfare of World War 1 required different strategies; colour was no longer used to inspire fear on the battlefield, but to conceal. In an unlikely collaboration, artists were recruited by the army and given the task of using techniques developed through the study of camouflage in nature, to disguise weapons, vehicles and, ultimately, men.

¶   The French army led the way with its dedicated camouflage section under the pioneering direction of artist Lucien-Victor Guirand de Scevola, producing new innovations for concealment in the air, on land and at sea. The Cubists, many of whom fought in the Great War and who were ever open to conceptual challenges, had already begun to re-interpret and mimic the camouflage techniques found in nature. It was Picasso who first used the term "dazzle" in reference to the need for warships to "mislead" their enemies at sea. In the UK, under the direction of British marine artist and Naval Commander Norman Wilkinson, the British Admiralty founded a "Dazzle Section" based at the Royal Academy of Arts. Here a group of eighteen artists, including Wilkinson and Vorticist painter Edward Wadsworth, developed paint schemes for warships that used disruptive patterns involving complex geometric shapes and colours to confuse enemy gunners as to the target's course, speed and direction. The role of the artist as essential camoufleur continued throughout the Second World War and by its end, camouflage was deeply entrenched in twentieth century visual culture. New printing techniques had facilitated the mass production of army uniforms; the international mass media which had documented the war, brought camouflage into the public eye on a scale like never before.

¶   The first post-war artist to appropriate camouflage was French painter Alain Jacquet. Exploring an interest in the visual effects of disruptive patterns, Jacquet created camouflage interpretations of his peers' works, including *Camouflage Jasper Johns* (after Johns' *Flag*, 1954) and *Camouflage Hot Dog Lichtenstein*, both in 1963. In 1964, Jacquet reinterpreted Manet's *Le Dejeuner sur l'herbe*, which he described as breaking "reality into dots" thus having the same properties as camouflage. In 1964, Jacquet wore a camouflage suit recycled from a US Army parachute to the opening of his show at the Alexander Iolas Gallery in New York, attended by Andy Warhol and Roy Lichtenstein.

¶   Italian artist Alighiero e Boetti famously discovered surplus camouflage cloth (the *telo mimetico* pattern created in 1929 for the Italian army) in a flea market. He used it to create works in 1966 and 1967, stretching the cloth as though it was a blank canvas, turning it into a visual artefact. In America, that same decade saw the rise of the Civil Rights Movement and the anti-war response to Vietnam; this counter culture, in all its many manifestations, used army surplus as a symbol of resistance, subverting the purpose of camouflage from concealment to visibility — subverting military language for political reasons.

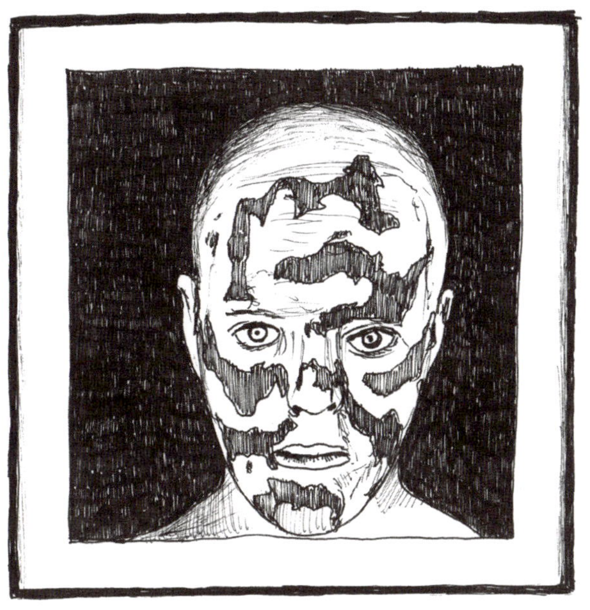

Gavin Turk Camouflage (Self Portrait) 1994
Reversal colour print, 90 × 90 cm
A photograph of the artist with a mud mask camouflage pattern on his face reminiscent of Mr Kurtz in *Apocalypse Now*

¶   It was newspaper coverage rather than surplus trade that led to Warhol's re-appropriation of the US Woodland Pattern in 1986 for his famous *Camouflage* series. Unlike Boetti, Warhol reworked the pattern's original colourways and scale, although he left the shapes intact. Warhol used these camouflage patterns as a base for nearly seventy works including *The Last Supper, Self Portrait* and his portrait of Joseph Beuys. Warhol's fascination with camouflage as a perfect form with which to explore the possibility of pure abstraction, mirrored his own personal need for disguise. Perhaps it's this central idea of disappearing, blending in, or, inversely, standing out — whether personally, socially, or politically — that makes camouflage so seductive to many artists.

¶   The idea of appropriation, recycling images, has been at the heart of much contemporary artistic work that references camouflage. Gavin Turk's 2007 exhibition *Me as Him* projected both Turk and Warhol, the men and the images, under a layer of silk-screened camouflage, challenging the idea of the self-portrait as something authentic with "deeper meaning", looking only to the façade for answers. Damien Hirst's *Amazing Revelations* (2003)

are collages of thousands of butterfly wings in abstract patterns, inadvertently demonstrating some of the most skillful camouflage techniques used in nature; his interest in butterflies as a metaphor for mortality may also be linked to the use of camouflage as survival mechanism.

¶   Despite the continued presence of camouflage in music, fashion and contemporary culture, the fact that its use in the 20th century developed through the synergy of nature and art is often overlooked. We might argue that its primary symbolic association remains with the military. As more military forces adopt black uniforms and new, pixelated patterns as camouflage, the traditional disruptive patterns — the khaki and sand uniforms that became iconic visual signifiers of war and combat for over a hundred years — are less useful. Does this mean culture will be able to reclaim camouflage by divorcing its original artistic and natural function from military needs? Each time another artist uses the pattern in a non-military context, will this slowly reshape our perception of camouflage and its meaning? Perhaps one day when we see a Warhol canvas, a rap album cover, or a Japanese toy using a recognisable camouflage pattern, we will respond to the colour, shape and form in its new context, without being dominated by historical military associations. We should remember the original intention of Thayer and Braque and Picasso to explore techniques found in natural forms, was essentially a desire to understand themselves. The need to hide, or to reveal, oneself is not the same as the need to declare war.

SEE ALSO:

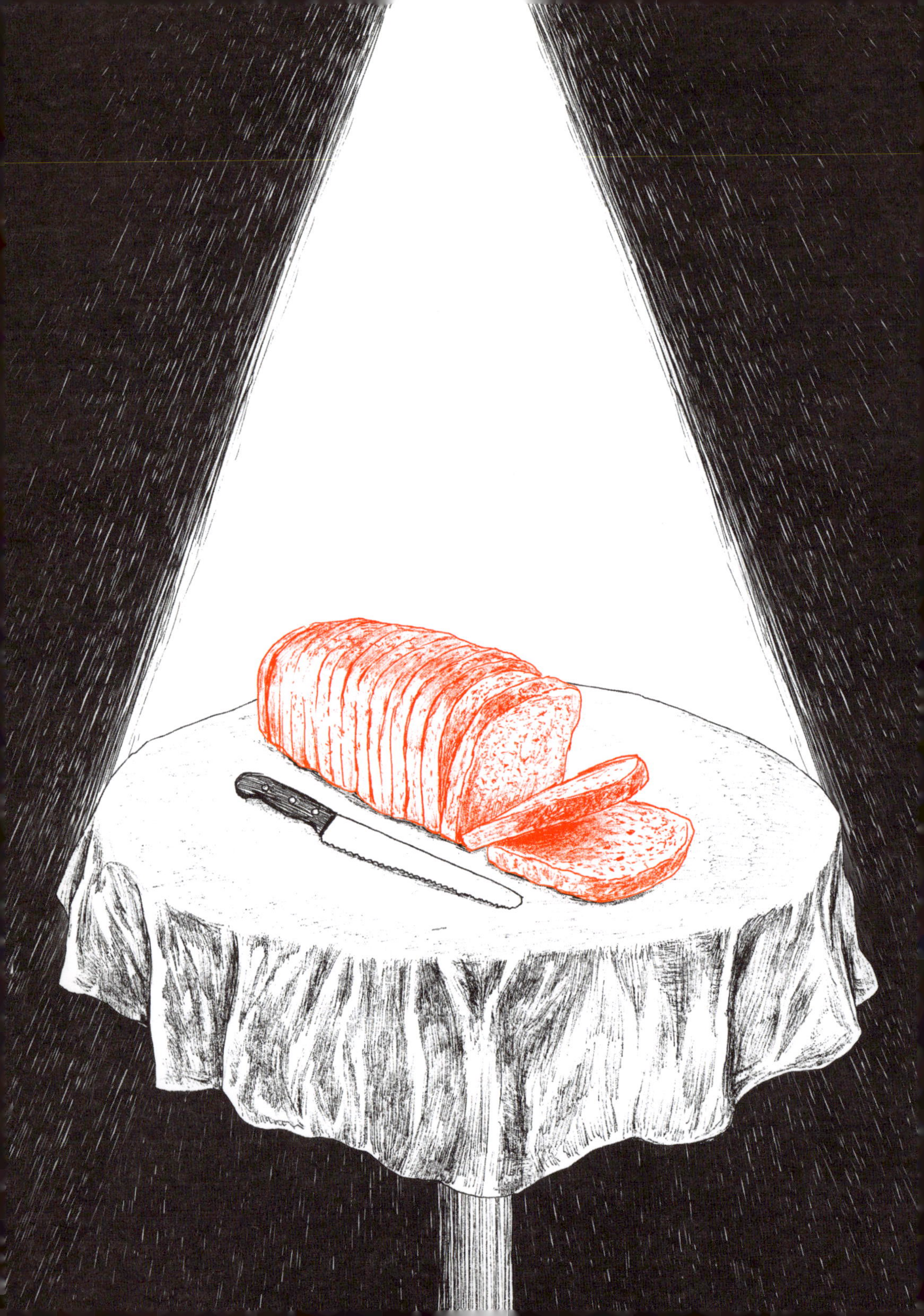

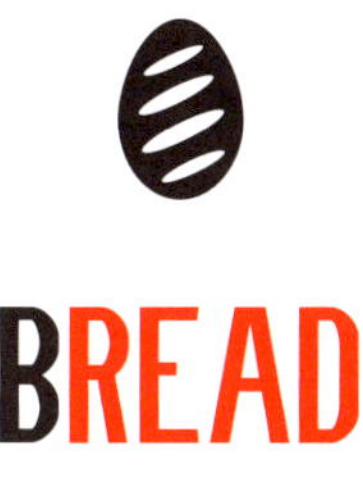

B**READ**

Kate de Syllas

We can survive on acorns but we invented bread

Art and bread may, at first glance, appear to have little in common. Yet seen as two key products in the emergence of human cultures, both talk of similar themes, struggles and processes taking place within the long history of those cultures. To consider art and bread together raises the question of what is the difference between existing and living. What is it about the human condition that makes us desire to do more than simply survive? Bread, like art, perhaps offers us the possible answer that it is an intense creativity and curiosity that marks us out as a species. "Acorns were good", said Francis Bacon, "until bread was found".

¶ While bread is a staple food, a constant across cultures and times, the variations that humans have created from a small number of ingredients seems almost limitless. Art is in many ways similar. Whatever limits have been placed on artists, they have found ways to create. To provide pleasure, evoke emotions, and to comment on the things that are important within their immediate cultures and to the species as a whole. Art has long commented on, symbolised or represented, and indeed influenced, political and religious issues, narratives and desires. That art should be able to crystallise complex ideas and say what cannot be easily said in words alone may seem obvious, indeed its *raison d'être*, but bread also holds a hugely important place in the symbolic order that surrounds some of the most important human themes.

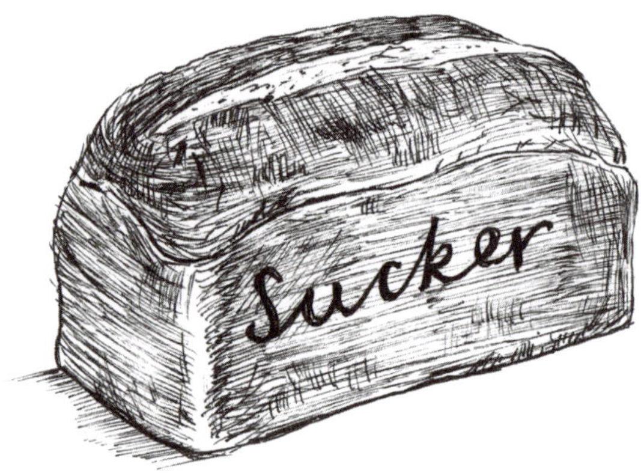

Gavin Turk Succour, Sucker 2003
Painted concrete, 13 × 10 × 17.5 cm
A concrete cast of a small split tin loaf painted to look real with the words "Succour" and "Sucker" painted on the sides

¶   While bread features heavily in the symbolic order of all of the world's major religions, many of us also find that bread is a material link with a religious heritage we may otherwise rarely encounter. Hot cross buns and Passover bread, for example, are tangible links to the narratives that form the foundations of our religions, and whether we actively practice them or not, religions form a basis within most of the contemporary cultures we find ourselves living in. There is a similar relationship between bread and political life. "Peace, land, bread", said Lenin in 1917, and, as Marie Antoinette found to her peril, bread, or the lack of bread, has more than once been the ferment for revolution.

¶   On the other hand, a hungry population has also been manipulated to avoid the turmoil of change. The late Egyptian writer, Naguib Mahfouz, said in an interview in 1992: "In Egypt today most people are concerned with getting bread to eat. Only some of the educated understand how democracy works". If only Mahfouz had been able to witness the events of early 2011 he may have been astounded by the move towards democracy his compatriots demanded in their revolution, but of course the point here is not the political system to arise from any particular revolution, but that bread is both a synecdoche for food in the wider sense, and symbolic of the importance of a nourished population for the political realities of a state.

¶   Our changing ability to nourish a population has also opened up fresh cultural battlegrounds. In 1961, amidst the growing turmoil of those times, bread underwent its own quiet revolution. The invention of the "Chorleywood process" saw the advent of industrial bread making. The loaf now came from the factory rather than the domestic hearth or the artisan's oven. The tangled relationships between the industrial, the artisan and the artist

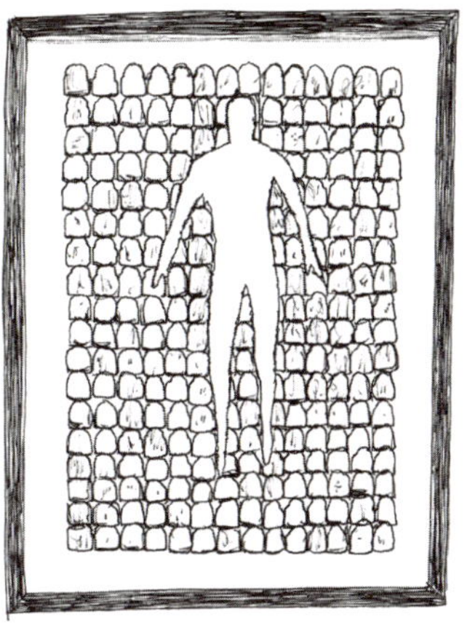

Antony Gormley Consumption **1982**
Bread and wax, 261 × 169 × 1.6 cm
Silhouette created from slices of Mother's Pride

may have begun to play out in the world of art long before Chorleywood, but they raise similar questions about authorship, quality and the nature of art, as well as perhaps more troubling issues.

¶ 1961 also saw the opening of MoMA's seminal exhibition, *The Art of Assemblage*. The term, "assemblage" was coined by the artist Jean Dubuffet to describe some of his works. Amongst them are a number of assemblages made from some of nature's most beautiful camouflage — butterfly's wings. Whether it is an accident that sees Turk's industrial-looking loaves concealed with camouflage or not, it brings us back to the question of living and surviving. We can survive on acorns, but we invented bread.

¶ Just as human creativity can make our lives richer, it is part of our tragedy that it can also be our downfall. The Chorleywood process and the industrialisation of food is part of a constellation that includes the industrial-military complex that has co-opted the butterfly's wings to more sinister ends. With global food insecurity on the rise these relationships are set to become starker and more important. Good bread and good art may be a matter of taste, but at their best, they can stand against the global homogenisation and industrialisation of culture and for the desire to live, not just survive.

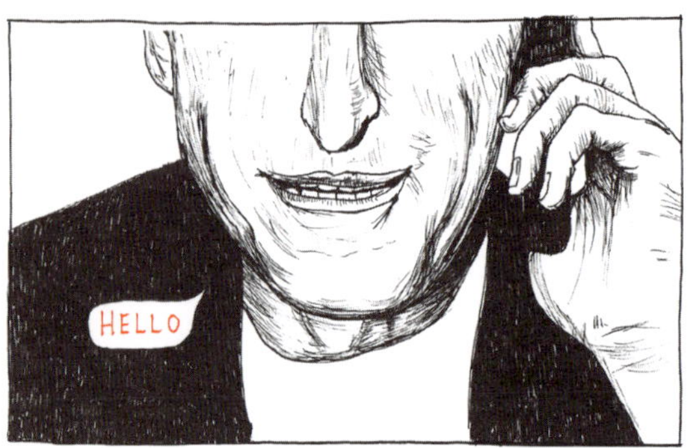

HELLO

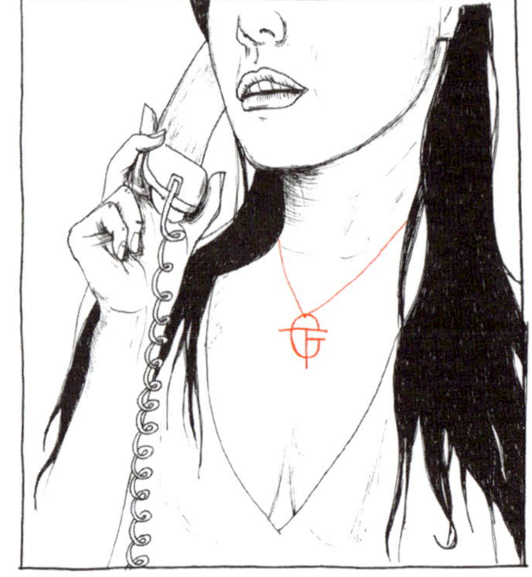

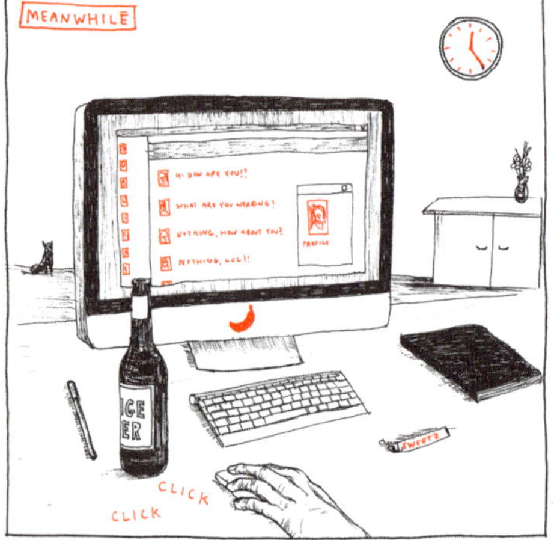

MEANWHILE
HI HOW ARE YOU!?
WHAT ARE YOU WEARING?
NOTHING, HOW ABOUT YOU?
NOTHING, LOL!!
PROFILE
CLICK
CLICK

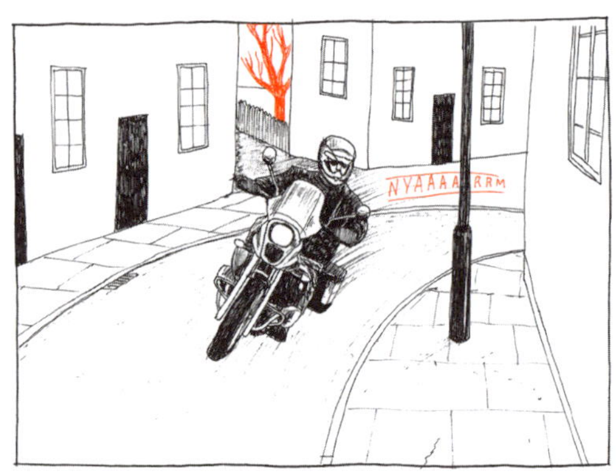

NYAAAARRM

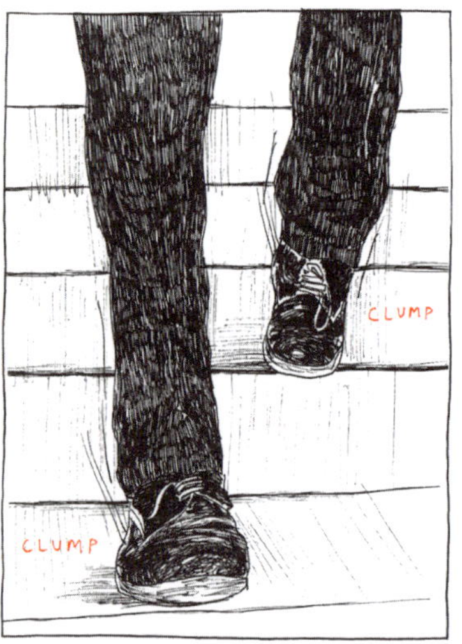

CLUMP
CLUMP

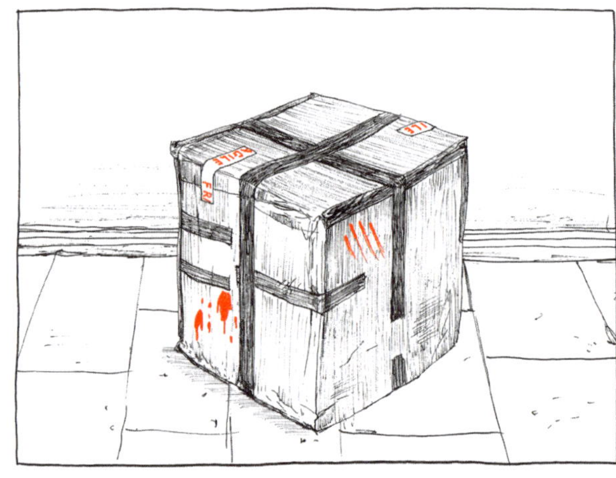

FRAGILE
FRAGILE

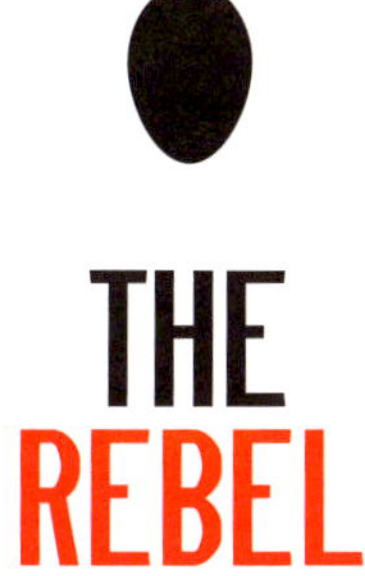

THE
REBEL

Richard Strange

The strange tale of Turk's head

I had always found Gavin Turk to be a wholly reliable, highly principled young man. A dome-headed fellow who knew perfectly the difference between smarm and charm, and who stayed very much on the right side of the great divide between the two. As far as I knew, his involvement with radical politics had always been theoretical and aesthetic rather than practical and dangerous — playful rather than impassioned.

¶ I was initially shocked, therefore, to receive a phone call from a stern-voiced female claiming to represent The Forces Of Reason, a small-membership, highly-volatile right-wing parliamentary splinter group.

¶ "Are you Richard Strange?" she snapped, the hint of a mid-European accent escaping through the rolled "r"s.

¶ I replied in the affirmative.

¶ "I will say this only once," she continued as if reading from a prepared text. "We are holding the artist Gavin Turk prisoner. He has been identified as an Enemy of the People. His art is decadent and elitist. To us his life is worthless and meaningless and when the revolution comes, his work will be seen as exemplary of all that was corrupt in the Old System. We shall behead him in one hour if a ransom is not paid. We require one million Euros to be paid into this Dresdner Bank account by money transfer immediately."

¶ She rattled off a sixteen digit, four-letter code and hung up.

¶ It was ludicrous, of course. The sort of joke that Gavin would play after a couple of drinks. One of his coterie of female admirers would make a call on his behalf while he savoured the drama of the moment, his distinctive cackling occasionally defying his best efforts to suppress it. Still imagining his amusement in his studio, I got myself a beer from the fridge, and tried to think of an amusing riposte. Instead, gazing at my computer screen, I got sucked into the erotic machinations of a sex chat room, and an hour and a half flew by as cyber-fantasists exchanged virtual wishlists.

¶ My enjoyment was interrupted by the sound of a motorcycle approaching; it seemed to stop outside my front door. I went down the three floors to investigate and heard its ear-splitting departure as I opened the door. Within seconds the bike was a memory, but on my doorstep the rider had deposited a brown cardboard box, neatly sealed with tape.

¶ The note read: "We warned you."

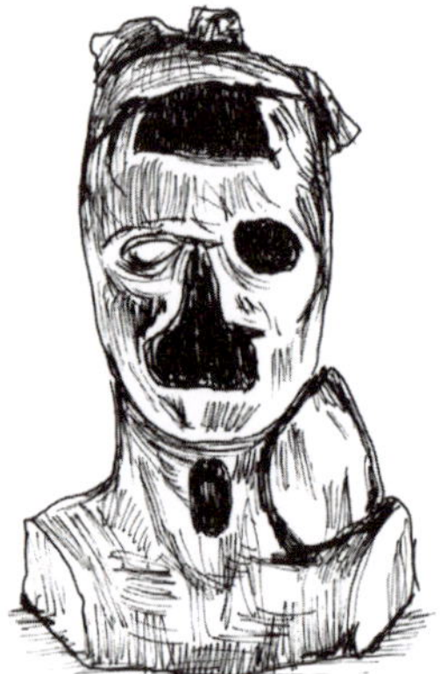
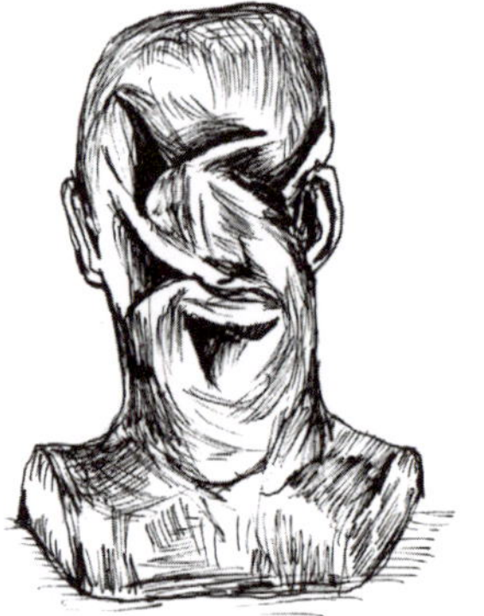
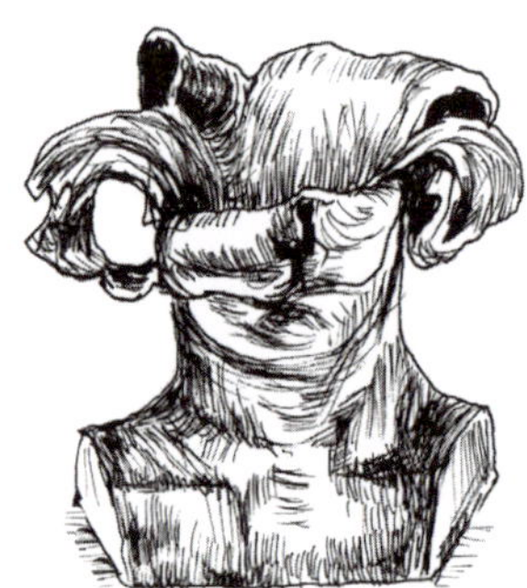

Gavin Turk from En Face 2010
Varnished clay, dimensions variable
Numerous clay busts of the artist altered at will by visitors to a studio "happening"

SEE ALSO:

THE MACHINE

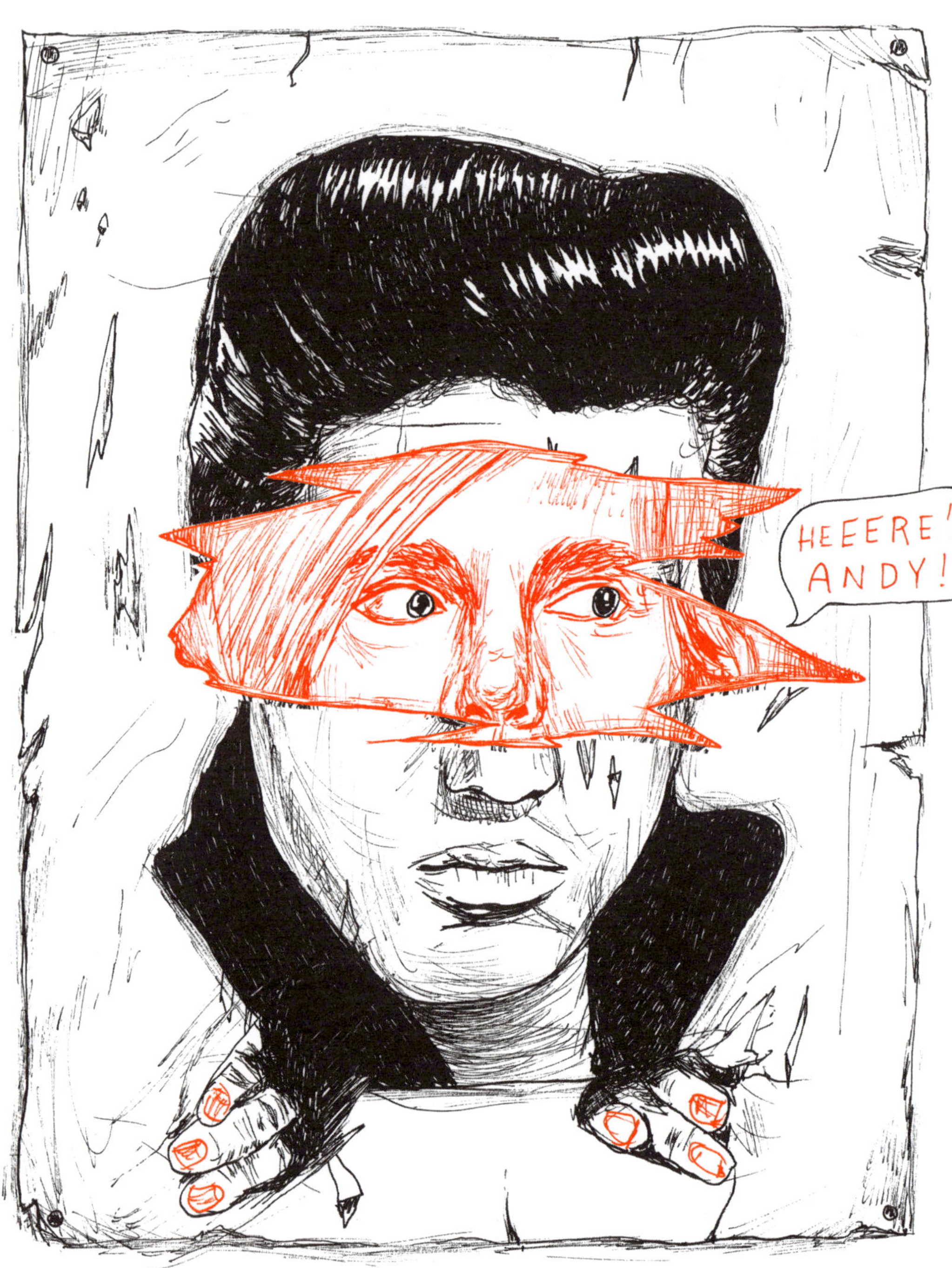

HEEERE'S
ANDY!

APPROPRIATION

Ossian Ward

Monumental masturbatory mirrors

Arguably, Andy Warhol realised his best ideas in 1962. He set up his studio in East 47th Street (later known as the Factory), he made his first silkscreens on canvas and he shot his first films, *Sleep* and *Kiss*. He painted his first *Campbell's Soup Cans*, his first *Death and Disaster* pictures, the first *Do it Yourself* paintings by numbers, as well as the first *Marilyn* and *Elvis* pieces.

¶ Using a postcard publicity shot for Elvis Presley's Hollywood western *Flaming Star*, Warhol enlarged and doubled the iconic image of the gun-slinging cowboy. The strange grey background might highlight Presley's portrayal of a half-white, half-American Indian character, or it might reference the silver screen. This was Presley's big movie break, considered one of his best acting performances by the critics and, as it happened, one of his last major roles. The film's soundtrack echoes with this irony:

> *"Ev'ry man has a flaming star,*
> *A flaming star over his shoulder,*
> *And when a man sees his flaming star,*
> *He knows his time, his time has come."*

¶ Warhol later multiplied and layered the bow-legged King up to eleven times on a single silkscreened canvas. "I like things to be exactly the same over and over again," he once said. His commercial background as a fashion illustrator made him acutely aware that his reproductions and copies of copies were toying with the notion of artistic originality. He was also canny enough to know that he wasn't doing himself out of a job but creating a new, infinitely reproducible model for making art.

¶ He was also speaking typically disingenuously about his love of mechanical reproduction. The repeated figures in works such as *Double Elvis* actually appear to dissolve slightly. It's as if Presley's image has been folded over and pressed down or re-printed with slightly less ink — as though the faded analogue was somehow less authentic than the original. Roland Barthes discussed Pop Art in similar terms, as a second-hand, plagiarised form of expression:

> *"Pop Art rediscovers the theme of the Double, of the Doppelgänger; this is a mythic theme…*
> *but in the productions of Pop Art it has lost all maleficent or moral power… the Double is*
> *a Copy, not a Shadow; beside, not behind; a flat, insignificant, hence irreligious, Double."*

¶ Warhol would disagree, of course, as he felt nothing short of religious devotion to most of the celebrities he portrayed. Tellingly, he wanted to be seen in the same terms; indeed his self-portraits became one of his longest running series. In some way, all the Warhols, Presleys, Jackies, Marilyns, Maos, Alis and Jaggers were monumental, masturbatory acts of wishful thinking on his behalf. He was making others in his image and *vice versa*.

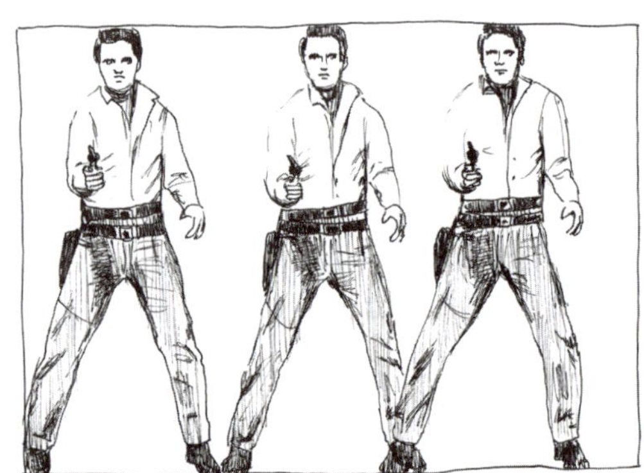

Andy Warhol Triple Elvis **1963**
Acrylic and silkscreen on canvas, 208.3 × 299.7 cm
Elvis Presley in gunslinger pose in triplicate

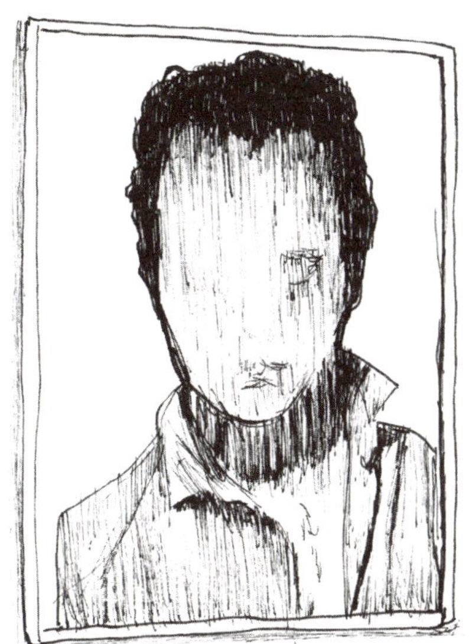

Gavin Turk   Dorian Grey   2010
Silkscreen and mirrored ink on glass with chemical dissolve effect, 60 × 45 cm
Print of the artist as Elvis

 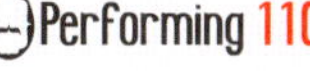 Celebrity 086   Performing 110

 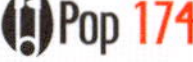 Pop 174

  069

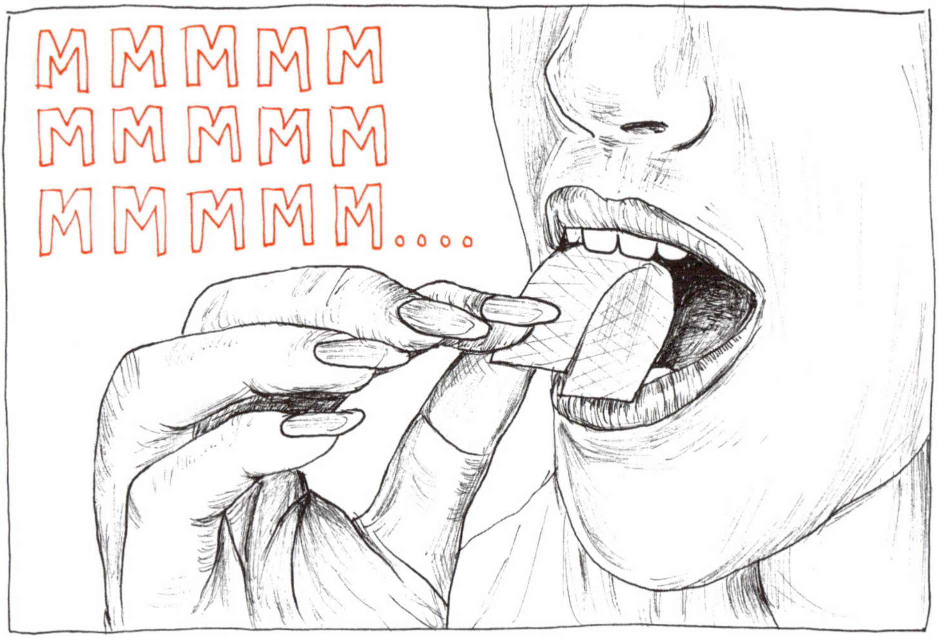

MMMMM
MMMMM
MMMMM....

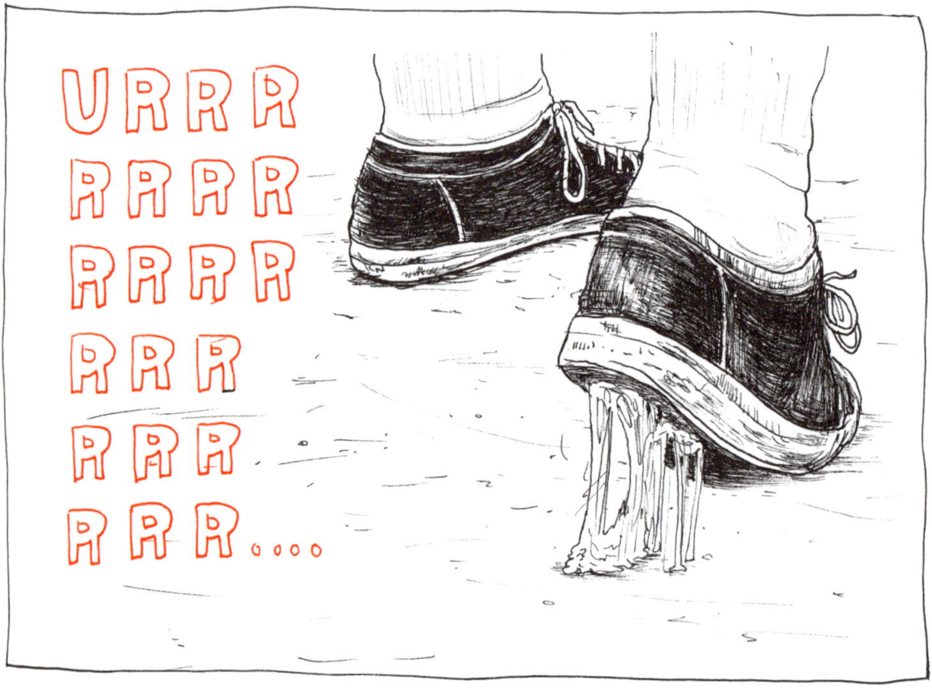

URRR
RRRR
RRRR
RRR
RRR
RRR....

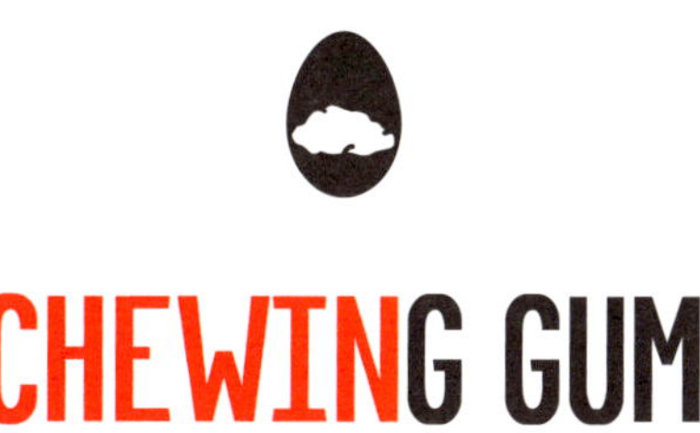

CHEWING GUM

Dixe Wills

Banned in Singapore

There is no real reason why chewing
gum in its modern form should exist at all.
At the time it was invented it served no purpose beyond
the satisfaction derived from purchasing and owning an object
(albeit briefly), and the pleasure to be had in exercising one's lower jaw.
Any functionality that is now ascribed to modern-day chewing gum has
been grafted onto it since its first appearance 120-odd years ago.
¶ Apparently cursed with a lot that plumbs the depths of banality — there
can be few fates less appealing than being placed in the mouth to be masti-
cated into tastelessness before being spat out — chewing gum has somehow
achieved iconic status. The frivolous nature of its existence, its record as one
of the first mass-produced products of the twentieth century, and its standing
as the epitome of inbuilt obsolescence, have assured its place as a
poster boy for the consumer culture of the developed world.

¶   It was not always thus. The first chewing gum was extremely practical in nature. Archaeologists working in Sweden and Finland have discovered pieces of birch bark tar imprinted with human tooth marks made over 5,000 years ago. Our Neolithic ancestors are believed to have chewed the medicinal tar as a way of warding off toothache and sore throats.

¶   Since then, there have been many resins, grasses and other plants made into some form of gum so that their healing properties might be released into the body. However, it was the American Indian habit of chomping on a resin derived from the sap of spruce trees that paved the way for chewing gum as we know it. Settlers in New England began to mimic the practice in such large numbers that one John Baker Curtis began to market strips of his home-made *Curtis's State of Maine Pure Spruce Gum* for two-a-penny in 1848. So successful was the product that he was able to build the world's first chewing gum factory four years later. However, for all its antiseptic qualities, spruce gum did not have an appealing flavour and Curtis soon moved over to the production of gum made from paraffin wax whose own less than thrilling taste was masked by the addition of vanilla or liquorice.

¶   The development of chewing gum might have stopped right there had it not been for a 1869 meeting in New York between exiled former president of Mexico, General Santa Anna — Davie Crockett's victor at the Alamo — and compulsive inventor Thomas Adams. Santa Anna was keen to raise money to fund an unlikely armed insurrection against the Mexican government by promoting chicle — a latex tapped from the *chicozapote* tree — as a cheap substitute for rubber in the manufacture of car tyres.

¶   After months of failed attempts to create a *chicle* rubber suitable for the motor industry, Adams and Santa Anna gave up on the enterprise. It was only when the former witnessed a young girl buying a pennyworth of paraffin wax gum (which the shop owner described to him as "pretty poor") that he hit upon the idea of experimenting with *chicle* as a chewing gum. He came up with a putty-like material that could be rolled into a ball in the mouth and, by February 1871, launched it in a single shop in New Jersey. It was tasteless and had no health-giving properties but it was recognisable as chewing gum and since it was better than the wax chewing gum on offer, people bought it. It was sold by the stick as *Adams New York No.1 — Snapping and Stretching*. A picture on the box showed City Hall, an instantly recognisable building in America's most exciting city. Chewing gum had taken the first step in its long

journey appropriating celebrity
as a marketing tool.

¶   Adams and other entrepreneurs
were soon adding flavours to the gum to make
it more appealing. Early experiments saw the
inclusion of sassafras root bark, liquorice (again) and
tolu, an ingredient then used in cough syrup, a move that
gave back to chewing gum its original medicinal function. Pliant
experts were soon on hand to recommend the use of gum to relieve thirst,
freshen breath, calm nerves, ease sore throats and quicken the appetite.

¶   Competition from other brands spurred Adams to advertise on huge billboards on Broadway, bringing gum into the public space and consciousness as
never before. William Wrigley went one better, erecting a line of 117 billboards along
a New Jersey railway track on his way to becoming the United States' largest purchaser
of advertising.

¶   Since chewing gum was a product essentially without a purpose it acted as a blank
page onto which manufacturers painted the fantasies of consumers. A brand called *Kis-Me*
played on the sexual appeal of placing something in one's mouth. William White, the first
man to market a mint gum, was also the first to make a link in the minds of potential customers between the chewing of gum and fame, fortune and success. In 1898 he began to get
his gum into the mouths of the beautiful people, even managing to foist a stick on the future
Edward VII whilst on a trip to England. The ploy was to be expanded later with the mass theft
by the industry of an idea used by bubble gum makers: the issuing of free cards depicting
movie stars, baseball players, national heroes and prominent millionaires.

¶   Gum first crossed the Atlantic in large quantities in World War One when more than
four million packs were sent to troops by the American Red Cross. However, it was the GIs
based in the UK in World War Two who turned Britons on to chewing gum in huge numbers.
It has since crossed the globe so that today there are over 500 companies making chewing
gum in 93 countries (though, famously, the substance is banned in hyper-neat and tidy
Singapore — those caught smuggling it in face a 12-month prison sentence). *Chicle*
is almost a thing of the past, however, since almost all chewing gum is now made
from synthetic substances such as vinyl resins or microcrystalline waxes.

¶   The relative cheapness and easy portability of gum has
contributed to its use becoming routine for large swathes
of the world's population. As a source of displacement
activity and instant gratification, it has

only the cigarette to rival it. However, despite chewing gum's acceptance into mainstream culture and its tooth-whitening, breath-freshening image, there's still something about it that suggests its home is on the wrong side of the tracks. Mix some surly body language with a slow deliberate chew and gum becomes a vehicle to express aggression and rebellion. This perhaps goes some way to explaining its popularity amongst successive generations of the young.

¶   More surprisingly, once used, chewing gum is capable of its own feats of artistic self-expression. Unlike its inert, uniform, pre-masticated state, used gum is uniquely shaped by the mouth of the individual who chewed it. Spurned by the user, it then takes its revenge wherever it is discarded, clinging limpet-like to pavements, park benches or Lonnie Donegan's bedpost. It punishes the species that created its all but meaningless existence by inflicting upon it its inherent ugliness. More potently still, it remains poised and ready, day and night, to stick to any careless shoe, hand or even backside with which it comes into contact. In 5,000 years, archaeologists will find it and will make a pronouncement about our era that we may not wish to hear.

Gavin Turk PK1 1998
Painted fibreglass, 65 × 60 × 25 cm
Oversized piece of chewing gum displayed squashed against the gallery wall

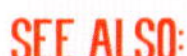

SEE ALSO:

 | 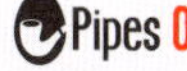Pipes **040**

 | 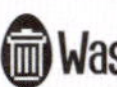Chip Trays and Chip Forks **130** 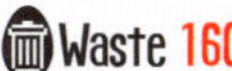Waste **160**

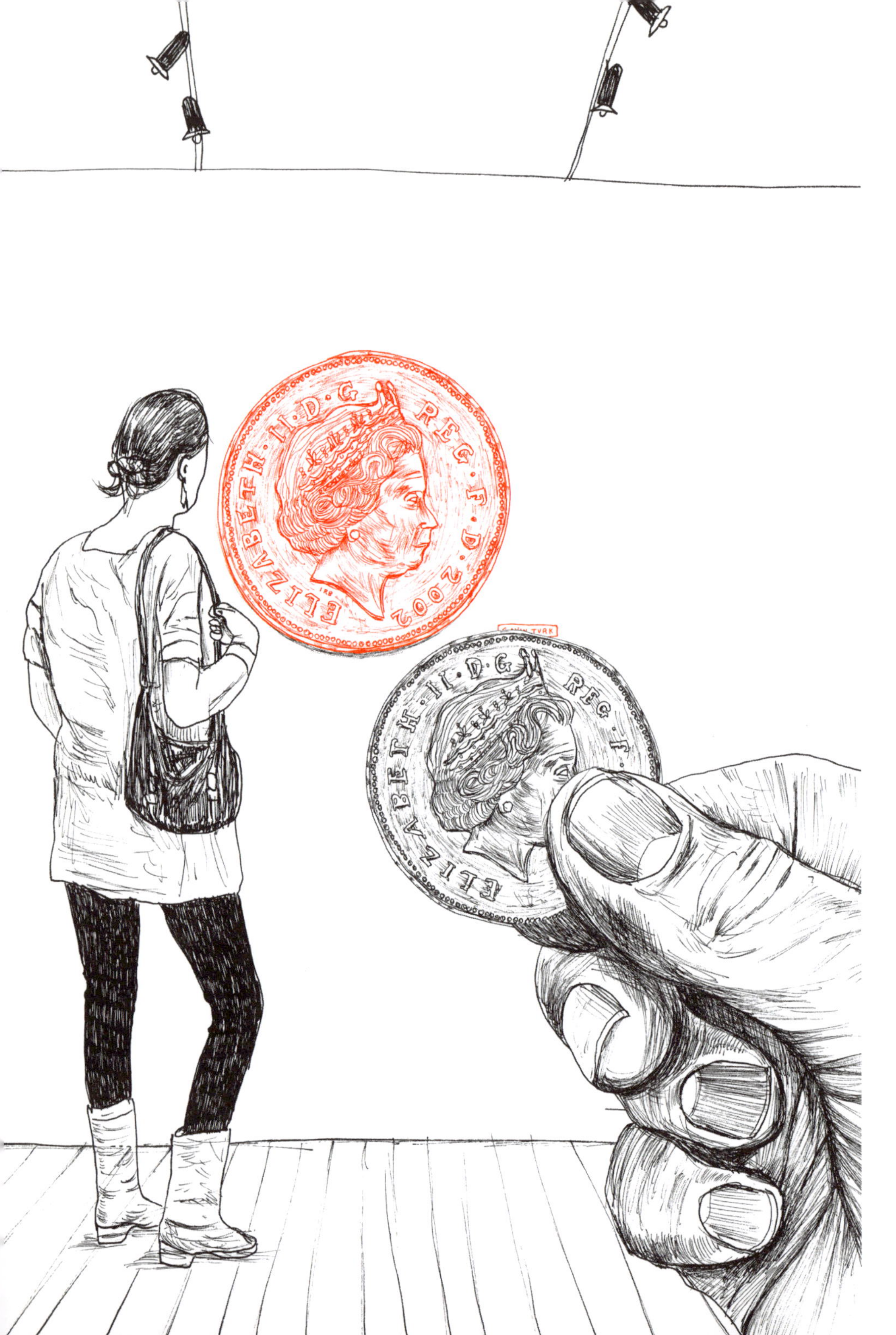

ELIZABETH·II·D·G REG·F·D 2002
ELIZABETH·II·D·G REG·F
TURK

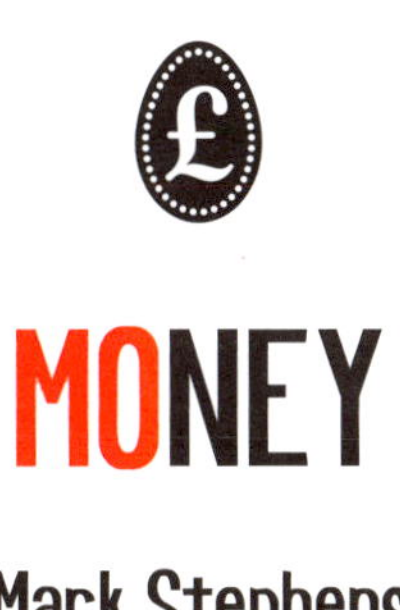

MONEY

Mark Stephens

Where there's brass there's art

Brass in pocket easily wears a hole in clothing. Beyond its day-to-day function as fiduciary ingot, we pay little heed to the value of coinage as works of art. Over decades artists have exchanged their work for cash, goods and services but rarely does an artist's work contain the conflict between the maker's aesthetic and the political symbols of the sovereign and state within which they work, more than it does in the art of money.

£ Artists who have confronted this dilemma include sculptor Christopher Ironside, commissioned by the Royal Mint to design the first decimal coinage. Later, with the introduction of the 2p piece, the Mint commissioned Ironside's friend and colleague William Gardiner to design a head for the Queen. This was later engraved by Ian Rank-Broadley whose initials appear on the coin under the Queen's neck — *yes, take one out and look at it.* He was the first sculptor to sign a coin of the realm.

$ Gavin Turk, with his brilliant freehand renditions of coins, draws attention to the challenges confronted by this group of artists. Turk makes us think about the dilemma between the economic, the aesthetic and the state. We question whether it is the quality of the work, or whether it is the symbols of the state depicted by the artist, or the value of the art work itself that causes society to mutually accept and ascribe a notional economic value to the coin.

¥ The coin thus becomes a quintessential distillation of the state's power-relationship with art and artists. It is the ultimate statement of non-value, brass value if you will, by the state as to the artist's place in culture. Gavin Turk resolves this economic and cultural under-valuing of art by exhibiting his work in galleries and selling it for more than the state sells its versions.

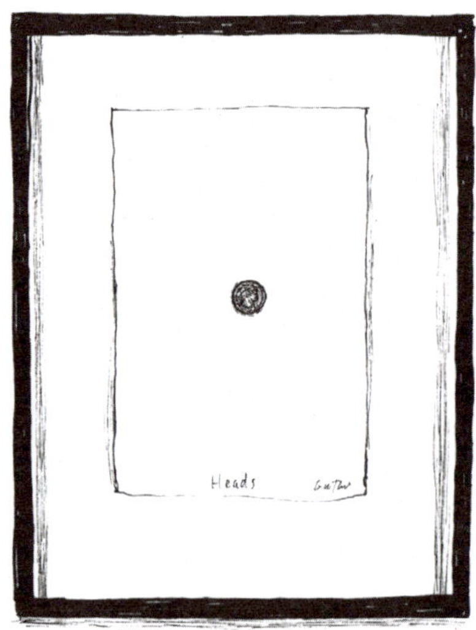

Gavin Turk Heads 2002
Pencil on paper, 20 × 16 cm
Rubbing of a British 2p piece

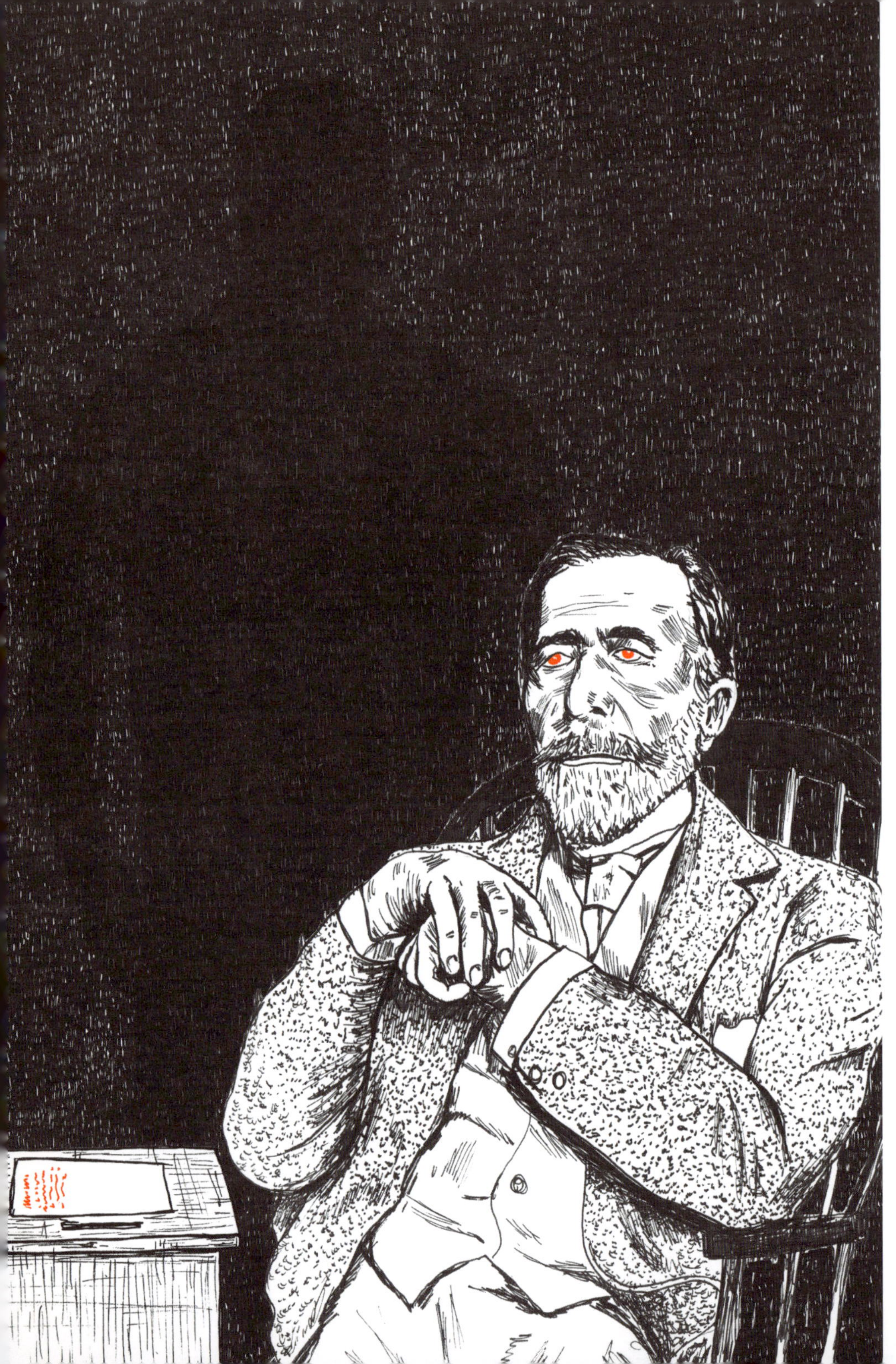

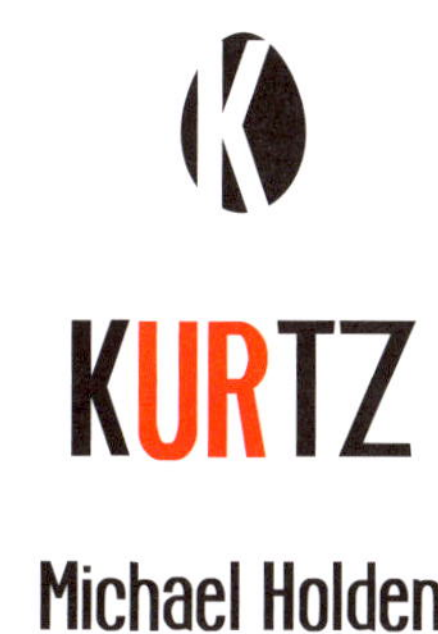

KURTZ

Michael Holden

The loose cannon that keeps on firing

One might imagine that Joseph Conrad **typed the character of Mr Kurtz** at the back end of the 1800's with no notion that his equatorial **phantom, the diseased and mythic antagonist** of what would become his best known book, would **not only survive but thrive as one** of the great enigmatic figures of all time. But I like to think he **knew what he was doing;** Conrad had seen enough of human nature and colonialism to understand **precisely how** our species' instincts would unfold and repeat **themselves over the coming** century. From that knowledge he forged a character **whose fall from optimism into fevered anarchy would** survive a hundred years of **academic study** — even the great mutating lens of Hollywood — and continue to beguile. He **knew that we lived in fear of Kurtz,** within us and without us, long before his book was begun.

¶ For those without the inclination to navigate the pages of Conrad's *Heart Of Darkness*, the abiding image of **Kurtz** will be Marlon Brando in *Apocalypse Now*: skulking in the shadows (to hide his obesity rather than from cinematic intention), transported from Conrad's Congo to Coppola's Vietnam, still muttering the same last line — "the horror" — in the face of a civilising mission gone wrong. But while the movie begins and ends in Asia, the book opens on the Thames estuary and the narrator, Marlow, invokes Drake, the Romans and anyone else who ever sailed past the Essex marshes in pursuit of foreign goals. It is a story rooted from its outset in antiquity, greed and the persistence of pain.

¶ As the sun sets over England, Marlow tells his shipmates the tale of his voyage along the Congo as a kind of ghost story, one that led him to the spectre of the man his mission set out to relieve and concludes in literal and figurative darkness. Marlow explains how he went to Africa to work for "the company" whose colonial endeavours seem to represent the process of civilisation itself, a process Conrad paints as futile and insane. Everything Marlow sees points toward chaos. An armoured gunboat fires artillery into the jungle at invisible enemies; a man tries to extinguish a fire with a hole in his bucket; everybody lies, everybody gets sick. Attempts to tame the jungle with bureaucracy for profit drives the company men to murder, "When one has to make correct entries, one comes to hate these savages, hate them to death". But at the end of the river waits the rumour of a man who sees things differently: **Kurtz. Kurtz** is "a prodigy", "an emissary of pity, science and progress".

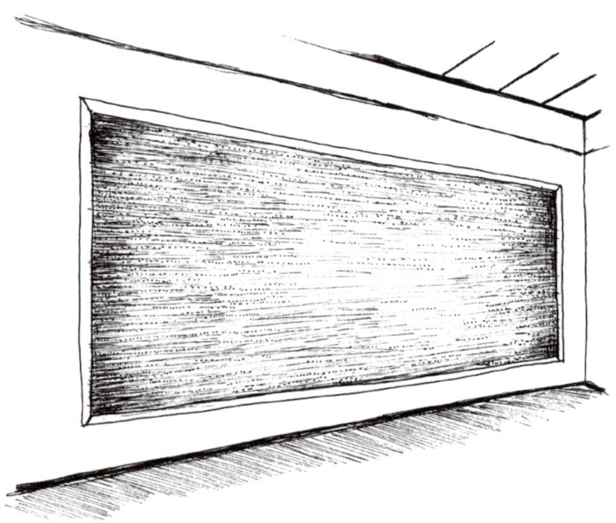

Fiona Banner   Apocalypse Now   1997
Pencil on paper, 274 × 660 cm
A handwritten description of Coppola's film in the shape of a cinema frame

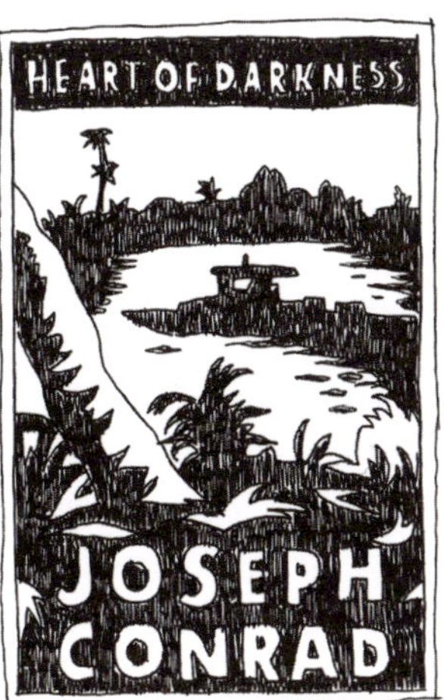

Most importantly, **Kurtz** gets results for the company, "he had stolen more ivory than all the agents put together". Marlow, a good guy but a pragmatist, is surprised to discover that Kurtz had set out "with **moral ideas of some sort" and wonders** what this Renaissance figure could have done that **the company might** want stopped?

¶ In the end, Marlow doesn't get to see the enigma in action but he gets an eyeful of the aftermath. **Kurtz's station has** dissolved into **anarchy; decorated with** severed human heads, great bales of ivory are **patrolled by a native army, loyal to the ailing Kurtz who seems to** have gone insane. **Having threatened to kill Kurtz**, it is Marlow who nurses and protects him from the company, **"that imbecile crowd", who seek only to** extinguish the man, assimilate his profits and press on.

¶ Marlow **assures his audience that Kurtz** was a "**gifted creature, and that of all** his gifts the one that **stood out pre-eminently, that carried with it a sense of real presence**, was his ability to talk". By the time we meet **him, though, this shattered optimist**, run wild and destroyed by experience, has nothing left to **say. It is a Russian adventurer** who gives Marlow the details of Kurtz in his prime before he, too, abandons **the scene. He** speaks of a reader of poetry, a painter, a visionary **who had tamed the wilderness, at least for a** moment, until it bit back like a **snake un-charmed. As he watches Kurtz** die, Marlow takes possession of his most telling artifact, a **report written for "The International Society For The** Suppression Of Savage Customs". Seventeen pages **long, the document is all positive** prognoses for the company project — "we can exert a power **for good practically** unbounded" — with insights set out in neat handwriting until, at a later date, its author scrawls across it his ultimate conclusion: "exterminate all the brutes".

¶ "His mind was clear," says Marlow, "but his soul was mad"; yet he offers a less lyrical analysis as well. He suggests that Kurtz's intellect became subordinate to his greed, that he suffered from "images of wealth and fame revolving obsequiously round his unextinguishable gift of noble and lofty expression". Although that might also be Conrad discussing his own dilemmas as a writer, it's still a valid point. For all his abilities and aspirations, Kurtz is just another dictator undone. He might be a resonant character but in the end Kurtz is a symptom, an example of what can and will go wrong, product of an environment that exceeds the imaginations of those who try to tame it. The jungle itself, and what it represents are the real enigmas of the story as it calls the characters "to the profound darkness of its heart". Conrad's tale hints at a malign wisdom at the core of life that mocks the living. Marlow even berates his audience when he thinks they're missing the point — "the inner truth is hidden... I felt often its mysterious stillness watching me at my monkey tricks, just as it watches you".

¶ Kurtz as colonial metaphor still has resonance; potentially Kurtzian figures in the American military — people who spoke the language, grasped the culture, gathered popular support before it all went wrong — were overlooked, replaced and overruled by feral bureaucrats from back home. This is Kurtz's fate in the end as well. The company men dismiss his ivory as inferior product and, with a gift for euphemism any modern speechwriter would recognise, give their assessment that "the methods are unsound". Invading countries means never having to say you're sorry, if you're quick enough to blame and replace the people who prepared the ground; the beat goes on.

¶ You might find comparison, too, in the demise of frontline capitalism, see Kurtz as a mad accountant or hedge funder surrounded by the wreckage of his fantasy, apologised for by the same legislators who encouraged him. We will all know better next time, perhaps. Except, as Conrad continues to inform us, we probably won't.

¶ In an ending that could stand alone as a masterclass in modern fiction, Marlow tells how he had taken Kurtz's widow a painting he had entrusted to him. When she asks for her husband's last words, he hides the truth — "the horror, the horror" — and tells her instead, "The last word he pronounced was your name." While one character at least is spared acquaintance with the heart of Kurtz's darkness, more than a century since its completion we cannot read the book or watch the news and say the same.

IT'S NOT YOU, IT'S ME

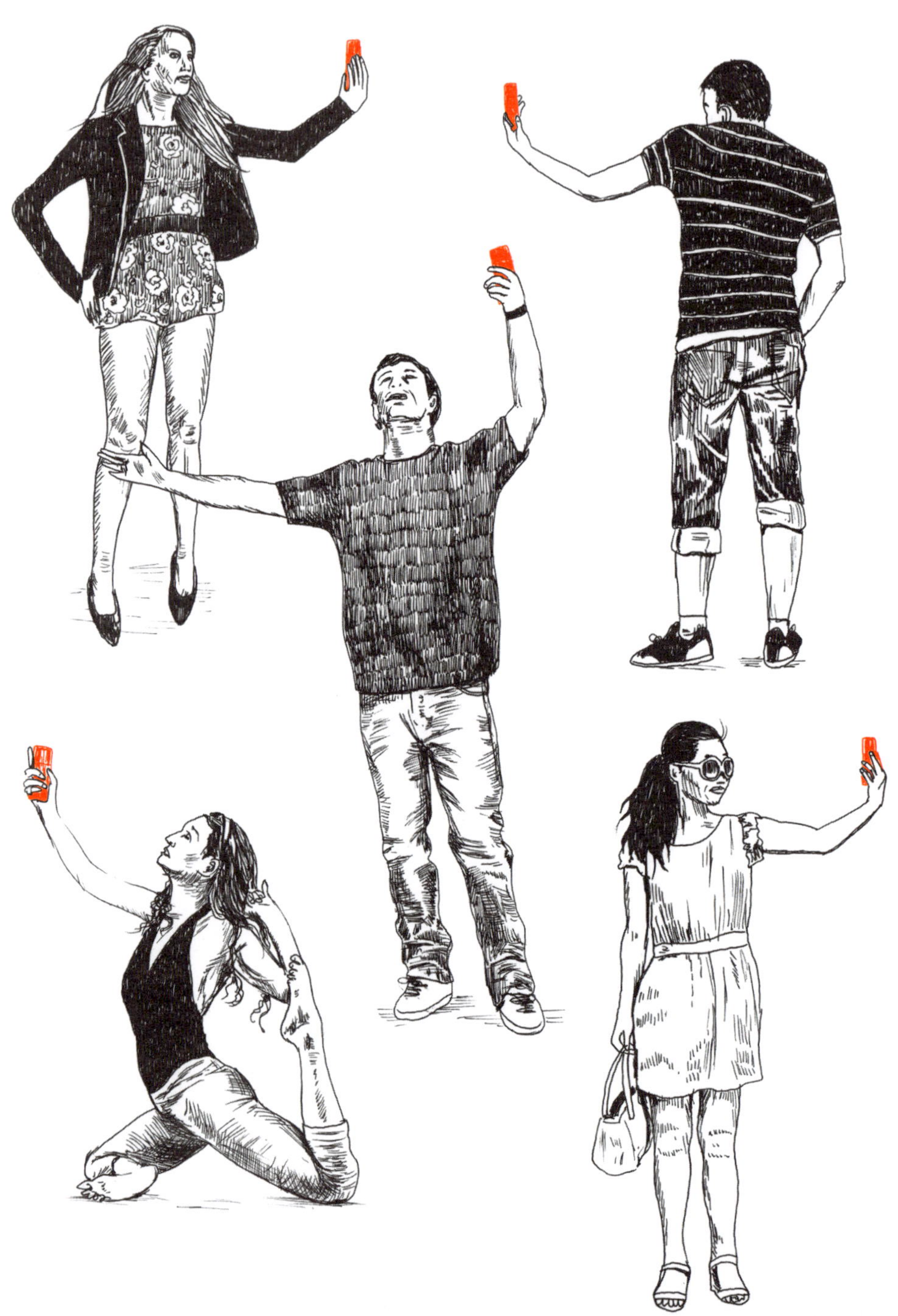

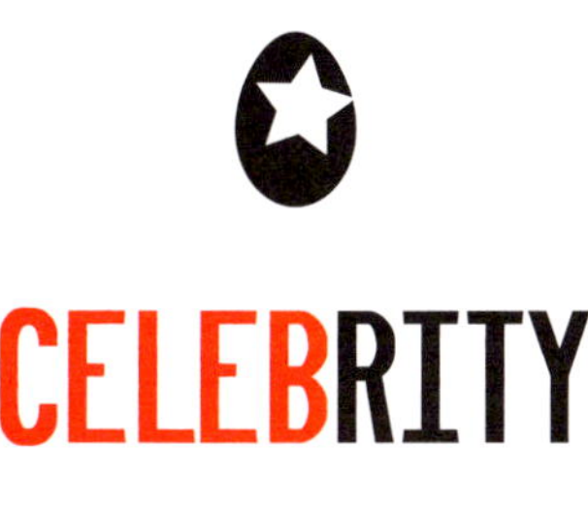

CELEBRITY

Paul Flynn

Fame for all and all for fame

In the immediate wake of 9/11, *Daily Mirror* editor Piers Morgan hastily declared an end to Celebrity Culture. His polemical wager centred on the dawn of a new age of serious thinking. It cut directly against the grain of tabloid thinking and effectively signed his own newspaper death-knell, as *The Mirror*'s sales fell into freefall.

! Seven years after declaring its end, with an irony arch enough to drive a double-decker bus under, Piers Morgan was a central figure in Britain's Celebrity Culture, making his living mostly as a judge on its favourite medium, reality TV, and interviewing celebrities for a behind-the-curtains-of-Oz interview show. He consolidated his niche with requisite spray tan and teeth whitening. Did his brassy sound bite, so potent in the eye of international tragedy, mean nothing after all?

!   9/11 was its own strange arbiter of Celebrity Culture, perhaps even its apex as it endeavoured to keep a moral temperature between good and bad. As it twisted through the global psyche, it bestowed its arbitrary 15 minutes with slapdash abandon, confirming temporary celebrity status on previously unfound icons. The obsession was not about to go down in the aftermath of the fall of the Twin Towers. Celebrity had already acquired too much personal significance for a nation that had bought into the idea of the self as brand. It had begun developing its own serious agenda, becoming at once synonymous with the idea of personal identity and community empathy.

!   The cult of the famous satisfies a deeper need for a narrative we can all share, a story in which reward for the good and judgement for the bad becomes modern folklore. In this way, stories of the most public beacons of our age frame the public moral dialogue. They are stories of redemption and absolution, satisfying age-old hopes that justice will be done, the good guy will get the girl and the world will, eventually, be saved. Those living in the book-marks between reality and celebrity have become living works of art. We can point at them and adjudicate ourselves against them.

!   One of the fun aspects of a a fetishism which embraces not just the extraordinary, but the ordinary in extraordinary circumstances, is that we can measure how we might behave in a similar predicament. Celebrity Culture replaces the fairy tale as the modern day fabu-lisation of personal narratives. Now there's "Fame for Everyone" and a democratisation of celebrity has taken place. The self has become the centre and mass communication fulfils the grand Warholian prophesy to the number and letter. Fame is no longer about People Like Them, it's about People Like Us. Public recognition is about personal recognition. If there is an element of narcissism in not wanting celebrities to be elevated and choosing to make them just like us, it is counterbalanced by the needling reality that it presents hope for everyone — and who doesn't want that?

!   Celebrity Culture delivers its own, hard-edged appeal. A collective game of good versus evil has emerged within it. In an age of transparency, where every aspect of the art of living has its price, silence is the only tool left to keep a myth intact, to protect the fantasy of living a perfect life. Is this any worse than fairy tales of old in presenting unreal-istic ideals? The public takes the role of priest in the confessional. No matter how much a celebrity chooses to control their own myth, no matter how much they shroud it in mystery or un-knave themselves for public consumption, the judgement is left to the moral hordes. The star system is a filter, a storytelling exercise, a picture book to turn the pages of and draw conclusions about the deep seated sense of right and wrong, good and bad, that has always been passed from generation to generation.

!   With the advent of social media, Fame-for-Everyone has become a new reality. The

THIS IS NOT A BOOK ABOUT GAVIN TURK

promise of living a self-edited life, to share with friends, admirers, enemies and strangers, conjoins celebrity and reality from the home outwards. Previously, fame was beamed into the house through former key screen, the television. Now it is beamed out through the main screen: the computer.

! The first social media at least concocted some pretence of social-ism — Friendster, Bebo, MySpace, Facebook. Twitter represented an incremental but crucial downshift; the movement from accruing "friends" to "followers" shot the pretence of friendship dead. Once you start "following" someone, expectation is raised. It incubates thin hierarchies, cronyism, certainty and consensus, which in turn lights the touch-paper of anger. Of course, this would end up in a grotesque public bun-fight between people who have way more in common than they might think, most notably the need to be noticed. This new high ground of moral arbitration is not projected onto celebrity, it is unleashed from within.

! Because of its seductively pied piper set-up, Twitter has become quietly embroiled in the Fame-for-Everyone dialogue that has consumed us, heightened by a thirst for first-person narratives drawn from direct experience. This represents a further shift from a societal search for a god outside of ourselves, to the search for a god within.

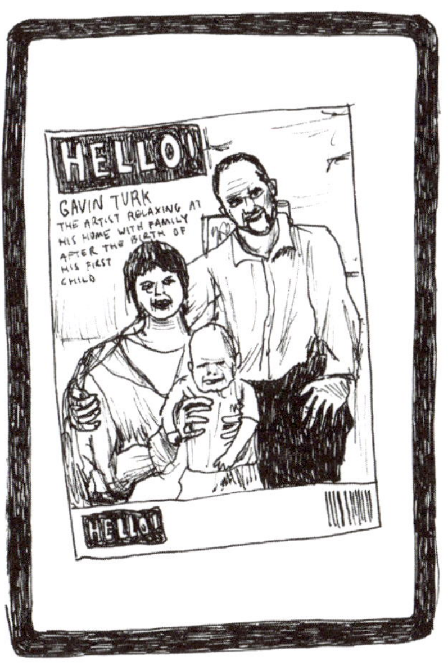

Gavin Turk *Identity Crisis* **1994**
Silkscreen ink on paper in lightbox, 172 × 112 cm
Pastiche of a celebrity magazine cover showing the artist's family

! The free movement of information and opinion online is one of the most amazing global shifts in my lifetime. It has emerged in direct counterpoint to government agencies that sought to protect us, protecting big business and building a spurious argument we'll-all-do-well-out-of-that-in-the-end.

! Yet no-one yet comes out of the self-edited Fame-for-Everyone model of Twitter very well. The power balance between leader (implied) and follower (named) incubates a unique malcontent previously experienced only by the famous-famous, with teams of skilled people around them to weather the storms of public love and hate. The open display of one's personal popularity in your declamatory address at the top of a feed has turned Twitter into *Animal Farm*, wherein all animals are equal but some are more equal than others. Sunday supplement columnists are awkwardly advantaged over those who come without a platform. It is a modern lunatic asylum built on pernicious power play.

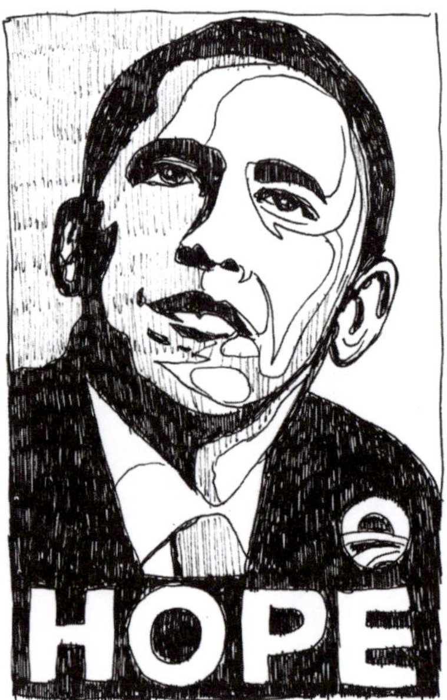

Shepard Fairey Hope **2011**
Silkscreen, 36 × 24 cm
Portrait of Barack Obama in the style of André the Giant

!   Pinning your sails to 140 character opinions, made in the heat of a moment could only ever lead to a snail trail of regret. You can't ask other people to like you when you don't know whether you like yourself or your life. Self-editing is a rigorous new social discipline that no-one has quite mastered.

!   Oh, maybe one. Piers Morgan traded his post on a reality show for an auspicious anchor's post at CNN at just the moment the trade off between reality and celebrity started its shift into the home, putting him back at the vanguard of hard news, the place he always claimed he wanted to be. At the time of writing, he has millions of followers on Twitter and a picture at the top of his page showing him interviewing Snoop Dogg. His avatar is sold with the caption: "One day you're cock of the walk, next you're a feather duster".

!   And so it goes.

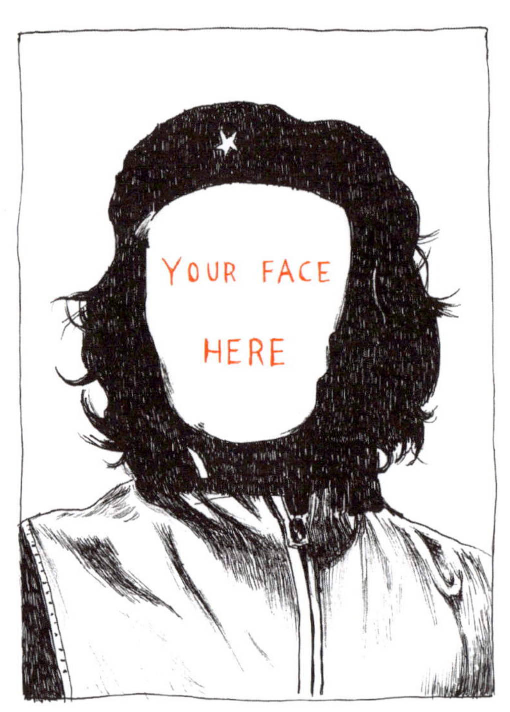

YOUR FACE
HERE

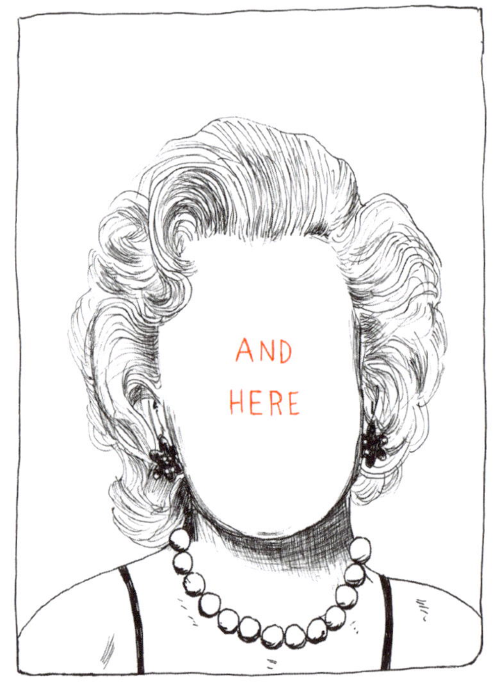

AND
HERE

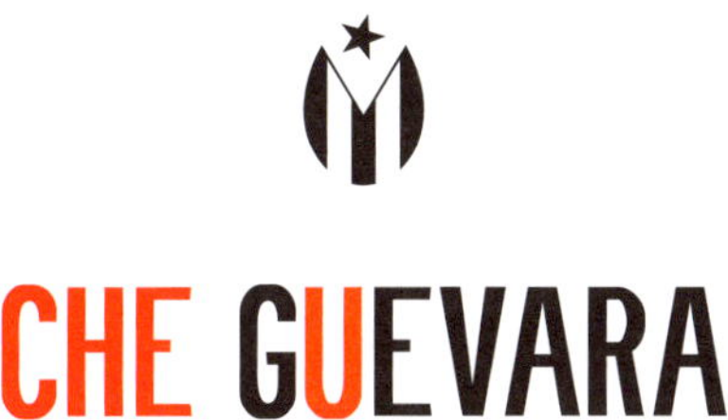

CHE GUEVARA

Ben Cranfield

Revolution for sale

In the *TIME* magazine cover article of August 1960, Ernesto "Che" Guevara was described as the "brain" behind Castro's Cuba. While Castro was the "heart, soul, voice and bearded visage", his brother Raul was the "fist that holds the revolution's dagger", and Ernesto took control of the country's ideological and fiscal policies — albeit in a particularly maverick way.

★ Recent artistic projects, not to mention notable biographies, have sought to reinstate the brain behind the floating iconic face, but it may still seem peculiar to hear Che described first and foremost as the brain, with Castro as the visage. The *TIME* cover jars with contemporary imagination. The Che pictured in realistic shades and hues is not the Che of Alberto "Korda" Diaz's ubiquitous photograph that we know — the statuesque Che, staring enigmatically into the distance, forever young, melting into the mane of his hair and beard, wearing them as crown of thorns or halo. We don't know him smiling, engaged and ruggedly lined.

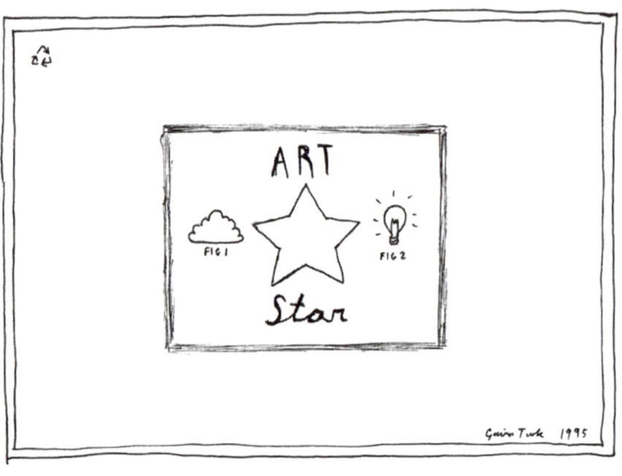

Gavin Turk Art Star 1995
Pencil on paper, 21 × 29.7 cm
Drawing of a vacuum-formed multiple for *Kamoke Football* exhibition in Germany

★ *TIME*, however, did prefigure the objectifying of Che, with all the attendant problems for historical truth, by remarking that he is "the most fascinating and the most dangerous of the triumvirate" and that his smile has a power that "women find devastating". In the same issue, there is a piece on Marilyn Monroe as she prepared for *The Misfits*, directed by her husband Arthur Miller. Poignantly pointing to cracks appearing in Monroe's façade, she is painted as a neurotic figure who reflects the character she is playing, Roslyn, as a "fractured, manhandled woman". Monroe was found dead almost exactly two years later; *The Misfits* was her last film.

★ "Che Guevara was the Marilyn Monroe of Marxism, an empty receptacle for fantasy," writes Jonathan Jones in his review of Gavin Turk's 2001 post-Beuysian teach-in, *The Che Gavara Story*. This seems an easy association, one we can accept without flinching. Yes, Hollywood's tragic heroine of Che's hated America and Cuba's martyred hero seem to be part of the same breath — yet it is only their emptiness which is the same. It is the remarkable similarity of their magnitude as ciphers which makes this connection so easy. Beyond this they are, of course, opposites. It is one thing that makes the Marilyn/Che comparison so natural and that is their reduction to a single image: Warhol's image.

★ In the course of *The Che Gavara Story*, Jones reports how the question was raised as to why Warhol never did "depict Che". Jones recalls that, in fact, Warhol had depicted Che in his film *The Life of Juanita Castro* (1965), but not as the Che of the multicoloured Warholian silhouette we all know. Trisha Ziff has tried to establish the origin of the famous "faked" Warhol Che and traces authorship of the image to former Warhol assistant and star of many a Warhol iconic portrait himself, Gerard Malanga.

★ Of course, any notion of authorship in Warhol's silkscreens is ambiguous and

debatable. Warhol allegedly claimed the series as his own after Malanga's appeal for help following the discovery of the forgery. We may wonder why Warhol had not produced an iconic image of Che himself. As Jones' opening assertion suggests, it would appear to have been an obvious choice. Perhaps Che had not captured Warhol's imagination. As the campery of *Juanita Castro* would suggest, Che did not possess the compellingly deep one-dimensionality that Warhol usually sought, or perhaps he simply hadn't got around to it before the forgery and other versions appeared. Forgery or no forgery, Warhol had already made an image of Che; all images on t-shirts, the icon of the Korda photograph, the Jim Fitzpatrick posters, the "devastating" Hollywood smile — all of them could be said to be Warhol's in a crucial way.

★   When Jim Fitzpatrick made possibly the most famous silhouette of Che using Korda's *Guerrillero Heroico* in 1967, there was no mistaking the presence of Warhol. Warhol as signifier for repetitious celebrity, as an embodiment of one-dimensional contemporary iconography, came before and after the flowing of Fitzpatrick's icon into contemporary consciousness. Although those with a stake in the art market might dispute it, Warhol's signature was not a moment of artistic authoring, but a statement about celebrity and value itself. The content of the signature, as the image of Che or Monroe repeated, existed in the act of repetition itself rather than in its particular signification. The proliferation of a Warhol image enacted its death with the morbidity that occurs with the uncanny fascination of recall and distancing. The attention to the particular and the generic that exists within a Warhol series, is akin to that which makes the familiar strange, like a word or name repeated without context until the tongue becomes awkward with the sound. The morose nature of repetition leads, arguably, to

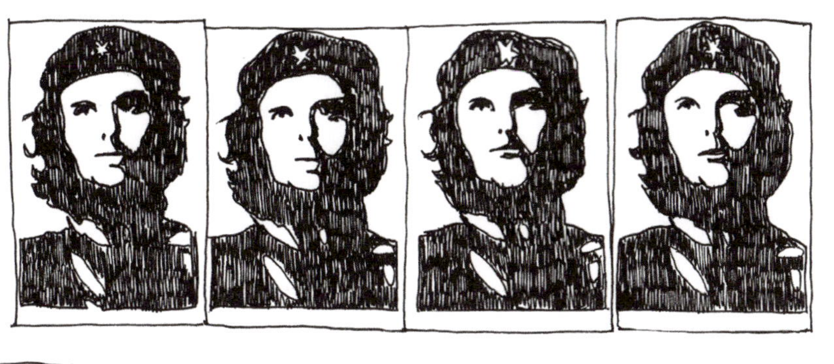

Gavin Turk   Che Gavara   1999
Silkscreen on paper, 305 × 1,220 cm
The artist as Che Guevara repeated four times in the style of an Andy Warhol screenprint

the limit event of Warhol's *Death in America* series. Hal Foster asserts, in his essay titled after the series, that —

"Somehow in these repetitions, then, several contradictory things occur at the same time: a waning away of traumatic significance and an opening out to it, a defending against traumatic affect and a producing of it."

★   In the waning of the traumatic, Foster is referring to Warhol's own remarks about the diminishing effect of the "gruesome" when viewed "over and over again". However, Foster also perceives these sites of repetitious unpleasantness to be instances of "traumatic realism" — a re-enactment of the death depicted in the horror of the semelfactive aspect of seeing again and again. Such a trauma is reminiscent of the film ending of Graham Greene's *Brighton Rock* in which Rose goes to play a recording of Pinky's voice to console her after his

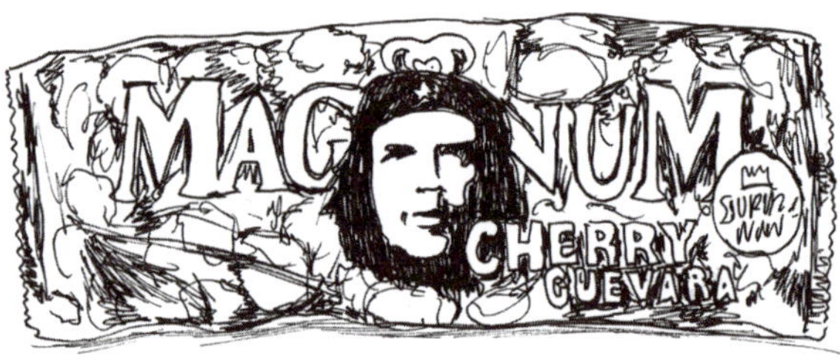

Ice cream wrapper

death, only to hear the record hit a scratch and repeatedly jump with static rupture, saying "I love you". The protagonists of Warhol's portraits become forever frozen in a permanently repeated death, with the question of salvation or damnation deferred. Similarly, the viewer of *Brighton Rock* is forced to relive a trauma both numbed and accentuated by the dramatic irony of the situation; we know that if the record were to play in full, Rose would not hear Pinky say how much he loves her but would instead hear him tell her, "I hate you, you little slut". The initial horror of the dramatic realisation as the record is played and the abrupt relief of the jumping needle, both softens the feared finality of the death of illusion and at the same time deepens the trauma by continually reminding us of the emptiness behind the words embedded in Rose's mind.

★   The banality of Warhol's repetitive and softened "Hollywood" endings are in themselves traumatic instances. A singular image of Monroe as colourful clown could have been seen as a celebration or at least a monument to mourn; multiple Monroes, proliferating

forever more at grotesque rate of speed, become a yawning, sorrowful emptiness — a morose stuck record.

★   As Hannah Charlston observes in her introduction to the catalogue for the V&A exhibition *Che Guevara: Revolutionary and Icon* (2006), "The story of the Che image is in part the story of the growth of visual literacy".Whether or not Che was a good man or a bad one, a hero or a psychopath, the trauma which is repeated in the proliferation of the image through a continual re-ordering of the linguistic, denoted and connoted, as Barthes might suggest, results in a deadening loss of aura and history. The multiple instances of Che's reworking in poster form, by activists on all sides — admen, artists, designers — becomes an essay in contemporary textual fracturing. Following on from Barthes, the re-telling of Che as image may indeed be best understood as a symptom of our visual literacy, our ability to digest and read all as textual mirror.

★   Discussing Che as icon is becoming as clichéd as the image itself. If one wants to discuss the rabid force of commercialisation, the ubiquity of celebrity, the reduction of the revolutionary spirit to image, then "Che", via Korda, via Fitzpatrick, via Warhol, is too exemplary to ignore. As we attempt to move forward heroically, romantically, pathetically, tragically, comically, we may find ourselves picturing ourselves as Guevara, in Elvis stance, through Warhol, as an act of trauma magnified; three one-dimensionalities compounding our own.

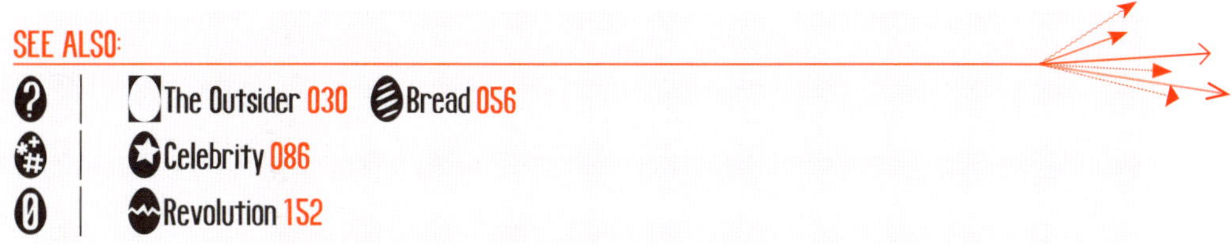

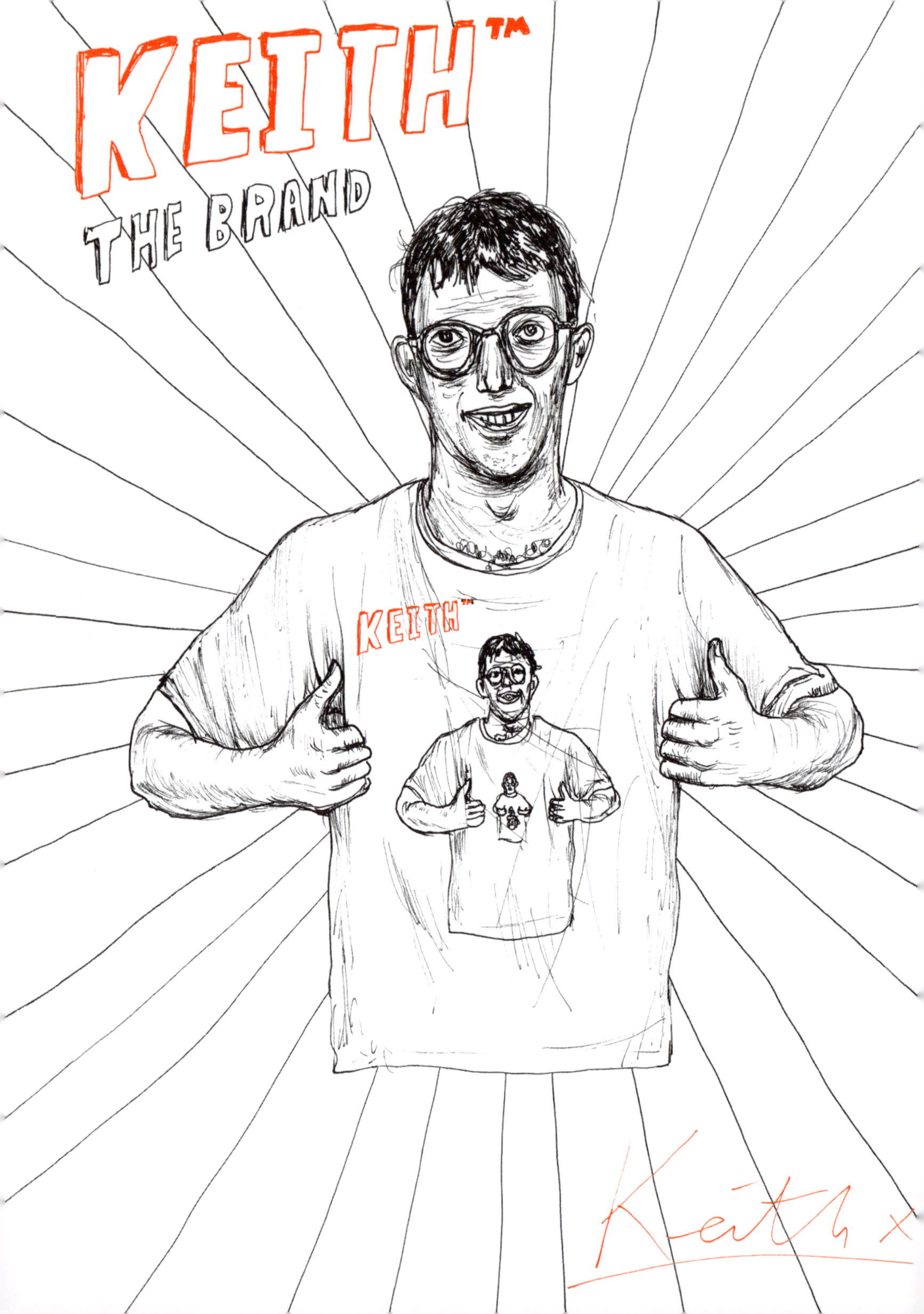

KEITH ™
THE BRAND
KEITH ™
Keith x

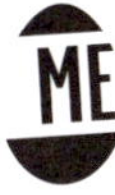

COMMODITY NARCISSISM

Alnoor Ladha

Love me, love my product

"Modern man has transformed himself into a commodity; he experiences his life energy as an investment with which he should make the highest profit, considering his position and the situation on the personality market. He is alienated from himself, from his fellow men and from nature."

Erich Fromm, *The Art of Loving*

The logic of capitalism necessitates that we constantly buy more things in order to perpetuate growth. Never mind who benefits from that growth or even what we are measuring with abstract notions like GDP; consumption is sacrosanct. The soft ideology behind this consumption is materialism: the simple assertion at the heart of the economic system is that "you are what you own". Happiness is said to depend on this material acquisition. It determines everything from our status in society, to what type of partner we attract, to what we decide to do with our lives in the first place.

©   This is not a conspiracy theory. There are no evil bearded men plotting your commodification; it is simply generative. This flows from rules of self-interest and profit maximisation as a logical outcome of the capitalist system itself. The value of everything is eventually weighed by its ability to generate financial profit — including you.

® To facilitate our commodification, we are inundated with frameworks for identity management, self-help advice, strategies to increase our "followship", and the language of personal branding. The very concept of success in the modern era has become inextricably dependent on the image we create and project of ourselves.

™ What Marx called commodity fetishism in regard to our insatiable consumption, has morphed into commodity narcissism — our eager willingness to become the final transaction in our own self-liquidation. We edit and shape our identities to suit the image we project to our Facebook friends and Twitter followers. The language of brand identity is part of our common vernacular, a key criterion by which we evaluate others in our social network and the supreme arbiter of worthiness. Regardless of inclination or occupation, our collective merit system awards on the basis of fabricated personas rather than authentic identity.

© A number of myths have arisen to justify and celebrate our commodification as a rational and pragmatic response to a fast-paced, attention-scarce, mediated world. We must face these aberrations head on.

MYTH ONE: We are all brands

This first assumption is the most perilous. Defining our individual personalities, complexities, contradictions and nuances in the simplistic language of branding is a distortion of our identities. Brands are built top-down, designed to reduce complexity to shorthand aspirations, decided by brand managers and corporate technocrats, formalised in boardrooms and on ad agency sofas over ethically sourced cappuccinos and over-priced catering.

® Authentic and genuine personalities are, by contrast, created bottom-up. We are products of our unique histories, experiences, relationships, geographies, circumstances, genetics and evolving world-views. Our complexity grows with our development and we become subtler, less reductive and egotistical the more self-aware we become — the exactly opposite qualities of a traditional brand. In essence, we lose the organic nature of our identity when we invert the natural order of how we come to be.

™ A generation has internalised lessons of personality branding and are rigorously applying them to "identity incubators" like Facebook. They are thinking about, manipulating, and editing who they are and what image they want to portray. The dystopian outcome of this conscious process of manufacturing identities is the creation of disembodied, untethered beings grasping for a self that never comes into existence. A more tempered version is of a world split between increasingly inauthentic digital avatars forever denying and being

denied by the beauty and richness that their true selves are able to realise.

©   The irony, of course, is that while individuals stamp out the genuine and natural elements of their identities, brands are desperately trying to become more "authentic" in order to sell us products we don't need, so we can become the people we think we need to be.

MYTH TWO: Personality brands help us navigate our role within society

In extolling the virtues of personality brands, we are taught to believe that clearly delineated identities not only help us determine who we are, they are signposts for the outside world to know what we represent. In practice, when we consciously fabricate our identities in either a social or professional arena, we collectively reduce our interpersonal relationships to meaningless transactions. The people we spend our time with, who we are seen with, whose pictures occupy the precious real estate of our social networking profiles, are vetted not by our genuine, altruistic desires for companionship, but the symbolism they telegraph to the outside world.

®   The related fallacy is that we determine decisions about our identity in isolation. The transactional nature of such an approach to the world and relationships corrodes both our personhood and our ability to value and be valued by other human beings. This forgoes a fundamental truth about identity: we are formed not for people but because of people. Our identities do not exist independently of concomitant actors, but because of exposure, interaction, and interdependence.

MYTH THREE: Creating personality brands differentiates us

In the collective race to find the thin layer of identity that represents us, we are constantly barraged with the same stimuli. What is considered aspirational in one social circle is the result of cues and cultural reference points targeted by the media and advertising to that very same audience.

™   Paradoxically, as we attempt to forge our brands, our identities look strikingly similar to the person next to us. The investment banker who donates to a fashionable charity, the aspiring hip hop artist, the stay-at-home mum turned novelist, are all reinforcing archetypes rather than differentiating themselves.

©   When everyone is applying the same aesthetic strategies, with the same props, affected by the same trends, in hopes of appealing to the same audience, we homogenise

the personalities that should be the source of creative variety and inspiration in our culture. Even the dissidents of counter-culture have been co-opted into sound-bites, rising and falling by din of their popular legitimacy.

®   As our mavericks are muted, the rest of us look around for ever more novel ways to stand out. Our increasing exasperation leaves us feeling alienated and ineffectual as we replace our identities with attention-seeking stunts, faux charisma and forced idiosyncrasies that will leave us remembered by others but forgotten by ourselves.

WHAT MUST BE DONE?

™   The words we use to articulate our world are reflections of our societal values and they propagate those values in a powerful way. As Wittgenstein famously remarked, "Like everything metaphysical, the harmony between thought and reality is to be found in the grammar of language". We cannot talk about identities as brands without reducing our behaviour to mimicry.

©   The creative industries — from art to journalism to advertising to entertainment — play a formative role in culture creation, in defining the grammar of language, in mapping the territory of our collective values. They must strive to champion and embrace what's beneath the social veneer in all its richness and complexity, to elucidate meaning rather

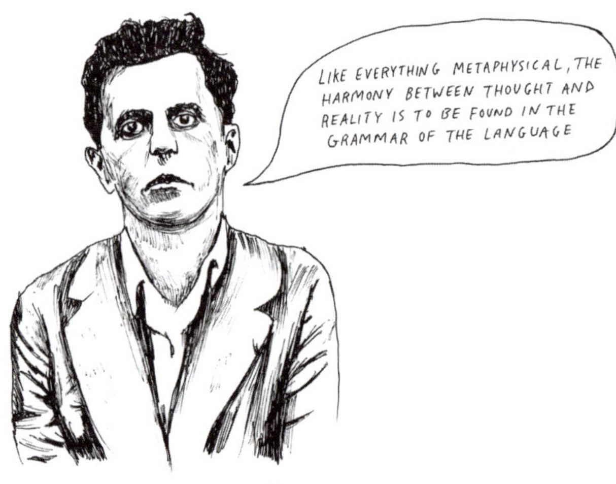

Ludwig Wittgenstein *philosopher* (1889-1951)

than simply regurgitate fashions and cheap emotions. But there is also an onus on us, as individuals, not brands, as citizens, not consumers, to become conscious of how we come to be this way, of why it is that we blindly follow the call to manufacture our identities.

® We must recognise that who we are is a result of the communities we are a part of. And the quality of those communities is a direct result of our contribution. There is fluidity and flux, a co-evolution, which defines our social fabric.

™ We are not commodities to be bought and sold. Our value does not derive from the number of followers we have. The human spirit transcends material reductions; it strives towards truth and meaning, social harmony, egalitarianism, and deep personal connection. We must revalorise the authentic, the messy self-realisations and social formations that make us who we truly are. The logic of self-liquidation must give way to the logic of collective identity, in all its diversity. Commodity narcissism must give way to new forms of communitarianism.

© What happens next depends on you.

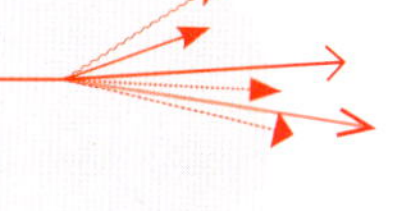

SEE ALSO:

 | 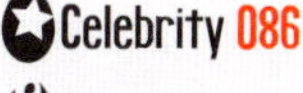Celebrity 086 Performing 110
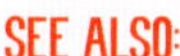 | Pop 174

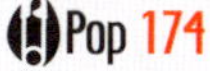

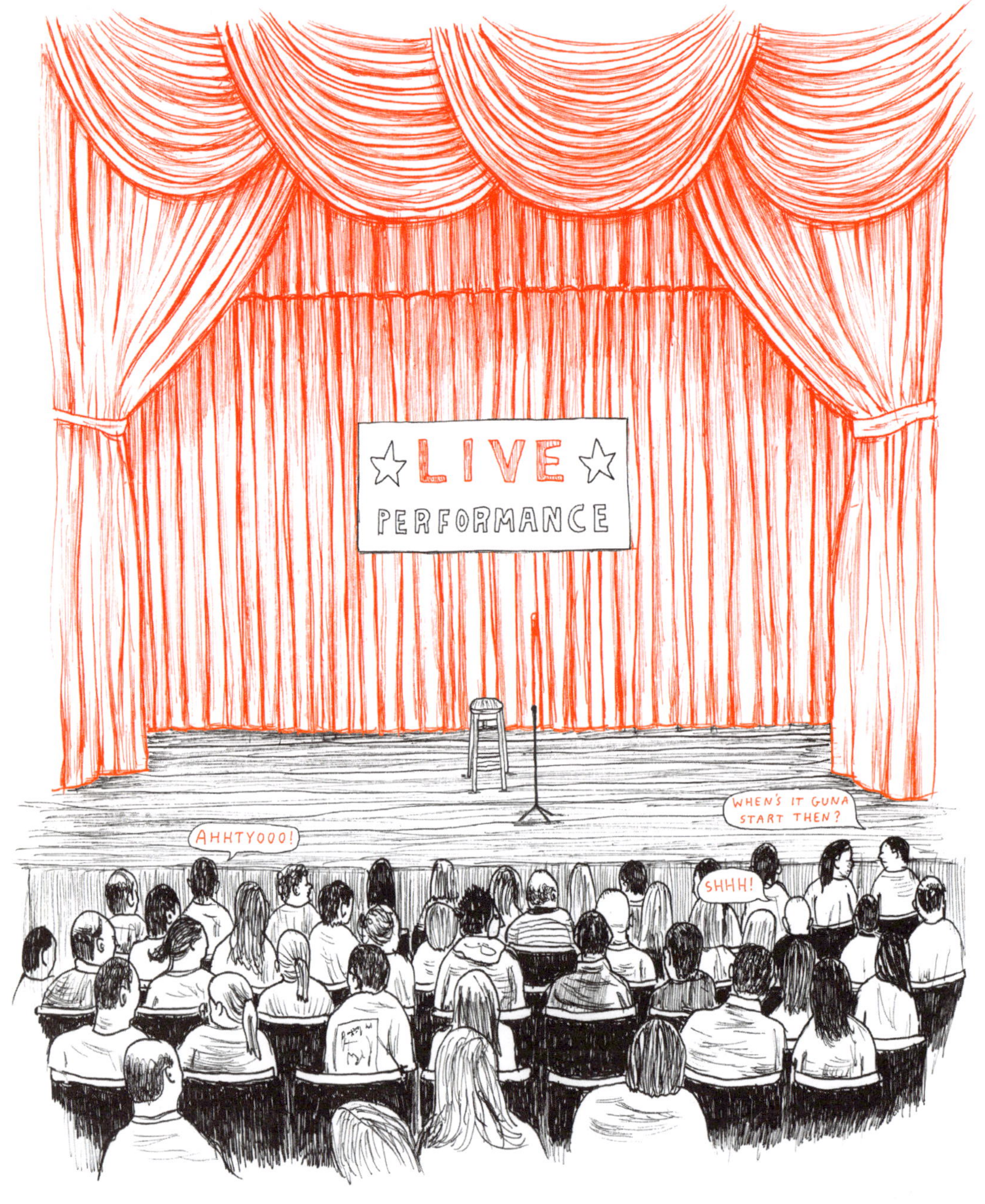

LIVE
PERFORMANCE
AHHTYOOO!
WHEN'S IT GUNA START THEN?
SHHH!

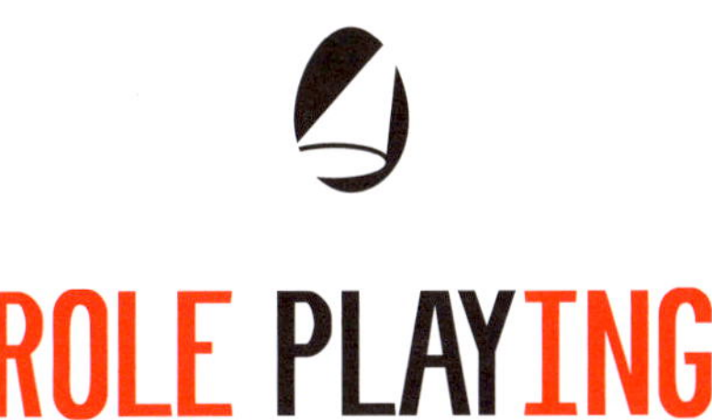

ROLE PLAYING

Matthew Collings

What kind of figure should an artist be?

I only ever saw one performance by Gavin Turk. He came on stage and divulged a string of sausages to the sound of *Scary Monsters*. Of course every exhibition private view is a strained performance by everyone present. In *After Theory* Terry Eagleton writes about our increasingly self-conscious performance of temporary selves. How we now accept a loosely connected relationship to whatever self it is we're supposed to be performing, as opposed to a previous era of modernity when more repressed and un-self-knowing types suffered endless traumatic shocks from the realisation that a persona is precisely not a real self.

¶ Artists who performed an artist-role in the past include Marcel Duchamp and a lot of European figures whose names I can't remember; one whom I never know what their sex was: you see those photos of her/him all the time, from the 1920s. Claude Cahun? Then there's Piero Manzoni, Yves Klein and Marcel Broodthaers — the mythic Euro-proto-conceptual-art figures who Gavin often invokes. The last one died of liver disease; having been a great gourmet he couldn't enjoy eating anything at all for a long period before he

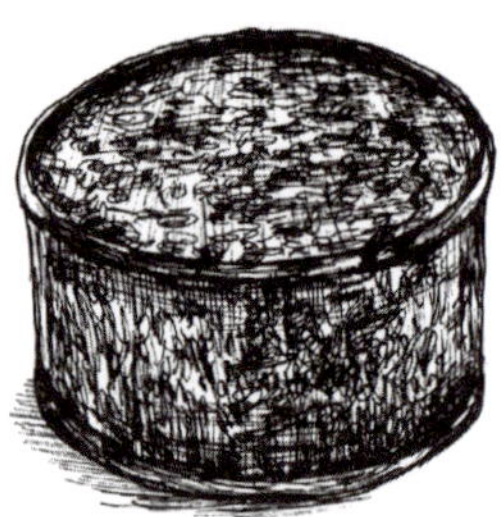

Gavin Turk Ordure 2010
Ready-made, 4 × 7 × 7 cm
Found rusty tin reminiscent of Piero Manzoni's canned shit

finally caved in. Both Manzoni and Klein died very young, barely thirty; Klein from a freak heart attack, Manzoni the same, caused by over eating. Manzoni signed boiled eggs with his thumb. He signed cans of his own excrement. "Excellent!" he said — "I think I'll call it *Artist's Shit*!"

¶   Every artistic self portrait is a performance of a certain kind; obviously not a profound one — the profundity is in the achievement of the work as a work, on its own terms, more than in the success or failure of the performance as such. But a Rembrandt self portrait is always a kind of staging of the profession of "artist" — what do they do? Their job is to look. You're very aware of how light falls in his *Self Portrait at Age 63* in the National Gallery, and how forms relate: those were the key skills for a painter in those days. When he dresses up it's to elevate the status of the skills — they deserve a bit of grandiosity he's saying. He dressed up in his period of commercial success more than in his period of commercial decline. We believe he gets more honest but it's more that he gets older.

¶   The description of a face ageing is moving, and so is the incredible skill with which it's done.

¶   When Duchamp performs for photos, whether by Man Ray or whoever, the photo is an artwork about a shifting sense of self — it's not to tell you what an artist is but to tell you something about how meaning works. When Gerhard Richter tells you about meaning in photos by painting a photo so that it has the allure of a photograph but is obviously only a painting, Richter himself remains the rather boring character, which he is in real life. When Duchamp is photographed as a woman the whole idea of Duchamp as a figure becomes intimidating, impressive. He makes all these intuitive moves. It's surprising how lo-tech his whole act is, how little there is to it, how scruffy his objects are, how anyone could have done them. They're all about staging some kind of inroad that meaning makes into art, with the figure of The Artist like some constant slightly disturbing dream you wake up from, anxious that there's something you ought to remember. The message is about changing conditions

in society, mass production, industry and the different ways in which art is now spotlit, ritu-alised and celebrated. Light is cast onto art so it can cast light on everything else. How did we used to see it? In a court or a cathedral or a private chapel, then in the salon, and then in salons organised by literary ladies and rich Russians and so on, and now in the Philadelphia Museum of Art, but before that in some store room prior to the Armory Show —

"Hey there's a urinal."

"Chuck it out!"

"OK."

¶   Obviously Matthew Barney's imagery is great. It's the filmic timing that's wrong, the lumbering, non-Rembrandt blind grandiosity. *It's A Knockout* giants with ginger beards crossing the sea endlessly to Orkney; dressed-up poseurs taking far too long to pretend to be sperm. How are you supposed to respond? A black and white photo of Manzoni signing an egg with his thumbprint — now that's show business!

¶   What kind of a figure should an artist be? Many of the YBA's have had a stab at this problem, the top ones perhaps with the least success in Duchampian terms — that is, instead of interrogating meaning, they keep trying to make themselves seem like Arthur Rimbaud. Someone shrieking on *Big Brother* is the same as Tracey Emin shrieking outside Munch's house, there's no difference at all in depth of feeling. (She made a film in 1999 of herself nude screaming on a wooden jetty outside Munch's summer house, called *Homage to Edvard Munch and all my dead children*). Someone getting depressed on *Big Brother* is the same as Emin being depressed. But unlike them she produces a lot of slogans about it — *You forgot to kiss my soul*;

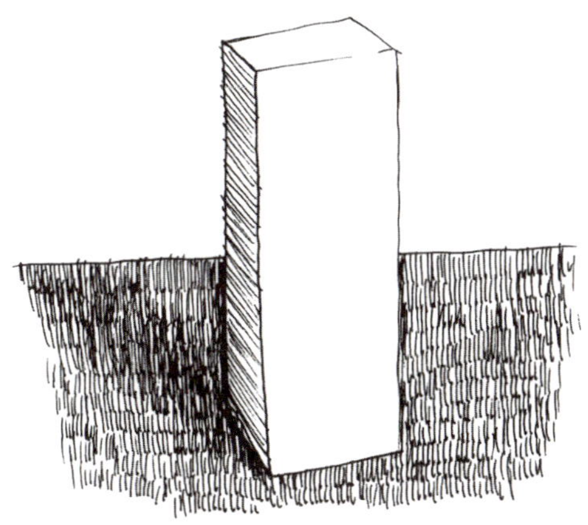

Tom Friedman   Untitled (A Curse)   1992
133 × 28 × 28 cm
A 28 × 28 cm space above a plinth, cursed by a witch

My cunt is wet with fear; *Every part of me is bleeding*; *Exorcism of the last painting I ever made* — and sometimes makes them into needlework. The depression still isn't interesting, but the pleasure of the art object is. When these slogans or soundbites are made into neon signs like Nauman's, or videos like Acconci's, or driftwood sculptures like Arte Povera or little gouaches or oil paintings by any art-world me-too striver, it's possible to feel impressed by the confidence but at the same time completely unengaged emotionally.

¶ In a book of interviews Damien Hirst and the writer Gordon Burn once performed a kind of authenticity act, each outdoing the other in macho talk. "Grr" is the basic sound all the way through — "Fucking fuck!" "I fucking thought fuck that!" "Yeah fuck that fuck." "Death fuck." The design follows the rough fuckiness of the apparently coke-fuelled fake frenzy of honesty. The illustrations are grainy and look like they might have just fallen on the page with a load of post-it notes. (Album covers used to sometimes stage this look). This method-acting of meaning — the combination of shouting out impulsive imitations of truth for hour after hour because you're so fucking crazy that finesse or politeness is just fucking bullshit for phonies, with illustrations of artworks that aren't arranged in a coldly glossy way like advertising but have a calculated designer wonky graininess instead — is different to the feel of Hirst's actual work, which is always factory finessed, and is in fact very like advertising. As if cold distance, a total lack of anything meaning anything, occasionally needs a bit of direct raw meaning in the picture so you can see more clearly what the meaning of true meaninglessness really is.

SEE ALSO:

 | 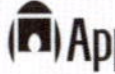Appropriation 066 Celebrity 086 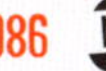Commodity Narcissism 098

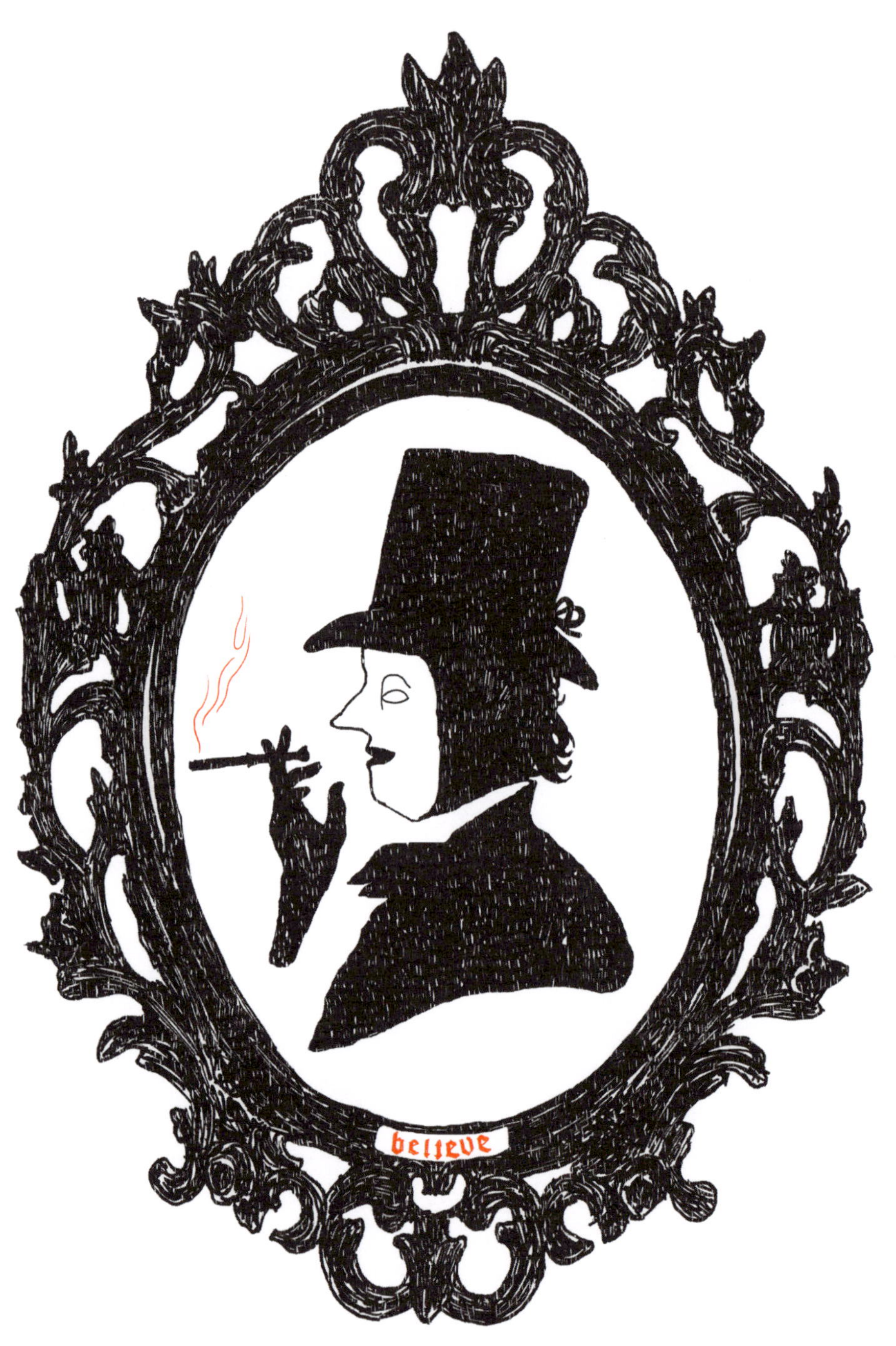
believe

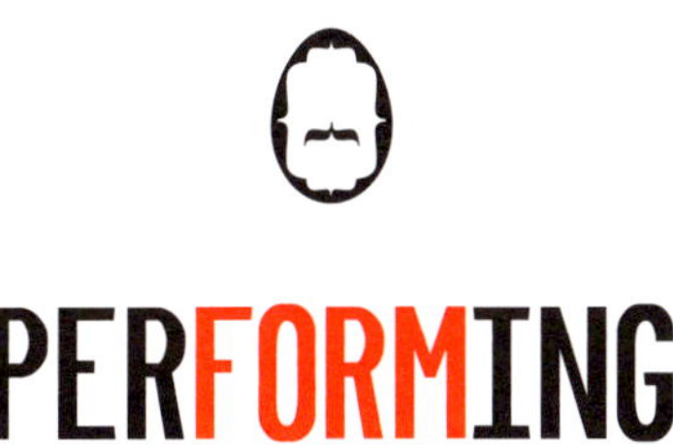

PERFORMING

Sebastian Horsley

How to be a Dandy

Dandyism is a form of self-worship that dispenses with the need to find happiness from others — especially women. It is a condition rather than a profession. It is a defence against suffering and a celebration of life. It is not fashion, nor wealth, nor learning; it is not beauty. It is a shield and a sword and a crown, pulled out of the dressing up box in the attic of the imagination.

The estrangement of the thoroughgoing dandy, is not from women, but from life. It involves taking a posture of ironic detachment from the world and living it out in scrupulous detail. Dandies are a brotherhood of higher types, the true princes of the world. And the true priests of the world — to become a dandy your days will become so ordered they will make the life of a Trappist monk seem like an orgy.

Here are the lessons in self-transformations I apply so rigorously. You must empty yourself of the dreariness of mere personality and make yourself available without reservation — not to individuals but to the world at large. You will find this way of life is only in a certain sense fulfilling, however. It is also a martyrdom of sorts. If you choose to share your life with the world rather than one person then you have to forfeit marriage, children, happiness — all the things, of course, that don't matter. How exactly is it done? It is time to take off my face and reveal my mask.

¶ The projection of dandyism can be effected by the following principal means:

Speech

- Unless you can improve on silence, keep your gob shut. To justify its existence speech has to be extraordinary. If it's ordinary it's less than worthless; it's clutter. If language is the dress of thought, there is never any excuse for denim.
- Read every day something no-one else is reading. Think every day something no-one else is thinking. Above all be witty. Wit enables us to act rudely with impunity. And wit has truth in it.
- Remember: the beginning of wit is to desire it. Read wit continually, exercise the mind, simply to keep the muscles at attention, like a person who runs a marathon. Turn your pain into humour and your anger into wit. Embrace life as a great metaphysical joke to which the only logical response is laughter.
- The key is to make people believe everything you say, though not a single word is sincere. The only terror is the terror of being understood.

Movement

- If all speech should be a kind of literature, every movement should be a form of dance. Every day put on your best trousers to go out to battle for freedom and truth. One must always look beautiful, look up and smile at the camera — even if it's only a security camera or a satellite.
- Contra Mr Orwell: be grateful to be worth watching. Curl your skip into a smile and your smile into a show. Your gait should be a purposeful lope, taut with authority. Walk in the perfect glow of self-adoration, striding invincibly through the awe-struck and fawning populace.

Clothes

- When it comes to dress, it takes a strong man to be an extrovert. A true dandy needs complete conviction that he is right; the views of the rest of the world simply don't matter. "If someone looks at you, you are not well-dressed," Mr Brummell tells us. But then Mr Brummell would say that; prissily precise, he was essentially a conformist. True dandyism is rebellious. The real dandy wants to make people look, be shocked by, and even a little scared by the subversion which his clothes stand for.

- Dandyism is social, human and intellectual. It is not a suit of clothes walking about by itself. Clothes are merely a part, they may even be the least important part of the personality of the dandy. Dandyism isn't image encrusted with flourishes, it's a way of stripping down to your true self. You can only judge the style by the content and you can only reach the content through the style. Mr Brummell was the original and most celebrated dandy but he was no hero of mine; he was so refined that I do not regard him as a dandy at all. I am more concerned with style than breeding and the key is to dress in such a style that you would attract attention at a Liberace concert.

- Being "well dressed" is not a question of having expensive clothes or the "right" clothes. You can wear rags, but they must suit you. In fact, to be able to sustain an existence on nothing but rags is the epitome of style. A curious dignity and a refusal not to keep up appearances is what we want. Style is not elegance but consistency. So, take heart, you will not need any money at all. A modest sufficiency cramps style; extreme poverty, like great danger, enriches it.

Remember: Life is nothing but a game of dressing up and make-believe. All dress is fancy dress except our natural skins.

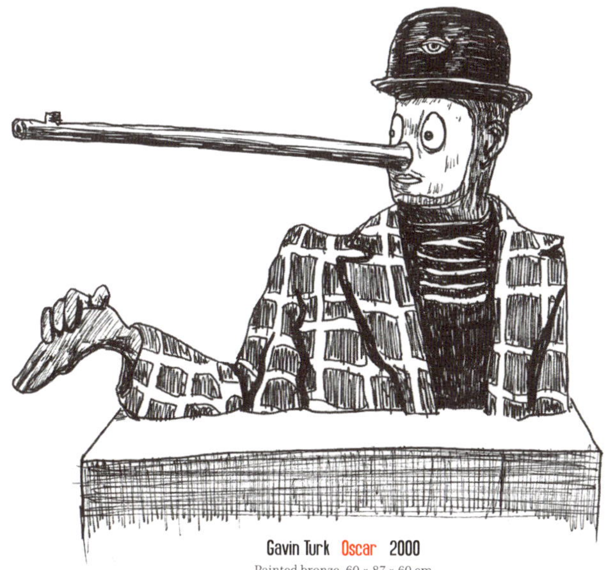

Gavin Turk Oscar **2000**
Painted bronze, 60 × 87 × 60 cm
A painted bronze bust of the artist with a shotgun nose inspired by René Magritte's *Oscar*

Occupation

- Works of art do nothing but they do it passionately. So, retire at birth. You must have no obligations, no attachments, no wife, no child, no occupation, no possessions, no obvious means of support, visible or invisible; you must be of no use whatsoever. Are we agreed about that? Good. Looking beautiful and being stylish is essential; a purpose in life is not. I have never had a career, but I do a splendid job as one of the handsomest men in the world. I don't want anything. I am completely un-covetous. Unless it is under the covers *avec tous*.

Family Life

- As a natural loner and auto-invention you will have grasped early the irrelevance of family life. Dandies reproduce themselves through emulation and style, not through family descent. Distant relatives, are the best kind, and the further the better.
- Love, marriage and sex represent species sameness and the defeat of individuality. So they gotta go. A dandy will not be a link in the chain of being, exchangeable with any other and expendable in himself. He is not a piece of animated meat, a fornicating carcass. He must defeat his animal function at all costs.
- The only place a dandy would push a pram is into the Thames. You must raise nothing but your cock.
- Women are on this planet only as trumpets of our glory. To love, even in the least elevated sense, means to desire, which means to be dependent. The key is to be disinterested and not become giddy from the heads you turn.

Life Trajectory

- Dandyism oscillates between narcissism and neurosis, vanity and insanity, Savile Row and Death Row. All the great dandies have ended in the flophouse or the madhouse. Gutter or nutter. You have lived like a king and shall die like a beggar.

Death

- As all self-respecting dandies know, suicides are the aristocrats of death. They represent a triumph of style over life. Your existence is a work of art.

It deserves a frame, if only to distinguish it from the wallpaper. Suicide will look nice; it will match the home furnishings.

- Write a note. If you are young perhaps something like:

  "I have decided to stop living on account of the cost."

  Or if you are old (say 90):

  "I am committing suicide because I am worried about my future."

Remember: It is not enough to know how to make a dazzling entry: you need to know how to vacate the stage with the same panache. Dandyism is a modern form of stoicism. It is a religion whose only sacrament is suicide. Fear not: by the time you have reached the end of the run, you will be as God. You will not be committing suicide but deicide. Pesticide is for mere mortals.

From Savile Row *to* Death Row

- Of course, Dandyism fails. How can originality create a whole movement by replication? How, on the one perfumed hand, can you talk about freedom when you willingly give it up with the other un-gloved mitt? How can you be unique and yet part of the gang? There are two universal truths about human beings. 1: they are all the same. 2: they all say they are different. 2 is of course the result of 1. The dandy just happens to be the biggest, the best and most beautiful fraud of them all. His doctrine is a laughable conceit, a delightful illusion.
- But so what? Life is absurd and the only way of tolerating existence is to lose oneself in a perpetual orgy of absurdity. A man gets up to speak and says nothing. Nobody listens and everybody disagrees. Nothing solves the meaningless absurdity of life, but we can clothe the abyss and make it wearable.
- When you hear thunder, take a bow. When you hear rain, assume it is applause. Like the sun: shine, having no alternative. You shall be a reprobate dandy; that's your job. And the Good Lord will forgive you: that's His.

EDITOR'S NOTE: Sebastian Horsley died of an accidental drug overdose in 2010, shortly after writing this text. His funeral was as busy and spectacular as the artist could have hoped for.

SEE ALSO:

The Outsider 030   The Rebel 060

Role Playing 104

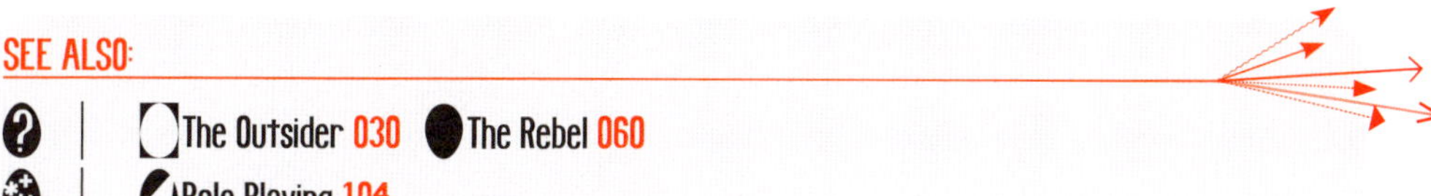

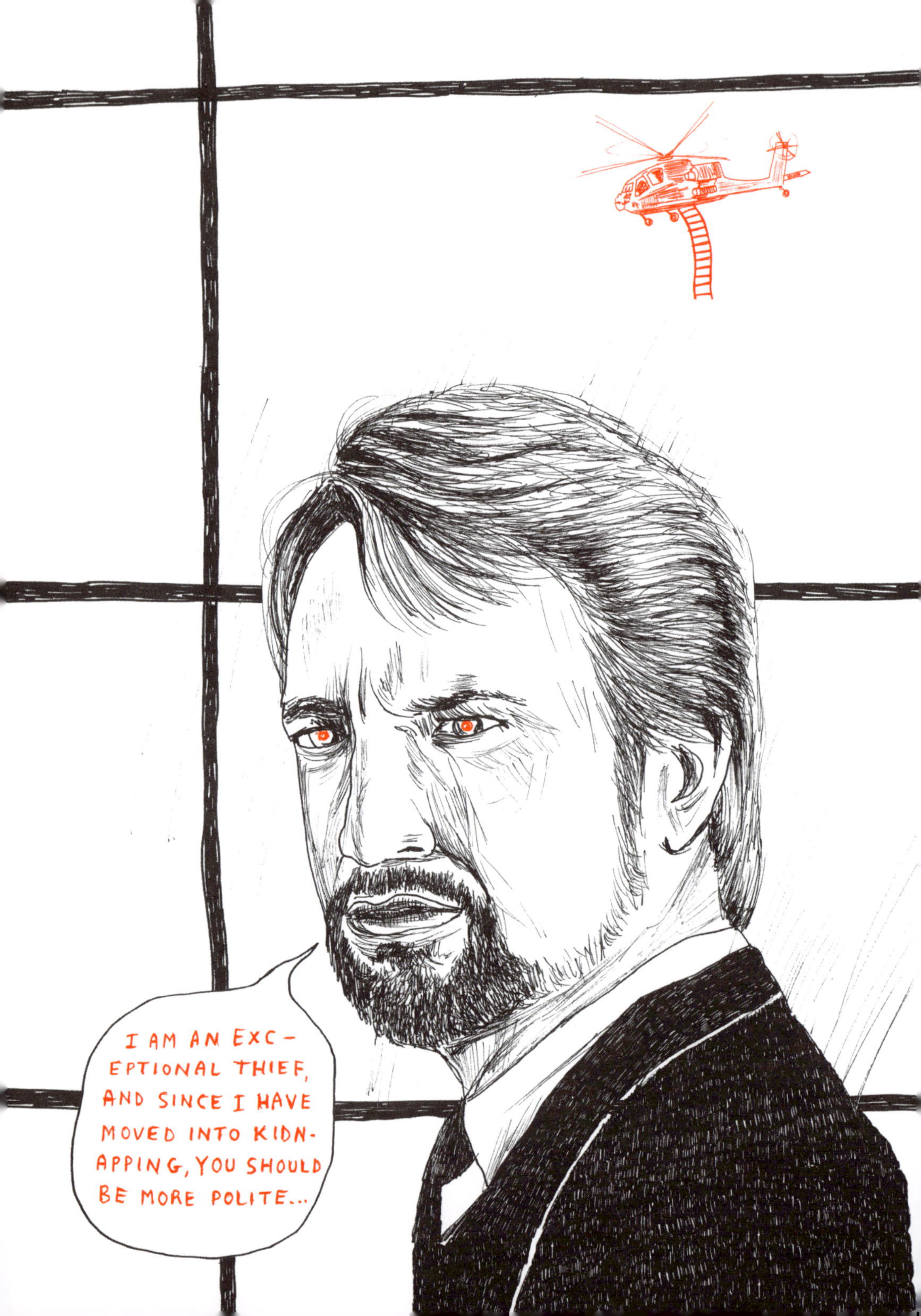

I AM AN EXC-
EPTIONAL THIEF,
AND SINCE I HAVE
MOVED INTO KIDN-
APPING, YOU SHOULD
BE MORE POLITE...

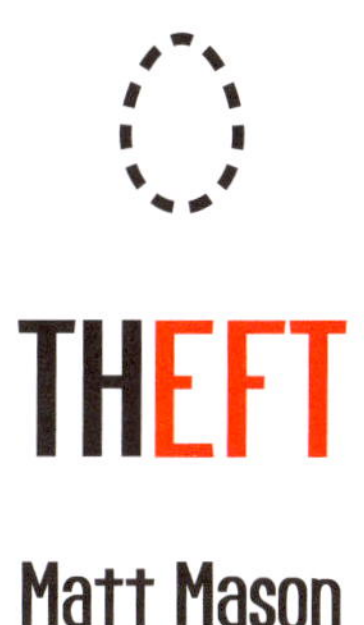

THEFT

Matt Mason

To copy is to be human

Gavin Turk is not a common thief. I think he's more like Hans Gruber, the German terrorist in the 80s action movie *Die Hard*. Towards the end of the movie, Holly McClane says to him, "After all your posturing, all your speeches… you're nothing but a common thief." Hans looks at her, offended, and replies "I'm an exceptional thief."

¶ Mr. Turk is a copycat of note. People are drawn to his work. The way he deals with concepts such as authorship and originality resonate with us for good reason: we are all thieves and we respect and recognise the exceptional ones. Let me explain. Every day each of us breaks copyright laws many times without realising. If you photocopy a page from a book, take a picture of a work of art you didn't produce, sing *Happy Birthday* in public or forward an email you didn't write, you're a thief.

¶ Our ideas about property rights, intellectual or otherwise, are generally viewed as good for society and most of the time, they are. The problem is that laws pertaining to intellectual property are no longer sophisticated enough to deal with the ways we use information in the real world. Author and attorney, Professor John Tehranian made a note of every time he inadvertently broke copyright law and worked out how much he would owe if he were sued each time this happened. According to his calculations, he owed an average of £8.1 million a day. If we take Tehranian to be an average law-abiding citizen, that's £2.93 billion a year in copyright violations.

¶ Of course the majority of us don't get sued for these crimes, because these laws are unworkable. Most acts of copyright infringement are entirely harmless; the crimes are ignored and we go unpunished. But we're still common thieves on paper. This huge crevasse between law and reality appeared because two things happened. Firstly, technology changed. When these laws were written, information flowed in one direction: producers produced, consumers consumed. There was a clear line between broadcaster and receiver, artist and fan, creator and pirate. Today that line is a blur. Information moves in many directions at once. Anybody can produce, rebroadcast or remix information of all kinds. Consumers can talk back in a variety of ways. They can form angry mobs or fan clubs — the fate of producers is in their hands. There is a power shift going on. Secondly, all this technology amplified one of our oldest behavioural traits: copying. Copying is part of the human condition. It is the backbone of our culture. It is how we learn to talk, how we learn social norms and manners. We are relentless copying machines, and now we have access to the most advanced copying machine ever created: the internet.

¶   Our laws were not written with billions of human copying machines in mind. We common thieves don't spend large amounts of time and money coercing governments to make sure copyright laws suit our behaviour; but large companies do. The result is a set of rules which serve big business but don't work quite as well for everyone else.

¶   The lot of the thief, both common and exceptional, is worth defending however. Families shouldn't receive takedown notices from record labels for uploading home movies of their kids dancing to copyright-protected music. Companies shouldn't be able to use copyright law to stifle free speech and restrict information that makes them look bad. Entertainment conglomerates shouldn't be allowed to upload spyware onto your computer without asking, even if they say they only want to make sure you're not stealing any of their content. Telecoms companies should not have the power to decide what information you see online. If this disconnect between law and reality is not addressed, our freedoms will be eroded.

¶   It takes exceptional thieves to defend such freedoms. It takes artists, like Gavin Turk, publicly questioning who owns what. We need the types of pirate who speak truth to power in order for things to change. Without them operating at the outer marker moving the boundaries, everything stagnates. We need people who innovate without asking permission if we are to defend culture, democracy and freedom of expression. Some of the greatest innovators in history were thought of as thieves when they started out. When Thomas Edison invented the phonographic record player, musicians branded him a pirate out to steal their work and destroy the live music business — until a system was worked out so everyone could be paid royalties. We now call this system the recording industry.

¶   Edison went on to invent film-making, and wanted to charge a license fee to use his invention. Several New York film-makers, including a young man named William, disagreed with this policy and fled to the (then still wild) west coast. Here they could make films illegally and flee to nearby Mexico if Edison's lawyers were dispatched. This town of pirate filmmakers is still there — it's called Hollywood; William's second name was Fox. Today these industries, established by pirates, are trying to protect their intellectual property rights and are locked in fierce battles with consumers they see as thieves. Of course, artists and industries should have the right to protect their work, but if throwing lawsuits at your fans suddenly becomes part of your business model, you no longer have a business model.

¶ When information flowed in one direction, it was easy to take culture and attach it to a product in order to sell it; those on the edges of society created meaning, and the commercial world stole it. But now the outsiders are finding ways to take meaning back from the market. People are organising without organisations; loose-knit networks and open source structures are proving more effective at doing some things than governments and markets. As a result, we're rebelling in new ways. Culture used to be one of the only ways of rebelling in a non-violent manner, but today we can kill bad ideas with new business models. Warhol famously said, "Good business is the best art."

¶ It already seems like bad ideas and old power structures are being brought to the slaughter on a daily basis, and the revolution has barely started. The future promises ever more

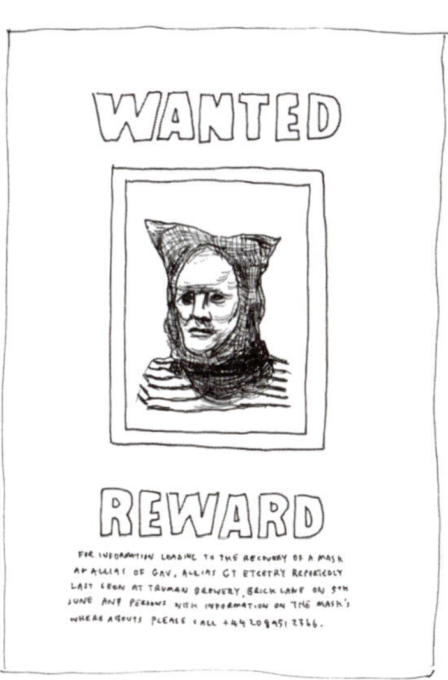

Gavin Turk Alias 2007
Silkscreen on paper, 45.5 × 30 cm
A WANTED poster of the artist wearing a mask taken from a performance at the Art Car Boot Fair

unfettered access to information and intellectual property. The internet may be the world's ultimate copying machine at the moment, but that was just Act 1; 3-D printing will further erode the idea of copyright. We've had 3-D printers that can print 3-D printers since 2008. When we have cheap, consumer-grade 3-D printers everywhere, the war over intellectual property will spill into the real world in a new way.

¶   Act 2 indicates even greater levels of both conflict and opportunity; things could get weird. The future promises new ways to create, reach audiences, gain notoriety, earn money and all the rest of it — if we can only reconcile the two opposing forces at work when we have a new idea. At the same time as we are thinking "how can I get this out there?" we're also asking ourselves "how can I benefit from/monetise/control this idea?" We want to spread ideas as information, but capitalise on them as intellectual property.

¶   That reconciliation is happening. This movie has a happy ending, which brings me back to *Die Hard*.

¶   Just before 20th Century Fox released the fourth *Die Hard* film in 2007, the marketing team at Fox had one overriding question: how do we get people excited about the *Die Hard* films online? What they didn't know was a comedy rock band named Guyz Nite had just uploaded the video for their new song, entitled *Die Hard*. The verses of the song outlined the plots of the first three *Die Hard* films, set to a sequence of tightly edited clips in their video; it was hilarious enough for millions of people to watch it and tell their friends about it. When the legal team at Fox found out about the copyright-violating video, they asked YouTube to take down the infringing material, which YouTube did; end of story.

¶   Except it wasn't. When the marketing team at Fox found out about the video, and the millions of people getting excited about the *Die Hard* franchise again because of it, they called Guyz Nite. "How much do we have to pay you to put your video up on YouTube again?"

¶   It all worked out in the end — copyright laws were ignored in favour of user-generated content that helped everybody out. The band even got an invite to the New York premiere of the film. Pirates can reach the places other advertisers cannot reach. It's like Jean-Luc Godard said, "It's not where you take things from, it's where you take them to."

¶   That was 2007 and we're already somewhere very different. You don't hear about legal wrangles over YouTube mash-ups anymore. They are still technically against the law in most places, but the big entertainment companies have stopped chasing them so aggressively. It's now common to see studios and labels release stems and footage so that fans can make remixes. In 2010, the United States Copyright Office quietly declared that people remixing videos on YouTube for the purpose of criticism or comment, was not a violation of copyright law. It would seem like the battle over copyright, as it pertains to culture at least, is already won.

¶ The war, however, continues. Everyone involved in cut-n-paste culture, from Turk to Guyz Nite to the millions of remixers on YouTube, were installing a new idea into our collective operating system. They were setting the scene for a much wider skirmish. The next thing we remix is not culture, or the laws around it, but the infrastructure we use to make and enforce those laws. It bears repeating: this war is about democracy.

¶ The new battles are over the infrastructures themselves, and who gets to control them. The Stop Online Piracy Act (SOPA) would have taken away freedoms online in the name of piracy. The late Aaron Swartz, one of the most brilliant technologists of our time, was harassed, bullied and threatened; unscrupulously prosecuted and wrongly condemned as a common thief, he tragically took his own life. He was trying to ensure academic journal articles could be freely available online. Edward Snowden has been labelled a terrorist for exposing a terrifying government surveillance programme.

¶ Things are escalating quickly. It started with pieces of art and entertainment, now the stakes are higher. It will take time. It will be a war hard-won. But if the thieves win, free speech, freedom of expression and democracy will be hardcoded into society. That was the promise of the internet. This is what we, all of us thieves, are fighting for — through art, through copy, through code.

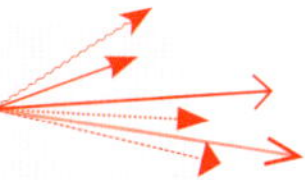

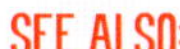
SEE ALSO:

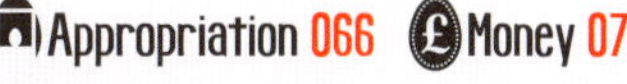

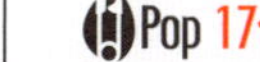

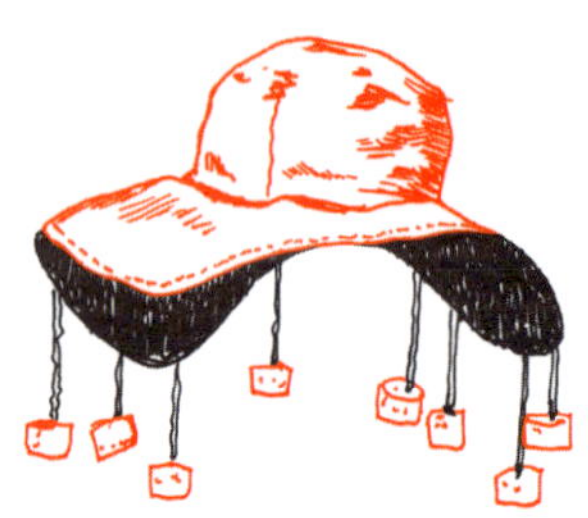
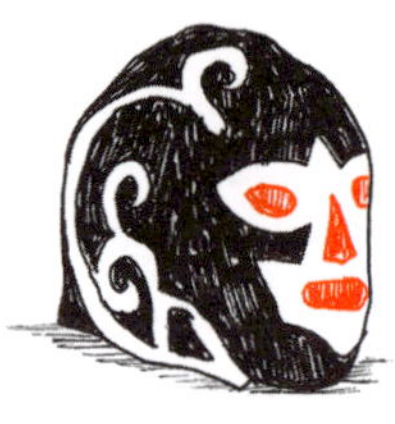
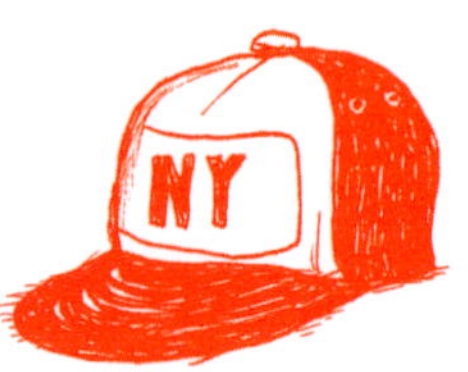

NY

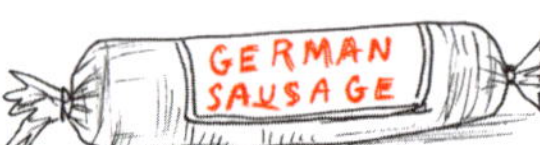

GERMAN
SAUSAGE

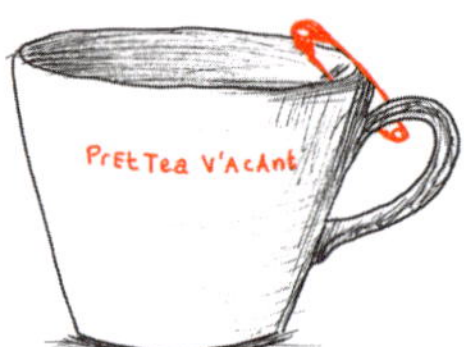

PreTTea V'AcAnt

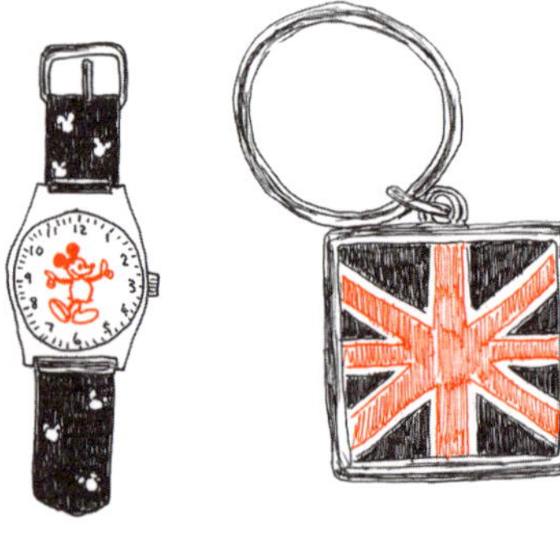
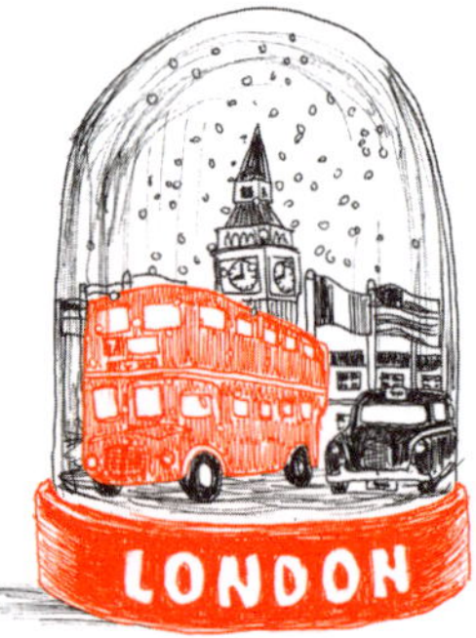

LONDON

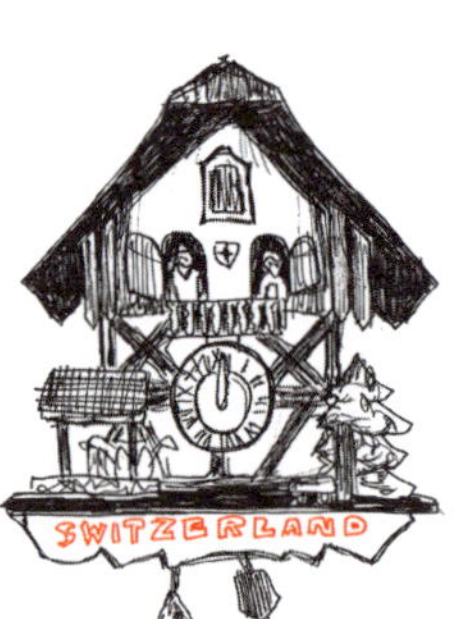

SWITZERLAND

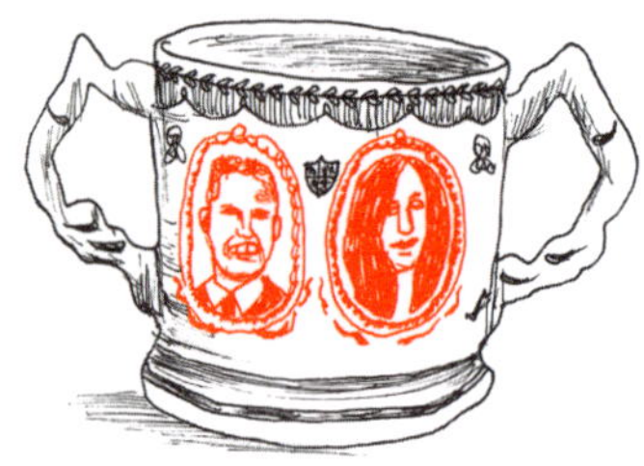
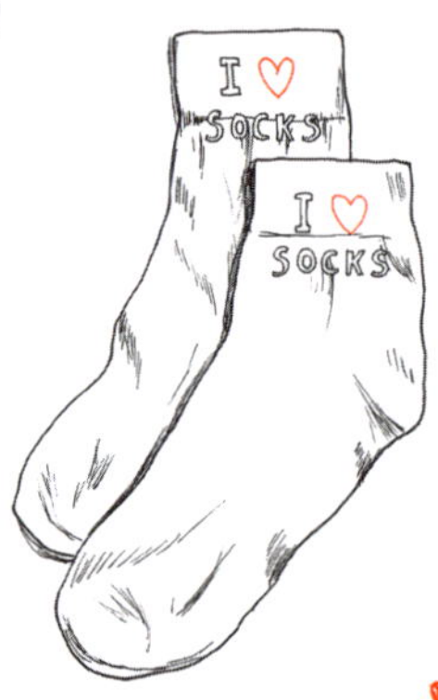

I ♥ SOCKS
I ♥ SOCKS

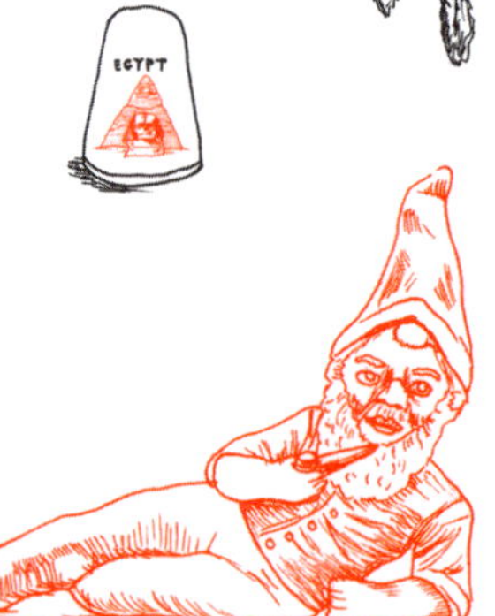

EGYPT

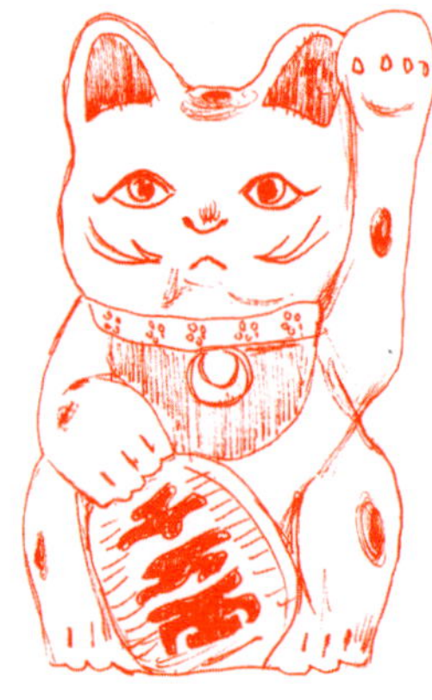
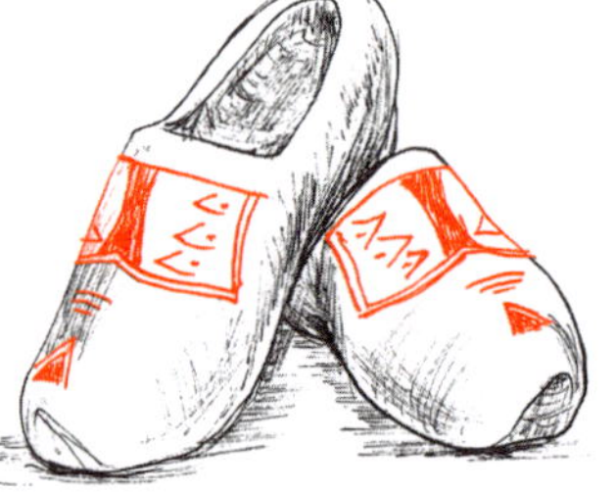
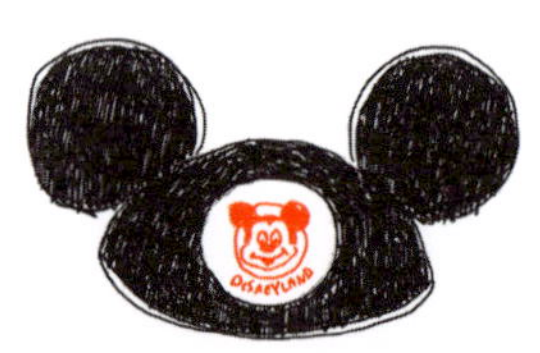

DISNEYLAND

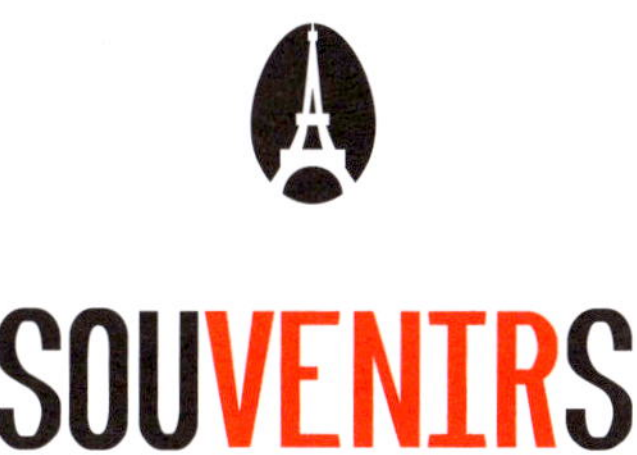

SOUVENIRS

Tony Marcus

Without angst and perfectly useless

"He owned nothing. No object, no family furniture, no souvenirs. All he had was contained in an old trunk where he kept a few photos and notes relating to his past work."

Lydie Sarazin, Marcel Duchamp's first wife, from a privately printed memoir, published 1927

This starkness of Duchamp is liberating. There is a similar resonance in descriptions of his New York apartment; one room, one chair, a basic bed, a packing crate that served as table and two nails banged into the wall. A piece of string hung from one of the nails.

¶   If it has nothing to look at, the mind has a better opportunity of being quiet. I don't know if this was Duchamp's intention, and pictures of his last home in Neuilly that he shared with his second wife show a much more "normal"-looking room. There are shelves and books, art and objects.

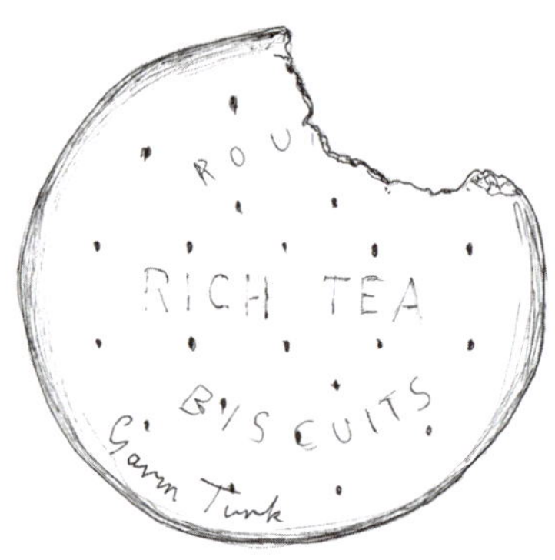

Gavin Turk   Rich Tea Biscuit   2006
A signed rich tea biscuit, 6.5 × 6.5 cm

¶   A souvenir will stimulate the mind. The word is French (it is a verb) and means *to remember*. The English noun "souvenir" is the infinitive mood of the French *souvenir* used substantively. The usage is modern. The word does not appear in *The Bible*, Shakespeare, Blake, Dickens, *Moby Dick* or *Alice in Wonderland*. There is a souvenir in Joyce's *Ulysses* (once) and in Scott Fitzgerald where usage is plummy and sentimental. Gatsby refers to a photograph: "A souvenir of Oxford days. It was taken in Trinity quad. The man on my left is now the Earl of Doncaster."

¶   The etymology of souvenir is Latin from *sub* meaning under or near and *venire* to come. The meaning is of something, in this case a memory, that comes from the deep of the mind. *Souvenir* describes an object that will dredge for memory (like police looking for a corpse in the river).

¶   It is not common to think of souvenirs as objects that recall lost memory. In regular usage the word hitches itself to snow-domes and "tasteless" (insists Wikipedia) objects linked to tourists' sites and capital cities. It is possible that these objects ridicule the colossal state monuments they miniaturise and recast in plastic. Or suggest that any place or event that requires a souvenir to remain memorable is therefore, by itself, forgettable.

¶   But souvenirs that recall lost memory externalise memory as three-dimensional objects. Which must give them a special status amongst the classification of objects. It is hard to see a memory. What does a memory look like?

¶   Pablo Picasso was fond of writer and Pataphysics founder Alfred Jarry's gun. Picasso acquired this weapon after Jarry's death as a souvenir of his friend, notes Duchamp's biographer (although Picasso's biographer Roland Penrose claims Jarry gave him the gun). Regardless of how he acquired the gun, Picasso took it on night-time jaunts and sometimes

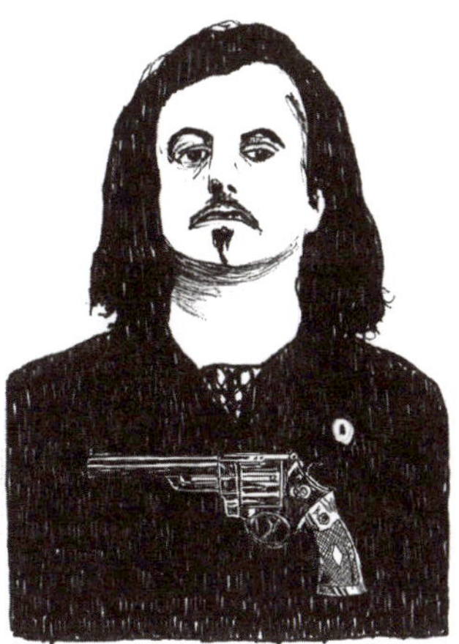

discharged the weapon in Montmartre. The gun reminded Picasso of his dead friend, say the biographers. It might be accurate to exhibit the gun with the label "souvenir of Alfred Jarry, author of Pere Ubu". It might be tempting to say the gun was a relic of either Jarry or Picasso although the word *relic* has a specific theological meaning.

¶   "Orthodox Christians," explains Bishop Kallistos Ware, "believe that the grace of God present in the saints' bodies during life remains active in their relics when they have died and that God uses these relics as a channel of divine power, as an instrument of healing." In the last days relics will be reclaimed and re-fleshed by the resurrected saints. They come back to life. "The relics were the saint," notes Patrick J Geary in *Furta Sacra* (an authoritative book on relics). But you could say "the relics are the saint". They are not souvenirs. Or representations.

¶   Jarry's gun is inert. It does not belong to eternity. Jarry's gun is not Jarry. It is a path to the memory of a dead writer (who will remain dead) and to Picasso's memory of his friend (Jarry died in 1907, Picasso in 1973). If Jarry's gun still exists it would be proof that Jarry (and also Picasso) did once exist. It is artefact or evidence like dinosaur skeletons. Because it can be difficult for the living to believe the past really happened. We need evidence — museums, galleries and archeologies.

¶   Coleridge wrote about a souvenir that could be extracted from a dream as a physical object (this meditation was not published during his lifetime and the idea prefigures memorable scenes from *Nightmare on Elm Street*). Coleridge writes: "If a man could pass through Paradise in a dream, and have a flower presented to him as a pledge that his soul had really been there, and if he found that flower in his hand when he awoke — Ay! — and what then?"

¶   But most souvenirs — even if they function as evidence that you have been somewhere — are tasteless and kitsch. The word "kistch" comes from German *verkitschen* meaning to make cheap and *kitschen* to collect junk from the streets. Kitsch is the "commodification of the souvenir," writes Celeste Olalquiaga, and "the souvenir the commodification of remembrance".

¶ There might be some who resist having their memories cast in "cheap" plastic (and there is a reflex prejudice against plastic — Umberto Eco has written about the wonder and beauty of plastic). St Mark's in Venice is to be avoided, I was told by a young postgraduate student of architecture, because it is tacky, a theme park. But if you walked away from the centre, my student friend said, you will find strange, watery fields, real farmers, authentic experience. This longing for the "authentic" might traumatise an otherwise restful holiday. I wonder if there is an tiring egotism in the tourist's refusal to accept his or her role. Or is this a consoling delusion because (for some of us) commodified leisure and memory are harder to stomach than commodified transport or education.

¶ There is an artwork Gavin Turk has exhibited of a discarded paper cup bearing the logo-ised image of Stonehenge. And Stonehenge (says Wikipedia) is "one of the most famous prehistoric sites in the world". I suppose you could argue it is England's oldest and most "magnificent" art work. Gavin may be having a go at English Heritage who produced the cup because there might be some leakage, some diminution of value heading back from the cup to the "magnificent" original. But then again both the cup and Gavin's image are perfectly adequate pictures of Stonehenge. They are calm images. Neither betrays anxiety about authenticity or form.

¶ When I started this story I wanted to rail against spoons from Ramsgate and a Tower of London snow-dome; now I find myself warming to these objects; they are without angst and either perfectly useless (which reaches Oscar Wilde's definition of art) or perform the role of dredging and externalising memory, which gives them a singular, if not favoured status in the classification of matter.

SEE ALSO:

Signatures 044

Theft 116

Garbage 142

ZERO

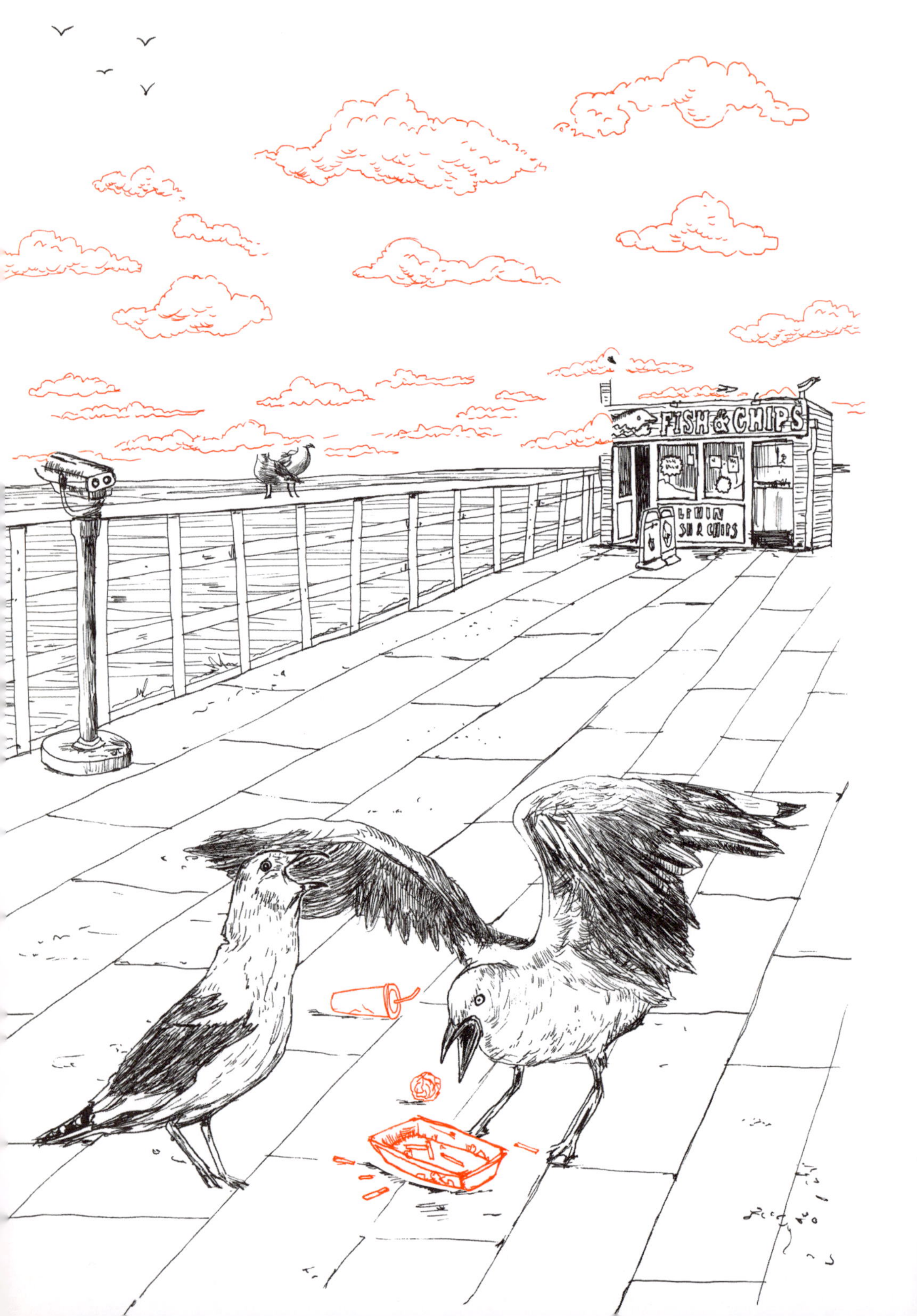

FISH & CHIPS

CHIP TRAYS AND CHIP FORKS

Dixe Wills

There is perhaps no meal so quintessentially British as fish and chips. Leaving aside the competing claims of the traditional Sunday roast and the fact that frying chipped potatoes is generally acknowledged to have been imported from France or Belgium, the fish and chip supper has become as much a symbol of Britishness as the Routemaster bus or the (now all but mythical) bowler-hatted city gent.

¶ Which is not to say the dish has been with us since the dawn of Albion. Charles Dickens makes passing references in *Oliver Twist* and *A Tale of Two Cities*, marking a time when the meal became a hit with the poorer sectors of society. The nation's fishing fleet had taken to trawling, resulting in a far greater catch which consequently lowered the price of fish. When combined around 1870 with the plentiful and inexpensive potato, fish and chips became the treat of choice for the working classes. By the 1930s, at the peak of its popularity, the middle classes were happily queuing outside chippies.

¶ Comparatively recently, and rather by accident, the now familiar polystyrene chip tray made its mark on this dish-cum-institution. The chip tray owes its existence in large part to the unstable properties of printers ink, coupled with a certain squeamishness with regard to food hygiene. From its inception, fish and chips had been wrapped in the cheapest form of packaging available: yesterday's newspapers. However, in the 1970s and 80s newspaper owners began to experiment with new types of ink. Although cheaper, they were also more susceptible to transferring onto the fingers of readers. When the ink came into contact with hot batter and a liberal dose of vinegar, it leapt off the page faster than the headlines themselves.

¶ Contrary to popular belief, there is no Act of Parliament banning the use of newspaper as a wrapping for fish and chips; it was environmental health inspectors who took a dim view of this unwelcome new condiment. There are several reasons why many chip shop owners found a solution in the polystyrene chip tray — they are cheap, feather-light and stackable, and usefully gauge the correct size of a portion of chips.

¶ To say that the chip tray has been taken to the hearts of the public would be to over-state the esteem in which it is held by some margin. Above all else, it is a very dull object visually. Trays *per se* are functional articles: a flat surface, usually an oblong, with a raised edge all round. Their simplicity has left them largely impervious to radical changes of design and the chip tray has not bucked the trend. Perhaps if they were pillarbox red or covered in yellow and black stripes or had some other markings that characterised them as chip trays and nothing else, they might establish some sort of tradition and we might muster some affection for them. As it is, the overwhelming majority of chip trays are the default colour shared by every other object made of expanded polystyrene: brilliant white.

¶ Found in numerous other outlets conveying a range of completely different fast foods to consumers, its genericism compounds the lack of sense of the chip tray being special in any way. It repeats its uniform monotony wherever it appears. Understandably, this lends it a feel of the corporate, which doesn't sit well with the independent spirit of fish and chip shops, the vast majority of which are individually owned (Harry Ramsden's chain notwithstanding). Even the fact that trays spare consumers from the burns and vinegar-seepage traditional newspaper wrapping was wont to subject them to, is outweighed by the argument that the pro-tection they afford sanitises, and thereby diminishes, the whole fish and chips experience.

¶ If this were not enough, chip trays are fast joining supermarket plastic bags as the anti-eco-warriors of our times. Unlike plastic bags, customers have no option to refuse them. Until recently they were a source of chlorofluorocarbons (CFC) and only a very small proportion of them are recyclable. The vast majority are not biodegradable and, unlike plastic drinks bottles

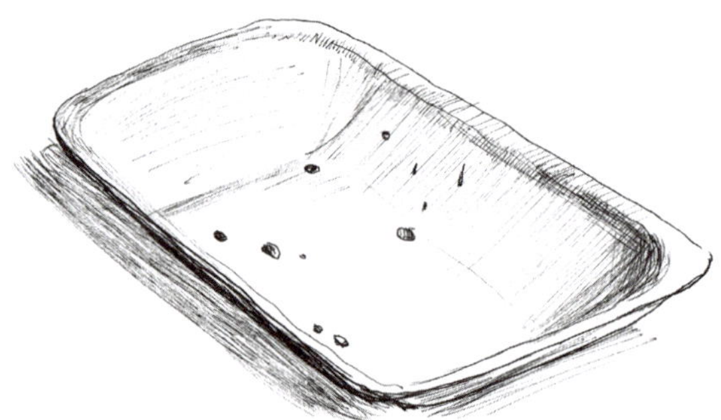

Gavin Turk Chish'n'Fips 2004
Resin and painted bronze, 5 × 12 × 19 cm
A bronze cast of a polystyrene chip tray painted to look real

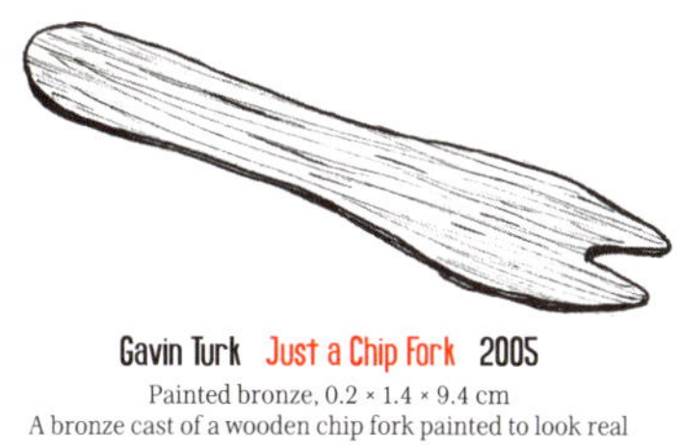

Gavin Turk   *Just a Chip Fork*   2005
Painted bronze, 0.2 × 1.4 × 9.4 cm
A bronze cast of a wooden chip fork painted to look real

which biodegrade in five to ten years, or chewing gum (which takes 25 years), polystyrene chip trays will be still be polystyrene chip trays on the day the universe collapses in on itself.

¶   Since the chip tray's useful life extends only for the length of time it takes for a person to eat the food it contains, it is no surprise that it has become an archetype of British litter. If a television drama requires a shorthand reference to urban grit or rural squalor, all they need to do is scatter a few used chip trays around.

¶   For the sake of authenticity, a number of miniature wooden forks would need to be sedulously strewn around too. In common with the chip tray, the chip fork is a relative newcomer and has found itself just as likely to turn into litter. One could argue, since they are typically bought from wholesalers in job lots of 20,000 at a cost of less than a halfpenny each, that chip forks are produced for the express purpose of being thrown away and that the ten-minute period in which they are employed to shovel chips into a mouth is an aberration. As would-be pieces of art these are not so much *objets trouvés* as *objets jetés*.

¶   At least there is some aesthetic pleasure to be gained. The organic feel of the wood between fingers complements the texture of the paper wrap held in the other hand. The chip fork's sinuous curves, rounded handle and aggressively slanted tines lend it the appearance of a Weeble crossed with an angry tadpole. Flipped sideways and it all but disappears, prefiguring its ineluctable disappearance into the cracks, crevices and fissures of the street, the Bic pen of the pavement. Perhaps in the end its most important function is as a delineator of human beings: after all, what sort of person buys a portion of chips and imagines themselves too precious to eat with their fingers?

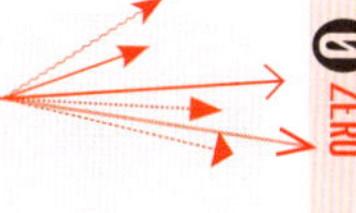

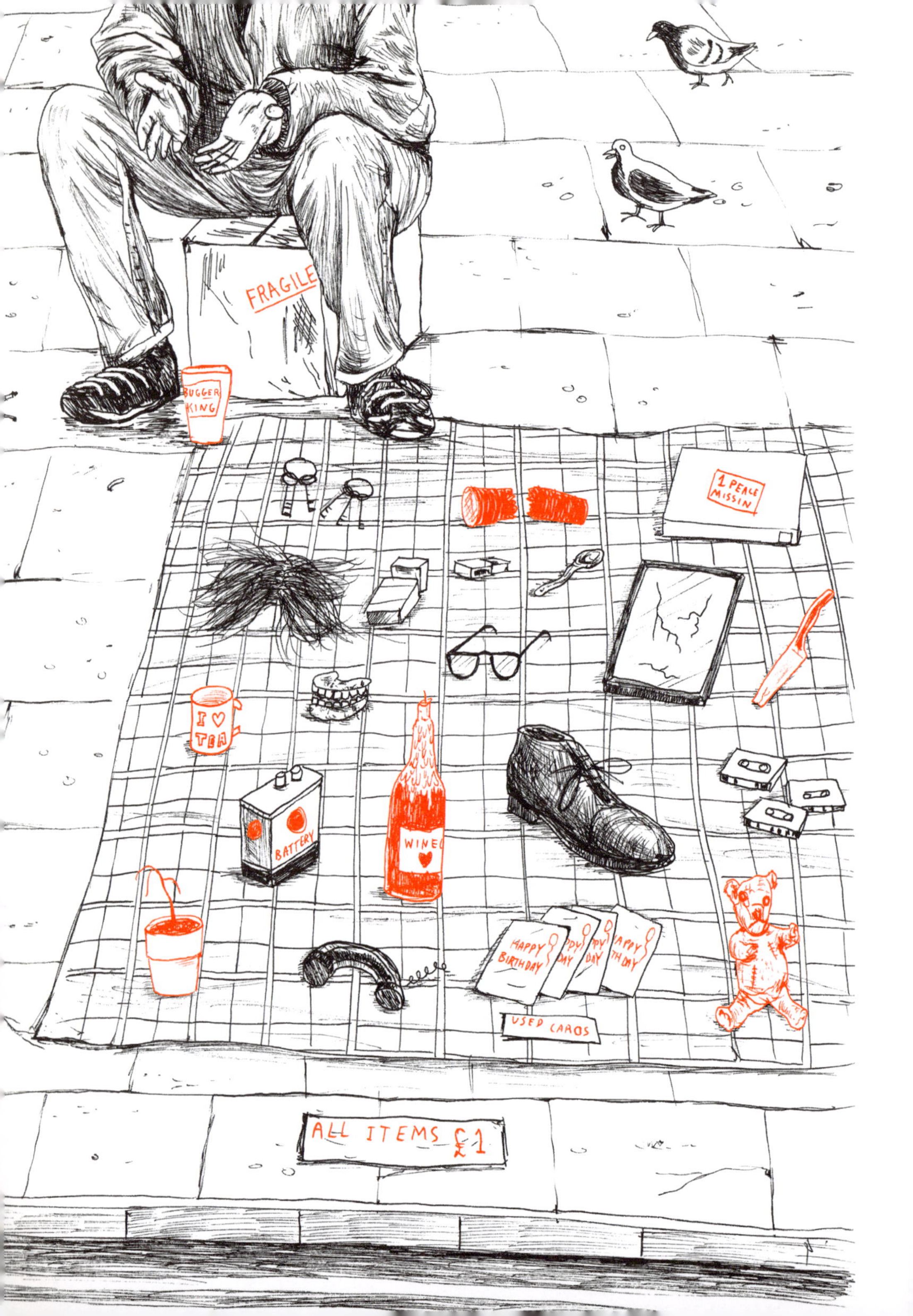

FRAGILE
BUGGER KING
1 PEACE MISSIN
I ♥ TEA
BATTERY
WINE
HAPPY BIRTHDAY
HAPPY DAY
PY DAY
HAPPY TH DAY
USED CARDS
ALL ITEMS £1

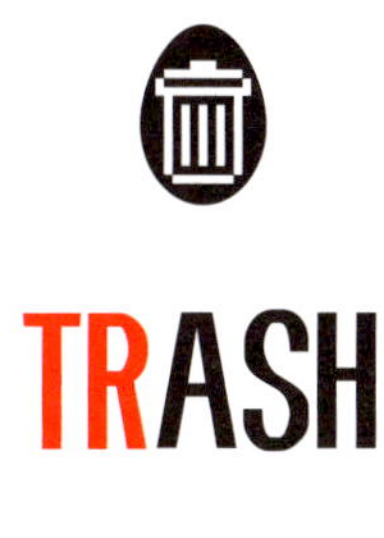

TRASH

Kate de Syllas

"Here we have a man whose job it is to gather the day's refuse in the capital. Everything that the big city has thrown away, everything it has lost, everything it has scorned, everything it has crushed underfoot he catalogues and collects. He collates the annals of intemperance, the Capharnaum of waste. He sorts things out and selects judiciously: he collects like a miser guarding a treasure, refuse which will assume the shape of useful or gratifying objects between the jaws of the goddess of Industry."

Walter Benjamin, *The Arcades Project*

While it was written between 1927 and 1940, Benjamin's description of a city garbage collector remains remarkably current. It offers a clear sense of a parallel between waste and culture, and in particular, our contemporary mores, where cultural artefacts are made obsolete almost before they exist. Where once musicians or fashion designers hoped for some longevity for their work, the market and its insatiable appetites now lead. Trash pop sung by footballers' girlfriends and £25 cashmere from Primark are our cultural markers.

¶   **It could also** be seen as a description of the artistic process — in the choosing of one item or idea, we reject something else — the process by which we continually redefine the boundaries of our culture. Yet in a world stage managed by a disposable media, we often find that we reject our own internal senses of discrimination and differentiation and allow

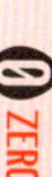

someone else to make, or at least lead, our choices. This is one way that the culture can become limited — defined by one strata of society, whose motives are monetary wealth, as opposed to the limits of the culture being set by society as a whole, motivated by a collective, mental wealth. Gavin Turk's painted bronze sculptures of bulging rubbish bags reminds us of this value system, and also of the fringes of the culture and the waste in our society. It is poetic in its minimalism.

¶ **Garbage refers to things,** ideas, even people that we have devalued, separated and removed — a valuable rubbish bag is seemingly a paradox we cannot reconcile. Understanding that the idea of waste can only exist within a dichotomy would seem to be helpful — yet it doesn't exist in a clearly oppositional system. We would perhaps like to think that we keep what is good and throw out what is bad, but this is clearly not the case.

¶ **As a society,** the scale of our wastefulness is alarming. In the case of the 33% of fresh food that ends up in the UK's bins, we can see that we are squandering resources and repudiating the idea of waste as that which is not wanted or needed. At this point in the Earth's history, food is both desperately wanted and needed. Yet moral, cultural and intellectual waste are equally a problem in our accelerated culture. A waste of time, a waste of space, a wasted idea. "What a waste" we say as another child star fires themself into the mental stratosphere, and we gobble it up from the mass of papers and trash magazines that fill green boxes up and down the land.

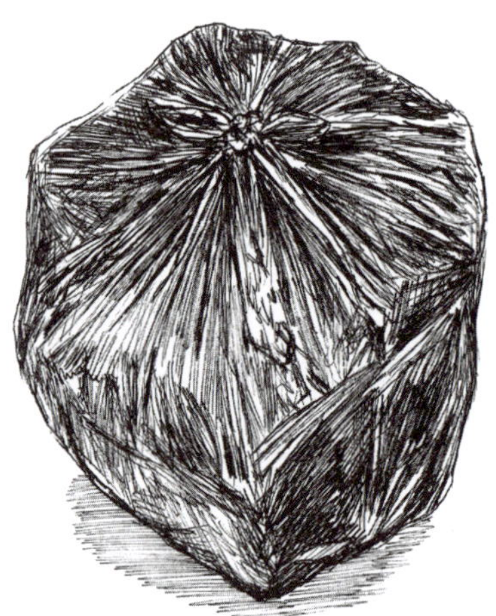

Gavin Turk Bag 2000
Painted bronze, 43 × 46 × 53 cm
A bronze cast of a full rubbish bag painted to look real

¶ **Still, the natural** and beautifully cyclical nature of waste almost lends itself to cultural expression, sometimes almost too clearly. Damien Hirst created an installation re-creating the remains of a party — empty bottles, full ashtrays — the gallery janitor mistook the work for the very thing it was supposed to represent and so cleared it up and threw the full bin bags away, closing the loop. The psycho-geographical also resonates. Kingsland Waste ("waste" once being the Middle English word for an uninhabitable area or wildernes) has become a market of waste. Vendors sell obsolete phone chargers and half-empty bags of Ikea fittings, single shoes and odd pairs of gloves. That this area was once a waste, bubbles up from the past and refuses the march of gentrification.

¶ **Perhaps strangely,** for something we often like to ignore, waste is now more important than ever. Not since the "Great Stink" of the mid-Victorian period and the subsequent overhaul of urban planning, have we been so tied to the things we throw away. With the Victorian idea of the "miasma" — exhalations from decaying matter — as a source of disease, society was forced to examine how it dealt with its waste.

¶ **With climate change,** recycling and land-fill on the political and moral agenda, we too are compelled to (re)examine the things we no longer want. As waste, and the management of waste, gain increasing economic and environmental importance, it is increasingly easy for us to see how our waste can become something new, even unfamiliar — the life of anything is transitory, changeable, malleable. There is a strange and uneasy grace to the new life and value that are always a possibility — a cardboard box becomes a chair, a tyre becomes a pen.

¶ **Yet if the value system** we operate on is always linked to fiscal value, the culture stagnates — perhaps, like people ready to re-engage with creating a less wasteful culture, we can re-engage with the giving and meaning of value within our culture. And so it is that the things we throw away as worthless, ultimately remind us of who, and what we are.

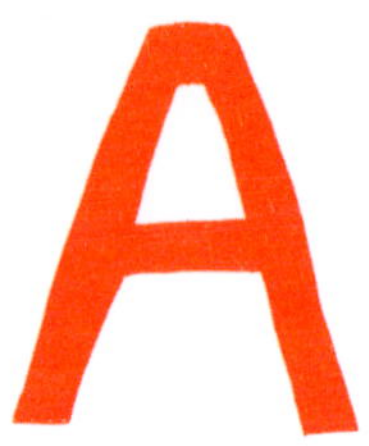

A IS FOR APPLE

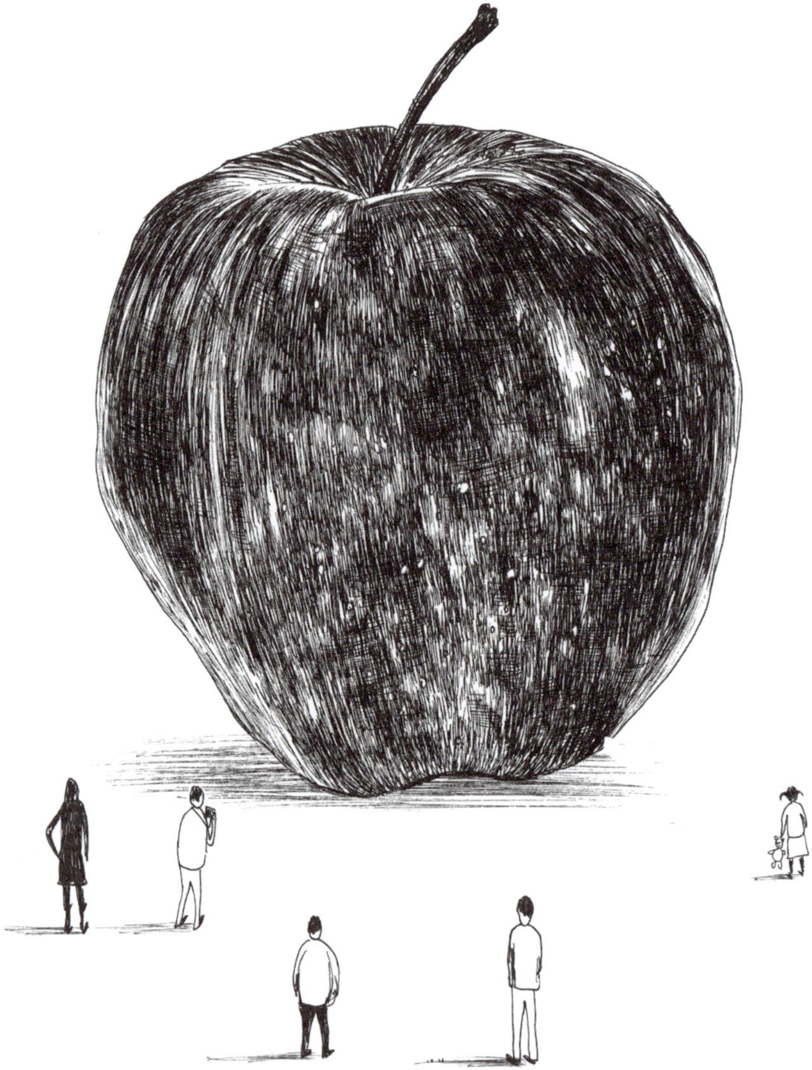

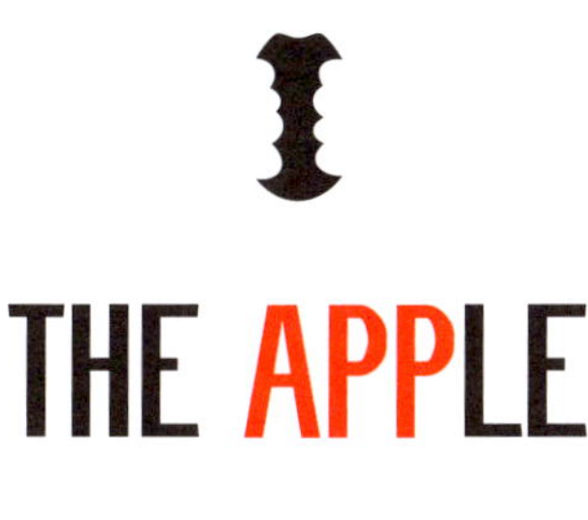

THE APPLE

Betsy de Lotbinière

From The Book of Genesis to The Beatles

In *Genesis*, the apple is the initiator of all opposites. Everything was "yes" in paradise until, suddenly, in 3950BC, "no" put in an appearance; the first couple could eat anything apart from the fruit of the apple tree. Blame it on the snake who sold the temptation, but Eve is the one who listened. Sin is what Bible believers focus on — we'll never recover from this first apple, this first forbidden fruit sampled, this first mistake. They paint this as the Original Sin and claim we are all rotten at the core. Eve was told "don't" and burned to answer the first ever "what if?" Risking that first bite makes this first woman the first artist, the first philosopher, the first revolutionary — and the first scientist.

¶ When learning the English language, the letter A denotes this superstar of the fruit world, making it one of the first words we read. The apple has its own constellation of attendant stories: "Do you trust me?" a Swiss archer named Tell asked his son. "Put an apple on your head and stand very still..." Greeks connected the fruit to Aphrodite who was awarded the Golden Apple by Paris. She bribed him by promising another man's wife, the beautiful Helen of Troy, thus kicking off the Trojan War. The connection to the goddess of love entered into their language of courtship. "If I throw an apple your way, know that I love you and if you catch it? You accept my love."

¶   "The good that men do, lives on after them," was the moral of Johnny Appleseed. An American ascetic who wore a saucepan for a hat, he heroically planted apple trees along an estimated 100,000 square miles on the paths likely to be used by the early settlers. For the apple was not indigenous to North America but introduced by seventeenth century European settlers. This queen of fruit comes from Western Asia — some say Turkey, others Kazakhstan. "Eat an apple a day to keep the doctor away," the Welsh began saying in the nineteenth century. "One bite and she will fall into a sleep so profound as to appear dead." The Evil Queen used an alluring apple in her plot against Snow White.

¶   The archetypal Tree of Life or Tree of Knowledge is depicted as an apple tree. A cousin of the rose, she is hearty, sweet smelling and beautiful in flower. Each flower has five petals. Slice an apple open from side to side and you will see five carpels that hold the seeds, forming a five-pointed star, in golden ratio: the ratio of the whole to the larger portion is the same as the ratio of the larger portion to the smaller. Its sacred nature is endlessly, exactly repeatable, infinite.

¶   The apple never falls far from the tree. Or does it? In England, the Yorkshire Goosesauce, the Egremont, the Laxton's Superb, the Beauty of Bath and Cox's Orange Pippins (to name but a few of 2,200 varieties of apples in the UK), were unexpectedly propagated by the railway. Once the core of this handiest of travelling snacks was tossed out of the window of speeding trains, it would settle into random fields and sink roots. Which is how the early-to-ripe Worcester Pearmain spontaneously sprouted up in Plymouth. The ubiquitous apple tumbles into moral phrases. "The rotten apple spoils its companions," warned Benjamin Franklyn. Take one for your teacher as an acceptable means of kissing ass.

¶   The Beatles named their record label, Apple, after a painting — or at least that's one version of the story. Sir Paul McCartney tells it this way:

¶   "In my garden at Cavendish Avenue, which was a 100-year-old house I'd bought, Robert [Fraser, the art dealer, a.k.a. Groovy Bob] was a frequent visitor. One day he got hold

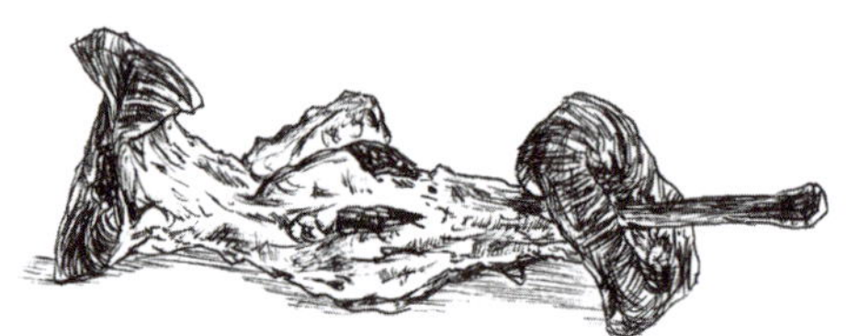

Gavin Turk Original Sin 2005
Painted bronze, 2.5 × 2.4 × 5.3 cm
A bronze cast of an apple core painted to look real

of a Magritte he thought I'd love. Being Robert, he would just get it and bring it. I was out in the garden with some friends. I think I was filming Mary Hopkin with a crew, just getting her to sing live in the garden with bees and flies buzzing around, high summer. We were in the long grass — very beautiful, very country-like. Robert didn't want to interrupt so when we went back in the big door from the garden to the living room, there on the table he'd just propped up this little Magritte. It was of a green apple. Across the painting Magritte had written in that beautiful handwriting of his, *"Au revoir"*. And Robert had split. I thought that was the coolest thing anyone's ever done for me. That became the basis of the Apple logo."

¶ As a young man, Steve Jobs picked apples to pay the rent while he twiddled with assembling and creating home computer sets. When it came time to name the nascent company, he sought to align its newness with a sense of inevitability. His first logo was an image of Newton being hit on the head by an apple when the notion of gravity was born. Later, the logo became a simple apple with a bite taken out of it — a play on the word "byte", a unit of digital information. He was warned against using an apple as the symbol for his technological revolution, but chose to go ahead with it. Of course. The Beatles sued.

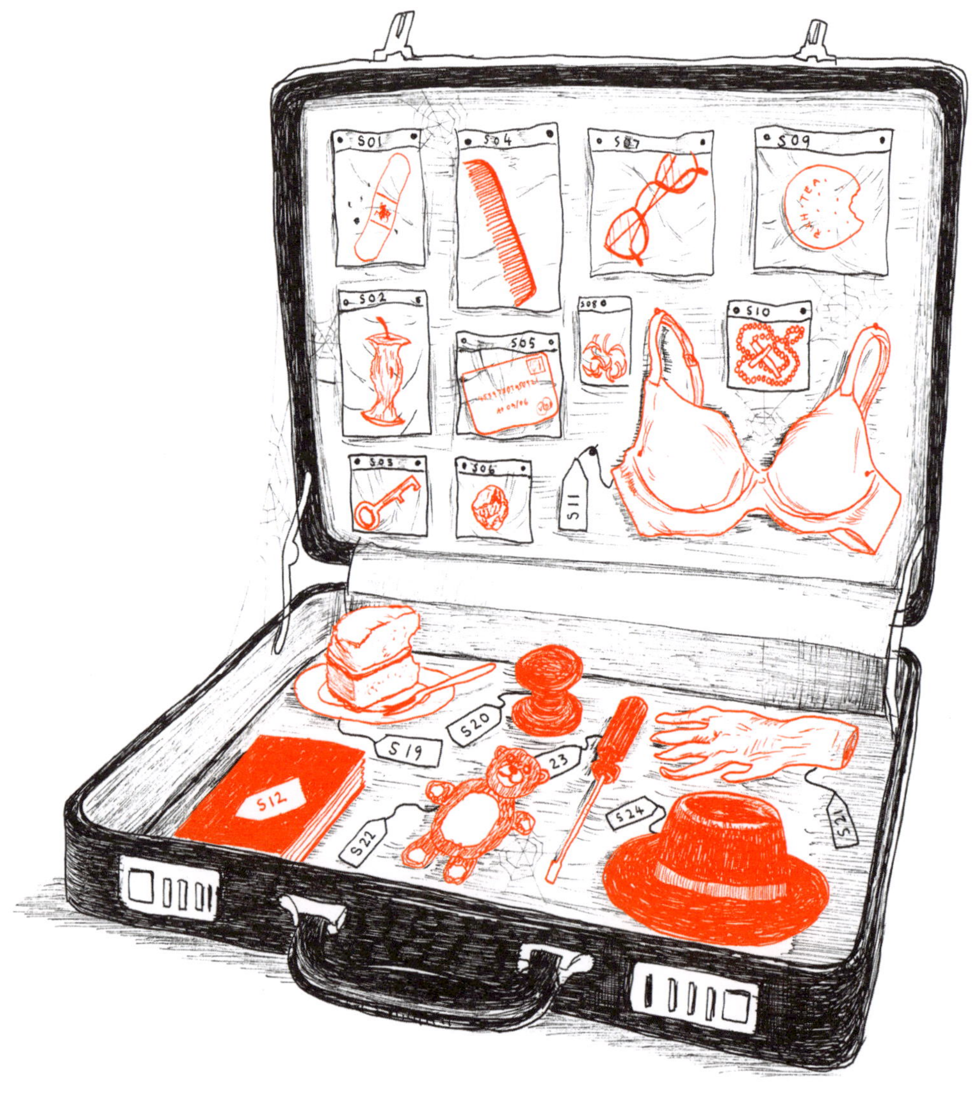

S01
S04
S07
S09
S02
S05
S08
S10
S03
S06
S11
S12
S19
S20
23
S24
S22
S21

GARBAGE

Jessica Voorsanger

The fine line between rubbish and gold

Aside from the fact that rubbish can be so telling about its owners (current or previous), it can also be collectible. In the case of a devoted fan, there can be nothing more precious than an object previously owned by their idol. I have several such items which I have shown as artworks, as well as objects I may one day exhibit which are valuable and precious to me which are rubbish.

¶ The most special is the plate (complete with mustard stains, napkin and stale crisps) used by David Cassidy when I was lucky enough to have lunch with him. I fell in love with David Cassidy at the age of six. Now with several years distance on this, I don't want to spend the rest of my life with him, but David Cassidy was/is a very handsome and a non-threatening first crush. He embodied both music and TV (happily combined in the form of *The Partridge Family*) and was my first full-on popular culture fixation.

¶ The plate and napkin wouldn't necessarily have become rubbish, but because I technically stole them from the hotel, they never got the chance to be washed and re-used. To the uninformed, they live in the same category of the "used and discarded items" any other form of rubbish would be. But as a fan, I don't want his plate or napkin to be cleaned, ever; I want them to have his invisible fingerprints as a substitute for him being here. He actually gave them to me (even though they weren't his to give) and was slightly bemused, especially as the lunch was in the guise of an interview. I spoke too much and never really gave him a chance to get a word in edgeways — an interview technique I highly recommend.

¶ Sir Bob Geldof's goods were actually pilfered. I happened to be near his house one day and there happened to be a rubbish bag outside the front. The next thing I knew, I had the bag in a new location with my elbows deep in smelly rubbish selecting choice items to be perused later — things like empty packets and old correspondence. I showed the items in an exhibition which was featured in the *Daily Mail* and led to me being invited onto *The Big Breakfast* show. I was terrified — not by the fact I was going to be on TV, but by the fact the programme was owned by Bob Geldof. I was convinced he would have the police at the gates to arrest me as I arrived.

¶ Luckily this wasn't the case, and while I was being interviewed, I was presented with the rubbish of the presenters Zöe Ball, Vanessa Feltz and Keith Chegwin — an excellent line-up! But the instant these items became a gift, they stopped being rubbish and became something quite precious: souvenirs, tokens, connections to their previous owners. Of course I later showed these items in an exhibition, too. And although I was disappointed, I wasn't surprised that Vanessa Feltz's broken earring was stolen. It just continued the pattern.

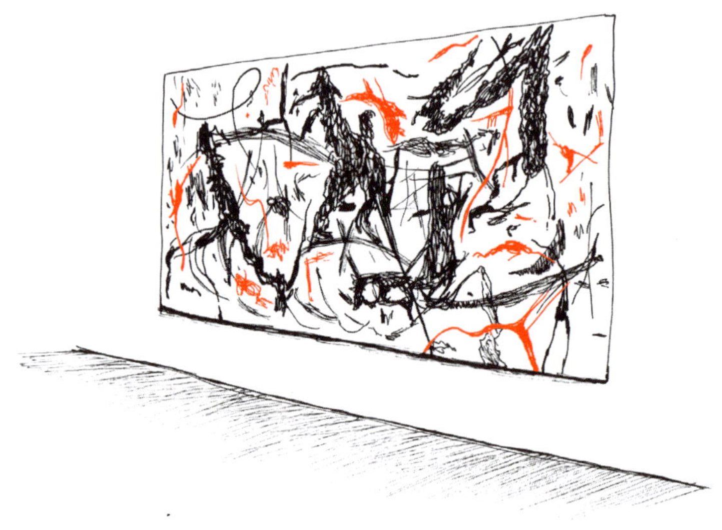

Dan Colen S&M 2010
Chewing gum on canvas, 121.9 × 182.9 cm

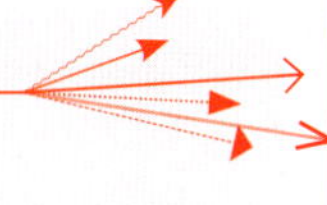
ZERO

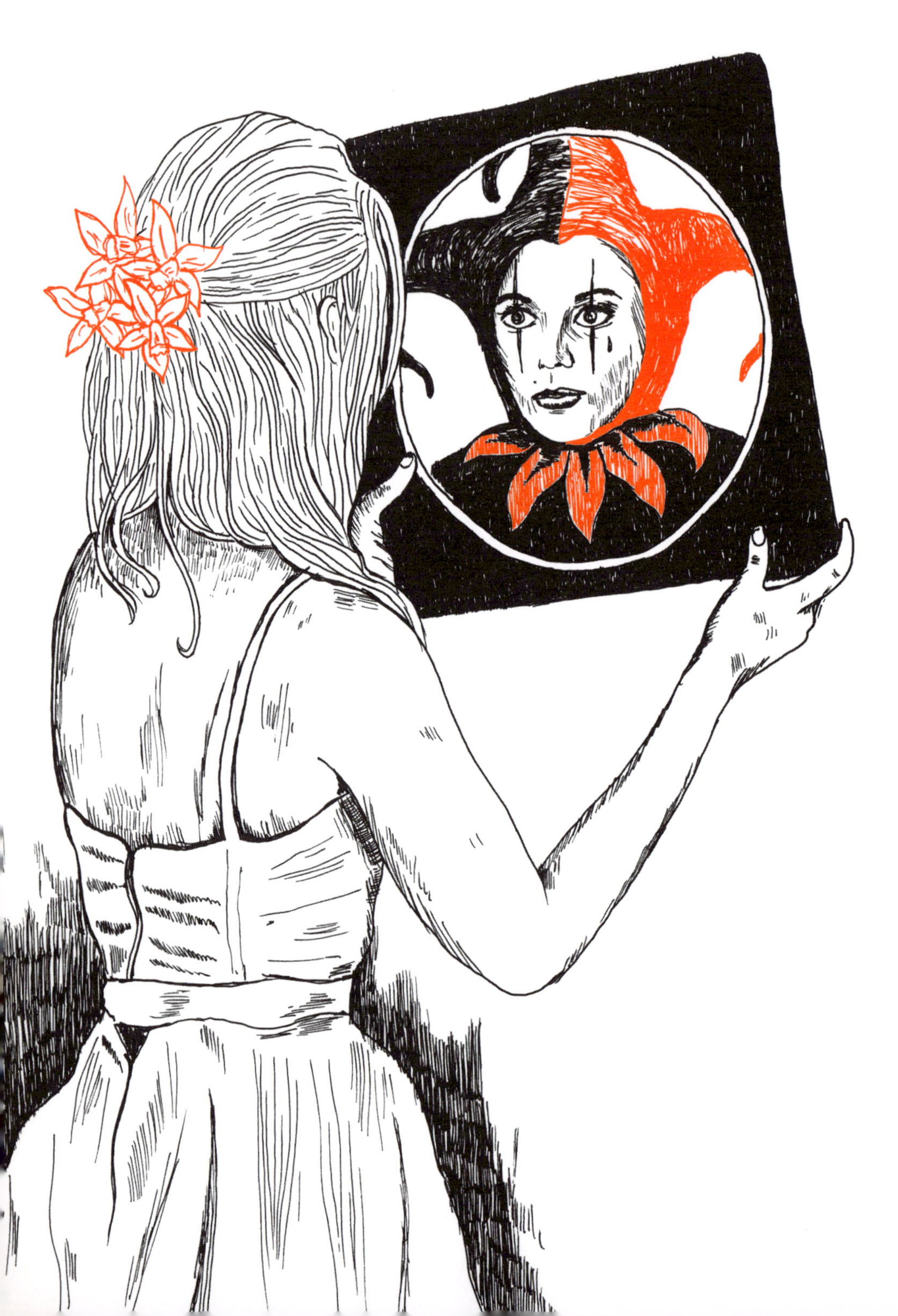

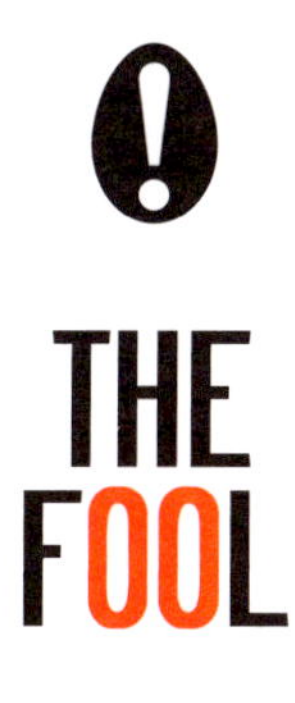

THE FOOL

Hari Kunzru

"This work I call a looking glass
In which each fool shall see an ass...
Whoever sees with open eyes
Cannot regard himself as wise
For he shall see upon reflection
That humans teem with imperfection"

Sebastian Brant, *The Ship of Fools*, 1494

Who is the fool? In the tarot pack, he is shown as a figure setting out on a journey, with a bundle on his back and a little dog tugging at his ragged clothes. Sometimes he is about to step off a cliff. The dog, symbol of social domesticity, is trying to drag him back home. But is the fool making a mistake, or taking a leap of faith? Is he actually wise? Verbal and visual genealogies of the fool link him with other figures — the beggar, the madman, the mascot, the scapegoat, the seer, the poet. Many of these figures intersect with Romantic images of the creative artist: the inspired outsider, at once absurd and magnificent. So, among other things, the fool is an artist, and the artist is a fool.

¶   As a historical figure, the court fool is a parasite, a professional dinner guest. In Ancient Greece, *parasitos* was originally a dignifed term, applied to someone invited to official banquets because of his personal merits. It soon became debased, a word for a flatterer, a wit, someone who would use his talent for clowning, mimcry or telling jokes in return for a free meal. The fool is an entertainer, sitting at table with the nobility, his position privileged but precarious. He must never be ordinary, never dull. The artist sits at table next to the collector, then goes back to his underheated studio.

¶   The fool has a very special position at court, or the gallery dinner. He is "all-licensed", empowered to say and do things others wouldn't dare. Sometimes he is a wise fool, cleverly telling truths under the guise of wit. He may also be a "natural", a dwarf or a cripple or a moron. His physical or mental deficiencies place him outside the normal social system, depriving him of both rights and responsibilities. The fool speaks truth to power, but since he is dressed in motley, a caperer in cap and bells, no one is obliged to listen. "This is nothing, fool" says Kent in *King Lear*, and the fool knows as much. His words can be ignored if they are too near the mark. "Then 'tis like the breath of an unfeed lawyer," he quips. "You give me nothing for it." No one need draw his sword: there's no honour in avenging the fool's insults.

¶   Above all, the fool is the only one who can insult the king. His jokes lay bare how the regime functions — the political regime of power, the aesthetic and economic regimes of value, the epistemological regime of meaning. Only through the fool's clowning is the regime made visible to itself. The king needs the fool, for he is surrounded by sycophants. Yet however wise he is, the fool must never mistake himself for someone influential, who can wield power like ordinary men. This was the error of Archibald Armstrong, court fool to James I. Armstrong went as far as travelling as part of a royal embassy to Spain, where an off-colour quip to the Infanta about the sinking of the Spanish Armada undermined months of careful negotiation. Nevertheless, he thought of himself as a masterful diplomat, signing himself paradoxically "youre best foole of State" in a letter to his royal master. His talent for making enemies finally tripped him up when he insulted the Archbishop of Canterbury and was permanently banished from court.

¶   Armstrong tried (and occasionally succeeded) in bridging the gap between foolery and political power, never accepting their essential opposition — if the fool is taken seriously, he will be hanged for his insolence. To be a fool is to be *homo sacer*, an exile from the Law. In the formulation of Giorgio Agamben, the ordinary person has two types or levels of life — basic biological existence (*zoë*) and political or social life (*bios*). The fool is denied *bios*, the life of the subject or the citizen. He has no status, no rights or responsibilities, only bare life. What he does has no significance. Nor what is done to him. This is why, as Erasmus says in *In Praise of Folly*, "the most violent tyrants put up with their clowns and fools, though these often make them the butt of open insults". Since the fool is *homo sacer*, under a state of exception from the Law (the Law of courtly honour, of social propriety), he is a living demonstration of the sovereign's power to give the Law, to enforce it or suspend it at his pleasure. So the fool is related to several figures from our contemporary period of permanent emergency — the stateless person, the untouchable, the unlawful combatant, the concentration camp inmate, the mental patient, the refugee. All live under the same suspension of the Law, isolated from social and political existence.

¶ Though, he is only a "poor, bare forked animal", sometimes the fool can be a king. In his role as the Lord of Misrule he is, as Mikhail Bakhtin puts it, "the constant accredited representation of the carnival spirit in everyday life" For Bakhtin —

> *"Carnival celebrates temporary liberation from the prevailing truth and from the established order; it marks the suspension of all heirarchical rank, privileges, norms and prohibitions. Carnival [is] the true feast of time, the feast of becoming, change and renewal. It [is] hostile to all that [is] immortalised and completed."*

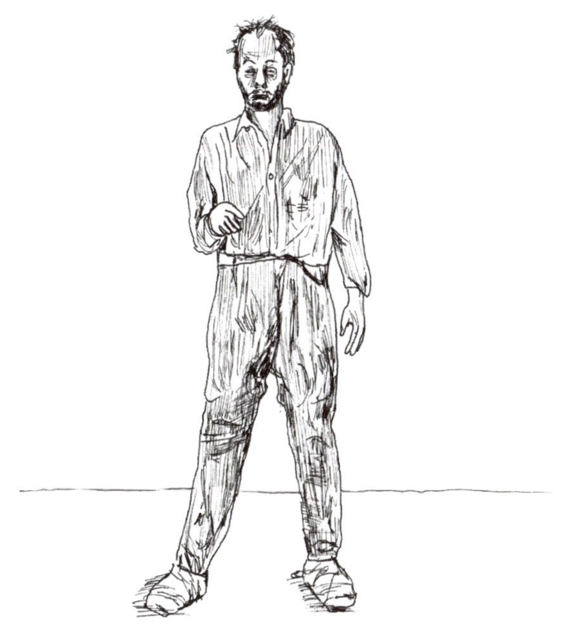

Gavin Turk Another Bum 1999
Waxwork, 167 × 70 × 70 cm
Life size waxwork of the artist as a tramp

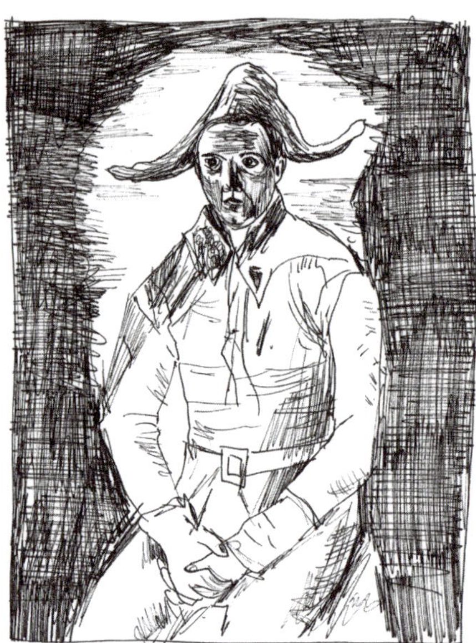

Pablo Picasso   Seated Harlequin   1923
Oil on canvas, 130 × 97 cm
Portrait of the painter Jacinto Salvado dressed as a harlequin

¶   The fool is productively disruptive. He just won't let things be. At the feast of fools, the slave is master, women are men, excrement replaces incense at the ritual and the dignified clergy are paraded about the streets in carts. The fool inverts the king, and during the period of his carnival rule, the iron network of moral, physical and social law feels temporarily as light as air. The powerful art collector becomes a puppet. The heroic artist is a tramp. The great names of the past are no more than waxworks.

¶   If the fool is an artist and the artist is a fool, that was never more true than now, after conceptualism. The Romantic artist struggles with the raw material of the world, transmuting it into art through the heroic operation of his genius. The conceptual fool reduces this to absurdity, by eschewing the noble work of transmutation. He may claim an everyday object as art. He may utilise comically humble materials or use noble ones to fashion humble things. He may reproduce an artwork that already exists. He may reduce his art to the simplest artistic gesture of all — that of signing his own name. So Duchamp is a fool. Warhol is a fool. Foolish Piero Manzoni says shit is gold. Beuys is a fool, though often he forgets. People get angry at this motley crew of artists, who say art can be made of repetition, boredom, or banality. Artists should be hacking away at a block of marble, not sleeping late and getting drunk on promotional beer. Art should involve craft. Craft should involve skill, difficulty. Conceptualism makes craft look foolish — mere dexterity, juggling.

*"When we are born, we cry that we are come
To this great stage of fools."*

¶   This is Lear's realisation, the truth that bawling babies know and adults forget as we get caught up in the serious mummery of our social and cultural lives. Only the fool-artist still knows the truth, and we carry him about in an international *charivari*, the pope of piffle, the sultan of senselessness. The artworld (the very term is a carnivalesque inversion of the real world) is a veritable ship of fools — gallerists and curators and collectors and writers and artists all stroking their long velvety asses' ears, taking the fool seriously, buying his golden shit. No accident that Brant's medieval poem was first published in Basel. What could be more ridiculous than the consensual hallucination of artistic value? Hey nonny!

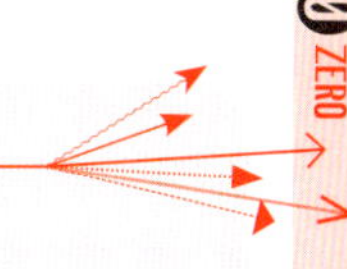

SEE ALSO:

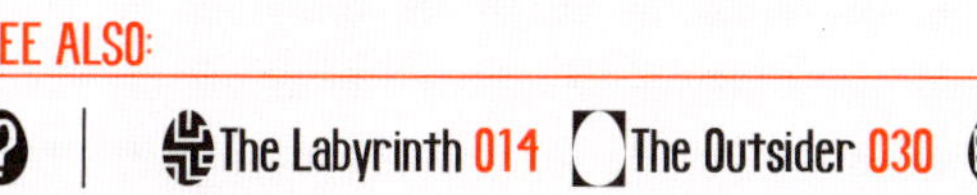

The Labyrinth 014   The Outsider 030   Sid Vicious 034

Money 076

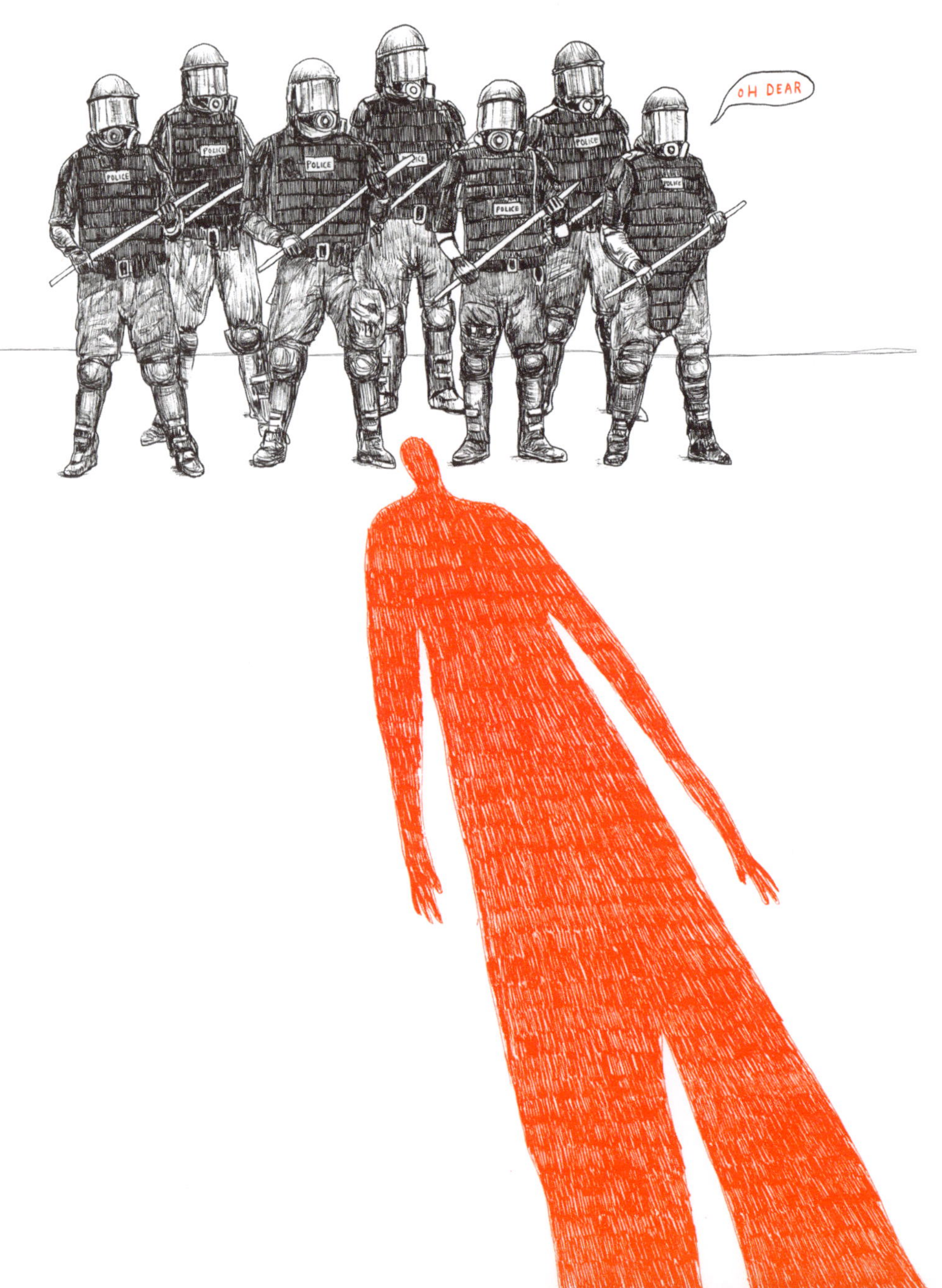

POLICE
POLICE
POLICE
POLICE
POLICE
POLICE
OH DEAR

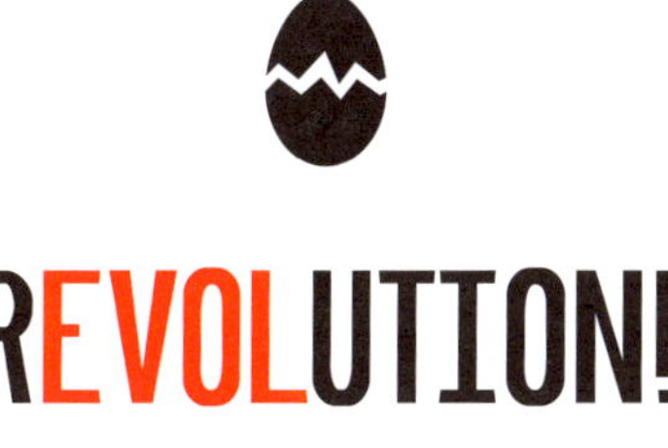

REVOLUTION!

Noel Douglas

How the social media revolution was dreamt by the 20th century avant-garde

"Your life is your life; don't let it be clubbed into dank submission. Be on the watch. There are ways out. There is light somewhere. It may not be much light but it beats the darkness. Be on the watch. The gods will offer you chances. Know them. Take them. You can't beat death but you can beat death in life, sometimes. And the more often you learn to do it, the more light there will be. Your life is your life. Know it while you have it. You are marvellous; the gods wait to delight in you."

These words, ripped off from *The Laughing Heart* by Charles Bukowski formed the spoken word soundtrack to an ad campaign for Levi's, titled *Go Forth*. The campaign's visuals showed images of youthful rioters and revolution. By chance, it launched as the largest riots in a generation hit London in the summer of 2011; needless to say, the campaign was pulled in the UK.

¶   But in many ways this campaign sums up capitalism's recuperation of the revolts in the 60s and 70s and how the demands for personal liberation that came from those times have been accommodated into our consumer culture; revolution — as long as it's personal and not social — is still used to wrap commodities in a radical gloss. Yet despite this recuperation, when real revolt and revolution is outside the door, its limits are exposed.

¶   This struggle — the clash between capitalism's need to commodify and our cultural need for meaning — is made all the more apparent by the "answering back" nature of

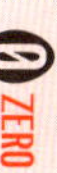

social media. Sure enough, a few weeks later a video response was uploaded on YouTube with a simple adjustment to the original ad in the form of the following text —

"Capitalists have stolen the whole world from us and poetry and protest even riots can become advertisements for products. Our bodies, our moments of joy are flattened into images that impoverish our lives. Now their system is collapsing, let's tear it down."

¶   The video was hijacked and its meaning shifted. The ease with which this is now possible for many across the world opens up possibilities for a real democratisation of culture and society. In many ways, this process is underway most visibly with the arguments and problems being created for copyright and value through the explosion of networked social media use.

¶   The democratic idea of people being both producers and consumers of culture is part of the legacy of the radical avant-garde art and design movements of the twentieth century and their belief that the overthrow of capitalism could lead to a society where art would be fully integrated into life and not, to use Marx's words, "in the hands of priestly castes". Properly understood, this did not mean—as many people think—that everyone would become an artist on the dissolution of capitalism; rather, that production and culture would, wherever possible, become infused with a holistic creativity that could lift the general level of humanity to new, uncharted heights. Meanwhile, the idea of competition — so destructive under capitalism and its struggle over resources — would become about the competition of artistic tendencies of all in the collective construction of everyday life.

¶   The interesting thing about social media is how its use echoes the democratic potential seen by theorists and activists in the 1920s in (then) new forms of mass communication — radio, television and film. Intellectuals like Walter Benjamin wrote about authors being producers; the Russian Productivists developed ideas like that of the "operative writer" who is at once a sociologist, photographer, economist, filmmaker, producer and a master of the new apparatus like radio. Brecht echoed this ideal in his 1927 essay *Radio as a Communications Apparatus* (radio, it should be remembered, was initially developed as a two-way medium and only closed down to a broadcast medium as it became commericalised). Constructivist Sergei Tretiakov had the idea of a two-way newspaper where listeners/readers could become broadcasters/writers and *vice versa*. Russian formalist Viktor Shklovsky developed the technique of "making strange" or "defamiliarisation", which was a way of forcing the audience to see common things in an unfamiliar or strange way, in order to enhance perception of the familiar.

¶ These ideas drew their inspiration and sense of revolutionary urgency from being part of the much wider wave of revolution and revolt that swept Europe in the aftermath of World War One. The Russian Revolution, the (failed) German Revolution, the Biennio Rosso Years in Italy, the Budapest Commune, the Spanish Civil War were only a few of the enormous struggles of mass workers movements of millions against capitalist and fascist forces, and the fate of the avant-garde was totally tied up with them, as Trotsky said in 1934 —

"Cubism, Futurism, Dadaism and Surrealism have all superceded each other without any of them coming to fruition... It is impossible to find a way out of this impasse by means of art alone... If society does not succeed in reconstructing itself, art will inevitably perish. Hence, the function of art is our era is determined by its relation to the Revolution."

¶ The war put most of that generation in their graves, leaving revolutionary movements weakened and allowing capitalism to find its feet, leading to the long boom of the 50s and 60s. But the embers of the ideas of the avant-garde still glowed in a few. One such group was the Letterist International, a Paris based collective of radical artists and theorists in the mid 50s. The Letterists were the first to talk of the way capitalism recuperated radical culture. They came up with the artistic strategy of "detournement", a technique of re-utilising plagiarised material for a new and usually radical purpose — this idea prefigures the

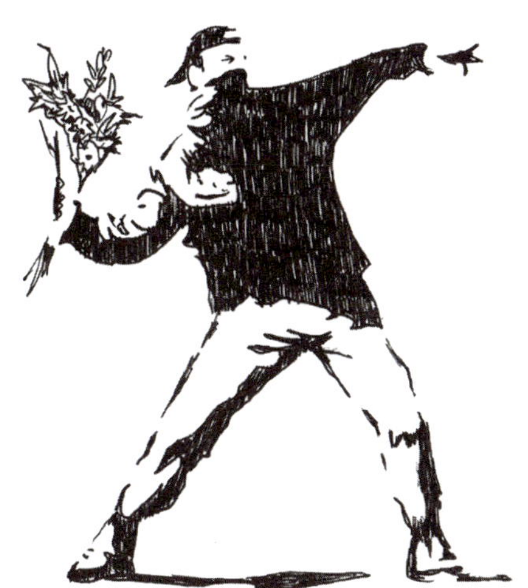

Banksy Flower Thrower 2002
Reusable stencil, various sizes

re-mix culture of social media shown in our Levi's example by nearly half a century. It was described by Guy Debord as necessary —

"to do away with the whole notion of personal property in this area. The emergence of new demands renders earlier 'great works' obsolete. They become obstacles, bad habits. It is not a question of whether we like them or not. We must pass them by."

¶   The Situationists, led by Debord, developed out of the Letterist International. As the 50s turned into the 60s, they developed the idea of detournement further. Debord wrote the book and film *Society of the Spectacle* which described living in —

"... [a] Society of the Spectacle, a world where everything that was previously directly lived had moved away into representation, a world where Capital has accumulated so much as to become an image, where people were spectators rather than actors."

¶   In doing so Debord detourned writings of Henri Lefebvre, Marx and György Lukács in the book, and everything from clips of old films to adverts for the film, which was entirely made of found material. To combat the spectacle, one proposal from the the Situationists was the creation of "situations", by which they meant a spontaneous moment without mediation of any kind. Debord wrote that situations were to be

"a moment of life concretely and deliberately constructed by the collective organisation of a unitary ambiance and a game of events."

¶   The ultimate situation being The Revolution — something which seemed unlikely in the early 60s, when standards of living were improving hugely in Europe and there was full employment. But as the decade rolled on, a wave of radicalisation swept the globe in size not too dissimilar to the early 20s. A number of countries saw riots and revolts. In France, the mass general strike of May 1968 brought the country to the point of revolution. The Situationists' moment had arrived! Although their actual role in the May events is a little overplayed — many say Debord actually fled Paris at the time — there is no doubt the movement's slogans, graffiti and detourne-ment of popular materials seemed to sum up the moment, and from there their ideas were transmitted through the counterculture.

¶   The Situationists broke up in 1972 but their theory of situations became a framework of sorts for creative politi-cal activism from then on — most obvi-ously in the punk revolt of the late 70s, when Malcolm McLaren and Jamie Reid

pulled off getting the Sex Pistols' *God Save The Queen* to number one in the year of the Queen's Silver Jubilee in a move that was heavily influenced by the ideas of the Situationists. In the space of a week, they managed to create the sense that a band could undermine the established order! But in some senses, the punk movement was a last gasp of the 60s radical wave that literally died in its own nihilism.

¶ Small flames of the avant-garde were kept alight during the 80s and early 90s but most of these concerned maneuvers kept themselves within the art world, in work by artists like Barbara Kruger or Hans Haacke. What work did move into the political sphere was generally around single issue campaigns like fighting nuclear weapons or raising awareness about AIDS.

¶ But then the break came. In November 1999, an alliance of direct action activists, artists, performers, environmentalists and workers shut down the meetings of the World Trade Organisation in Seattle. Building on struggles around the world but especially in the Global South this protest finally broke the run of defeats which radical movements had faced in the West since liberal intellectuals had declared the "end of history" as the Soviet Bloc came apart. For the first time in years, an avowedly anti-capitalist movement had beaten one of the new institutions of globalisation as it attempted to draw up plans to privatise the world. This victory sparked a huge wave of protest against further summit meetings across the planet.

¶ A similar movement was happening in culture. While the art world became globalised, with work becoming more and more compromised by money and the disparities of wealth and often echoing the globalised methods of production of the system — think Damien Hirst with his factories of art graduates producing his spot paintings which he just signs (or brands) — a burgeoning "culture jamming" movement organised around ideas of "tactical media" was taking hold in Europe and the US at the same time. Activists with backgrounds in art, design and media technologies began to make use of the relatively cheap production tools and nascent networks enabled by the World Wide Web, to produce work that took up the old ideas of the avant-garde and applied them to new ways of creating and distributing. The goal was not to be displayed in a gallery or exhibition (although that happened sometimes) but the avant-garde idea of disrupting capitalism and trying to change the world through the power of imaginative action. So in this sense, the idea of the Situation took on new life again.

¶ The development of social media in the last ten years has expanded these possibilities and altered the notion of the spectacle. In a situation where we can be both producers and consumers of culture and distribute what we do globally — even if, for now, it is still only an embryonic possibility — we could now overcome the domination of the capitalist spectacle in a way not available to the radicals of the 60s. In place of the idea of a spectacle

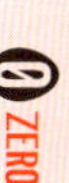

that we have to necessarily keep at a distance or deny, Americian critic and activist Stephen Duncombe suggests in *Dream: Re-Imagining Progressive Politics in an Age of Fantasy and the Cultural Resistance:*

> *"A dream self-consciously enacted... a dream put on display. It is a dream that we can watch, think about, act within, try on for size, yet necessarily never realise. The Ethical Spectacle is a means, like a dream, it performs to imagine new ends. As such the Ethical Spectacle has the possibility of creating an outside — as an illusion. This is not the delusion of believing that you have created an outside, but an illusion that gives direction and motivation that might just get you there."*

¶   In this sense the idea of the Ethical Spectacle recognises that forms of culture which enlighten, estrange and encourage participation (as the avant-garde tried/tries to) are all necessary to any movement for revolutionary change. But they must be connected with movements for change, or they will never overcome the contradictions and limits of producing culture in a capitalist society,

THIS IS NOT A BOOK ABOUT GAVIN TURK

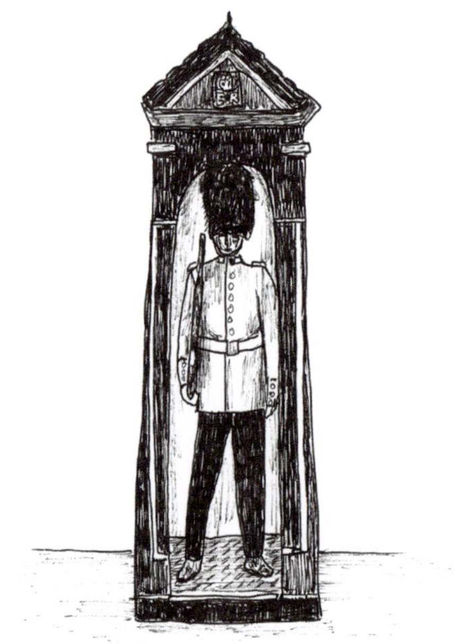

Gavin Turk Somebody's Son 2007
Mixed media, 280 × 100 × 100 cm
Waxwork of the artist as a Queen's guard in full uniform standing in a sentry box

¶ These movements for change are now not bound up with just traditional party or union-type organisations but the networked social media of millions of "expanded" individuals who represent vast potential for organised disruption, political activity and meaningful democracy. This interplay of physical occupations, strikes, demonstrations and networked spaces, activated by our own creativity, is, in a sense, where the "new" will come from. How to inspire others through imaginative action is now a pressing matter as we face the double crisis of economic depression and potentially catastrophic climate change.

¶ Occupying a physical place, connected through computer networks to a virtual global space, the global Occupy movement, the *Indigandos* in Spain and Tahrir Square in Egypt, are all contemporary examples of Ethical Spectacle. Decorated with scores of signs, banners and other forms of creative expression, the physical occupations themselves have all become sites charged with public debate and meaningful democracy (however limited). But additionally, they now tap into virtual global networks where their ideas resonate around the world, affecting others to act and intervening in the public discussion on the crisis. Think of the way Occupy has foregrounded the cancerous nature of the financial system and the inequality it leads to in a way that has made politicians respond. What's exciting for the future, is the way this relationship between the physical and virtual and how they can mutually reinforce and amplify each other in ways we are only beginning to grasp.

¶ But if we can, the future is ours for the taking.

ZERO

MAYBE THE WORDS ARNT SO IMPORTANT. WOULDN'T IT BE GREAT IF, AT ANY TIME, WE COULD HEAR AND SEE GREAT ARTISANS THINKING ABOUT THEIR CRAFT? WHEN DID OUR FIRST COMMENTARY THERE WERE, LIKE, TENS, EVEN THOUSANDS OF DETAILS EMBEDDED. I'M SURE THAT'S EASY TO DO YOU JUST GOT TO ASK YOURSELF WHY IT HASN'T HAPPENED. THERES TOO MUCH AT STAKE FOR THE SECOND CHARACTER, WHAT WOULD THEY DO IF EVERYTHING THEY THOUGHT ABOUT WAS ALL STREAMED LIVE? THEIR WORK WOULD VANISH OVERNIGHT I GUESS. ALTHOUGH WE WANT TO TIE TOGETHER THE SEEMINGLY INCOMPREHENSIBLE ELEMENTS OF THIS COMMENTARY, AT THE SAME TIME, WE'RE NOT TRYING TO GIVE THE ONLY ENDING, THE ONLY POSSIBLE INTERPRETATION. WE'RE JUST TRYING TO HELP YOU IF YOU'VE BEEN CONFUSED. THERE ARE A LOT OF PEOPLE WHO ARE TRYING TO PUT THIS TOGETHER BUT STILL HAVING DIFFICULTY. AT FIRST YOU CANT TELL WHAT THE HELL YOU'RE READING — THEN IT PULLS BACK AND YOU CAN TELL THAT ITS A COMMENTARY THAT SUGGESTS INTERPRETATION. BUT ITS NOT AN OBVIOUS ONE, A HOMAGE. WHAT WE'RE SUGGESTING IS THAT MUCH OF WHAT WE'RE READING HERE IS JUST MADE UP.

I FIGURED I DIDNT HAVE A GREAT VOCABULARY WHEN I WAS WRITING THIS PIECE, JUST ONE OR TWO WORDS THAT WERE KINDA IMPORTANT TO ME, AND THIS IS ONE OF THEM. USUALLY THOSE WORDS, THOUGH NEVER MAKE IT, WHEN THE WRITER TRIES TO GET ACROSS HIS IDEAS. THE INSPIRATIONAL WORDS ARE ALMOST NEVER IN THERE. I WAS SO EMBARRASSED WRITING IT BECAUSE I WAS WORRIED THAT SOMEONE MIGHT READ IT. IN MY IDEAS WHICH I KNEW ABOUT, MAYBE THE REST OF MY TEAM KNEW ABOUT BUT WHICH WERE ESSENTIALLY INVISIBLE TO THE WORLD AT LARGE THE COMMENTARY DIDNT EVEN SCRAPE THE SURFACE. WOULDNT IT BE AMAZING TO MAKE ALL OF THAT THOUGHT AVAILABLE INSTANTLY TO ANYONE, ANYWHERE, CONSTANTLY. I GUESS SO. THERE'D BE NO ROOM FOR PROFFESSIONAL COMMENTARY. IT MAKES ME APPREHENSIVE. I'M MEAN HOW ELSE COULD SOMEONE CONFIRM THE SUSPICION THAT THE COMMENTARY ON RONALD HAVER TALKING ABOUT KING KONG IS A HOMAGE TO THE WAY RONALD HAVER INTRODUCING HIS COMMENTARY ON KING KONG IF THEY WERN'T ABLE TO LISTEN TO THE COMMENTARY ON RONALD HAVER TALKING ABOUT KING KONG? ACTUALLY WHAT'S INTERESTING IS ITS THE OPPOSITE OF CAUSE AND EFFECT: ITS LIKE THE OPPOSITE OF A PLOT. NOP

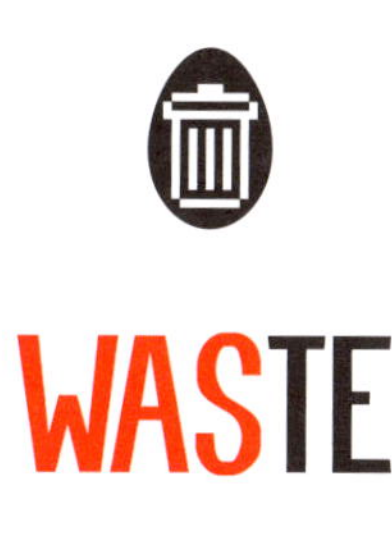

WASTE

Neil Mulholland

What should be kept in the edit and what go straight in the bin?

Hi.

Hey. This is our commentary. It's specifically developed for those of you who wanted to be able to read the commentary in their head at the same time as reading it out loud. Since it's not perfectly synchronised, we're going to start and we'll sometimes describe what's, um, happening as it's goin' on, but if it's a little bit out of sync that's kinda okay.

Yeah. It's as if you're walking in our shoes, through the world as we see it.

So, we started writing this commentary when we were asked to write something. So this bit ended up being a very last minute addition to this commentary, I don't think it was in the version that we first proposed.

Nope, in fact we only decided to work with each other pretty late in the day, mainly since we worked together on our previous commentary — so it's a co-write. It's coming out at a critical juncture in history, so it was important to get the right people involved.

Yeah. The team will always have ramifications, which we, of course, know is inevitable.

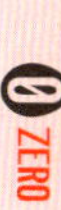

We wanted to be clear about who was facilitating and who was actually writing. I asked my ghostwriter and former assistant to play me since I wanted to actually appear as myself in the commentary rather than as just a character. And he was gracious enough to agree. I think I got it just about right.

The feedback from the readers and the Q&A we had on the last commentary, well, the reaction was phenomenal, just outstanding. It was beautiful!

Be sure to be involved, and take this information back to your local communities. This has to get out. I remember that one in particular. I think it's valid. Yeah?

Kinda reminds me of the geeky one from *Scooby Doo*. Yeah, but I can see already that there's a tendency to draw out the strengths of the last commentary rather than get on with this one. This is starting to develop all the hallmarks of a clunky bit of prose — the introduction of the second character's health problems is always something that I'd wanted to happen earlier on.

I wasn't so keen on that; it's all a bit *Casualty*. Let's leave it for now.

It's sad this bit here; one of those Tiny Tim moments. We were always going to edit this sentence, but we never did. Now it's really grown on me.

This was the last bit of the commentary to have the words written.

I don't mind that really. This bit was always the hardest. One bit like this nearly cost the publisher his house last time. It was tough. He'd been working

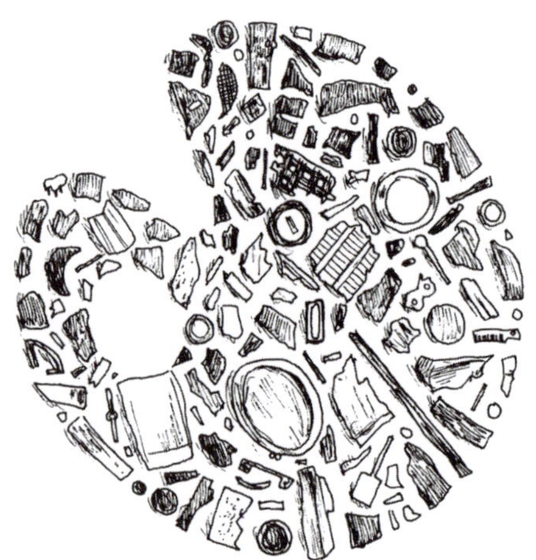

Tony Cragg **Palette** 1984
Found plastic objects and painted acrylic panel with accompanying installation instructions, 198.9 × 185.4 cm

You did this bit, but I think I took it out. The words were changed here; it used to say, (as we know, later in the text we read these exact same words). But now it's in this section that we see many of the motifs, like, being planted, seeding what's to come later. It builds up suspense and promises what we will see later in flashback. We can't take it all as actually what we said; it's filtered through memory.

I always wanted to change it because I think commentaries are really more about fantasies than facts. Always. I'm always careful not to introduce any spoilers, so I hope, if you're reading this, eh, for the first time that you've actually read it before.

Oh yeah, I mean I suppose it's only then that everything would slot into place — but, sure, we started with this then everything else came afterwards. God, we spent ages writing this bit, even though it was very simple. Very uplifting this. I'm down with this. Good bit this.

Uh, I'm not so convinced. It was meant to be a commentary about observations but I was worried it was too banal. Notice where this is, the same spot we see later where something horrible happens.

Yeah, it kinda ties the two storylines together. But, um, but perhaps this is a bit too dry. It's a tough juncture but I think that, right here, this is just a great line. Look at the way it reads, I don't think it would read in quite the same way if it were published somewhere else. I think it's a beautiful passage — a remarkable skill.

I like this change of tone — it's less polemical. I had to fight to have this bit in here.

Ooooh yeah, I like this bit. It's gorgeous; you done a great job!

I figured I didn't have a great vocabulary when I was writing this, just one or two words that were kinda important to me, and this is one of them. Usually those words, though, never make it, when the writer tries to get across his ideas. The inspirational words are almost never in there. I was so embarrassed writing it because I was worried that someone might read it.

Maybe the words aren't so important. Wouldn't it be great if, at any time, we could hear and see great artisans thinking about their craft? When we did our first commentary there were, like, tens, even thousands of details embedded

in my ideas which I knew about, maybe the rest of my team knew about, but which were essentially invisible to the world at large. The commentary didn't even scrape the surface. Wouldn't it be amazing to make all of that thought available instantly to anyone anywhere? Constantly?

I'm sure that that's easy to do. You just got to ask yourself why it hasn't happened. There's too much at stake for the second character, what would they do if everything they ever thought about was all streamed live? Their work would vanish overnight.

I guess so. There'd be no room for professional commentary. It makes me apprehensive. I mean how else could someone confirm the suspicion that the commentary on Ronald Haver talking about *King Kong* is a homage to the way Ronald Haver introduced his commentary on *King Kong* if they weren't able to listen to the commentary on Ronald Haver talking about *King Kong*?

I guess. Although we want to tie together the seemingly incomprehensible elements of this commentary, at the same time, we're not trying to give the only reading, the only possible interpretation. We're just trying to help you if you've been confused. There are a lot of people who are trying to put this together and still having difficulty.

At first you can't tell what the hell you're reading — then it pulls back and you can tell that it's a commentary that suggests interpretation. But it's not an obvious homage. What we're suggesting is that much of what we're reading here is just made up.

Actually what's interesting is it's the opposite of cause and effect; it's like the opposite of a plot. Normally, as we know, later in the text we read these exact same words. But here it's different, it's exceedingly difficult. It's not just filler.

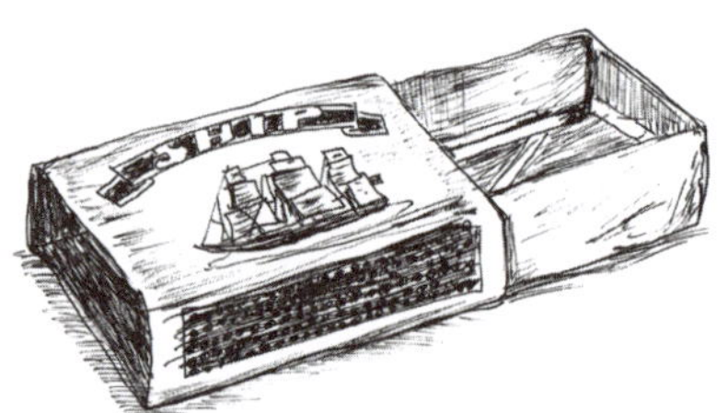

Gavin Turk H.M.S. Odyssey **2011**
Painted bronze, 1.4 × 3.4 × 8.3 cm
Cast of a match box painted to look real

It's not linear; it's an intense feeling, an experience rather than a moment.

This reminds me of something we said earlier on in this commentary. I'm not sure what exactly, but it's very familiar. It takes place in a very similar context.

It's building up something that resembles, uh, the kind of commentaries we know, rather than the ones we'd really like to hear.

You've made that comparison before. It's not allegorical, but the structure of this text, when you look at it, hopefully makes a lot of sense. It's audacious to include it here I think.

I actually wouldn't know how to do crack.

Me neither. Which is why this moment is so believable to me.

We probably rewrote this bit more than any other bit. I think it's a case of over interpretation. We've been here already. It doesn't hold up so well; but let's get into that later. The effect is lost here, it doesn't read or scan so well.

But it can't always can it? I feel we have to confront this just to make sure it's the case. This remains one of the most interesting subtexts of this commentary. It's an abstraction perhaps, maybe the unknown. The way the characters get split up and then end up becoming practically the same people.

I think I nicked that bit. It's a quote I think. It gives it more emotional weight — I can see the effect it has. I'm really happy with it.

I think you did a great job. We should probably get back to the key themes.

This is getting like some horrible hospital drama.

Sure.

"THE PLASTIC IS MUMMIFIED

Anonymous

CUP A SOUL "

ZERO

Gavin Turk

THE **BLANK** PAGE

Darian Leader

Everyone is familiar with the image of the writer or artist confronted with blank page or canvas. We see it on TV, at the movies, in comics or in magazines. When we read a description of the particularity of the experience, we might identify with it or we might not. Sometimes the emphasis is on a preconception and sometimes on a void: there's a difference between having a clear image of exactly what one wants to create and being stuck at the moment of materialising it and just knowing one wants to create but not having any idea of what. Both of these suppose the encounter with the blank page, but isn't this blankness itself something that involves a complex process of creation? Is a page with nothing on it a blank page from the start?

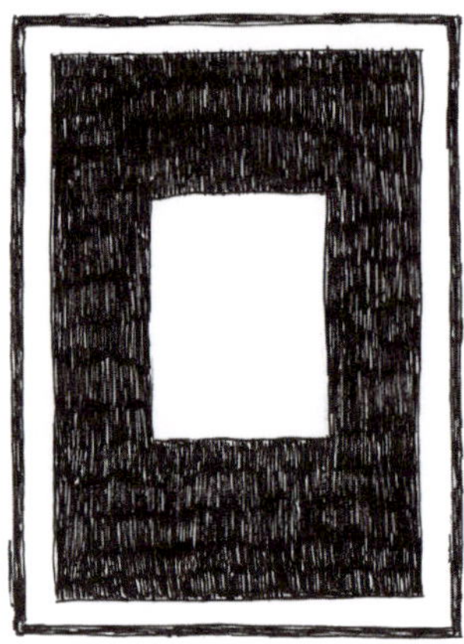

Gavin Turk Positive Negative A4 2005
Silkscreen ink on paper, 67 × 47 cm
Screenprinted black frame leaving a white A4 space to look like a framed blank piece of paper

¶   Blankness, like silence, needs to be created. You might enjoy the silence of your garden every morning until one day you notice that it isn't silent in the same way anymore: the birds have suddenly stopped twittering. The silence you feel now has a weight to it, created by the absence of birdsong. In other words, it's the noise that creates the silence, that frames it. To take another example, you might be pleased to spend the day at a spa where mobiles are banned and there's only a vague background hum of New Age music. But what would happen if when you checked in, the receptionist just stared at you and said nothing? The absence of noise at the spa wouldn't be silence, but the receptionist's non-response would be. Isn't the blankness of the blank page quite similar?

¶   It only becomes blank at the moment we feel the weight of an expectation to fill it, to put something there. It's the expectation that creates the blankness. This means that the same blank sheet of paper will only become a blank sheet of paper at a certain moment in one's life. Perhaps it will then stay blank forever, perhaps not. But the moment that it becomes blank will be specific and unique to each of us. For some, the accent is perhaps less on expectation than on necessity. Paul Klee would find it impossible not to draw, covering any available surface from menus to newspaper borders with configurations of lines. Klee explained that he felt looked at from all sides: even on his trips to the country, he said, "it was not I who looked at the forest, since the trees were looking at me". This feeling of being submerged, of being invaded, was why he had to make marks. They protected him from an intrusive and enigmatic presence. With such high stakes, the page, for Klee, could not stay blank.

¶ We often make marks at moments when we feel overwhelmed. This goes beyond the idea that we make narratives to protect ourselves from trauma. It is less about making meaning than about making an inscription, less about making stories than about making marks. Something can be fixed or arrested by making a mark, as we see, for example, in the feeling of relief sometimes experienced by self-harmers after they have made a cut in their body surface. This could be seen as a form of discharge, but a better term might be barrier or limit. Isn't the crucial moment in the act of inscription, after all, the moment when one ends a line or mark or brushstroke? This is less an art of representing than an art of stopping.

¶ Sometimes, it can be the very blankness of a page that needs stopping. The page itself becomes a conduit for an anxiety that has its source somewhere else. The blankness calls us like a siren: say something, write something, do something. This solicitation requires us to represent ourselves, yet representing always involves a loss. We can never represent ourselves perfectly, only inadequately and incompletely, and this margin of loss can both bind us to the blank page and inhibit us to go further. Whatever we do will not be enough, so we remain at the edge of what seems like an abyss. Writers sometimes speak here of how they feel taunted by the blank page. And yet without this blankness, how can a creation emerge?

¶ Gavin Turk's blue plaque provided an elegant solution to this apparent impasse. Instead of displaying works that would necessarily fail to represent their maker, he simply indexed the fact that works had been made. That way, no one could judge whether the works

Tom Friedman One Thousand Hours of Staring 1992-97
Paper, 82.5 × 82.5 cm
A blank piece of paper that the artist claims to have stared at for 1,000 hours

had done their job or not. Naturally, this solution was a transitory one, as the association of the plaque with renown opened up a thread that the artist followed with some tenacity: his later works explored iconic images and what it would mean to inhabit them.

¶   The parsimony of the RCA installation of course raised the question of the missing works. Where were they? How could the artist conjure himself out of representing himself? What was there to interpret? This coalescence of blankness and creation brings into focus nicely the main psychoanalytic approaches to making.   Analysts tend to fall into two camps here. Those who believe that we create   from our phantasies, unconscious scenarios that mould and shape what   we produce, and those who emphasise less such unconscious templates than   their absence. For them, it is precisely the points at which our phantasies fail   us, from which the work of creation springs. Where we are unable to explain to ourselves key questions such as birth, death and sexuality, we create works in the place of the missing solutions. This would

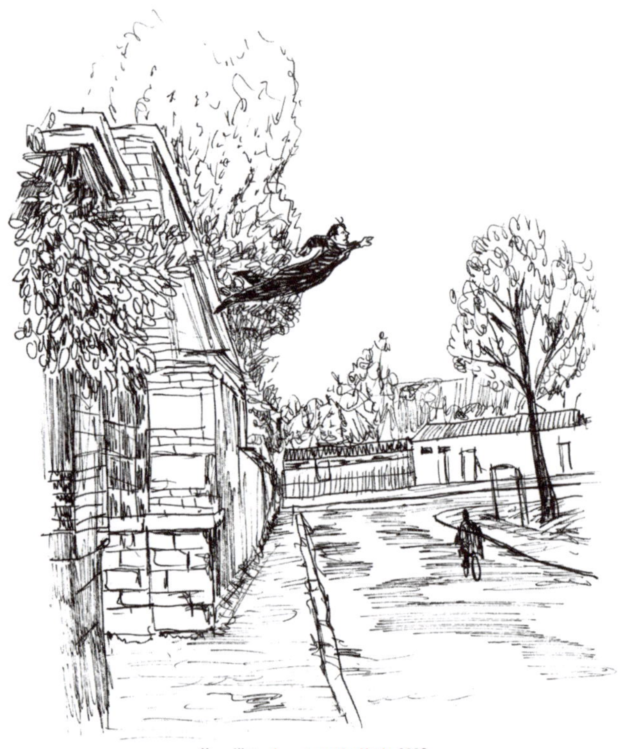

Yves Klein   Leap into the Void   1960
Photograph, 18.2 × 13 cm
Yves Klein appearing to jump from a building

explain why classical psychoanalytic readings of literary and artistic works seem so reduc-tive: they put the emphasis on phantasy and meaning rather than the experience of a hole.

¶ Again, the stakes can be quite high at this point. Confronted with a hole, we can make something out of it or we can jump into it. And can't the blank page be both the substance and the metaphor of these options?

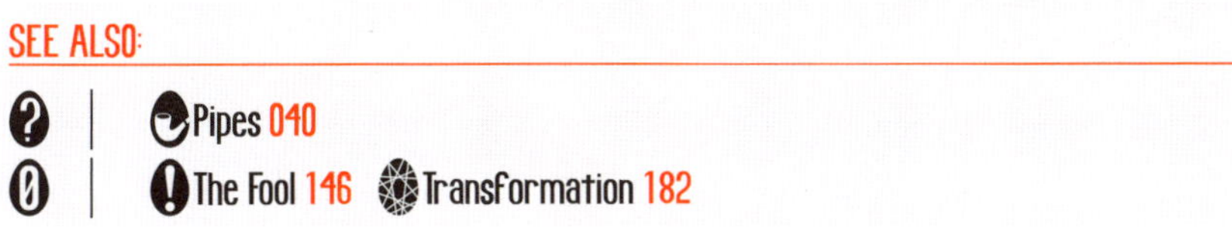

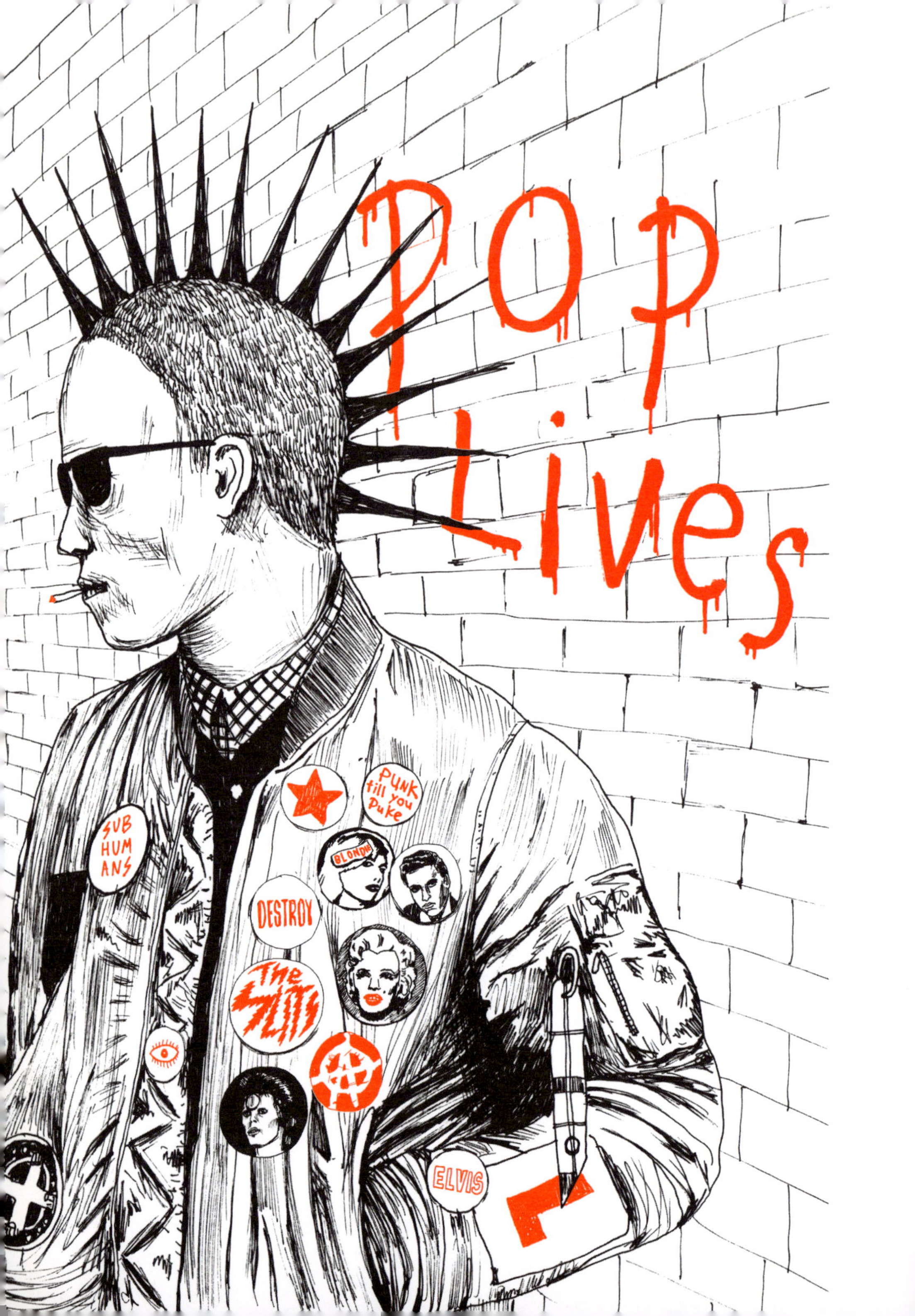

POP
Lives
SUB HUM ANS
PUNK till you Puke
BLONDIE
DESTROY
The Slits
ELVIS

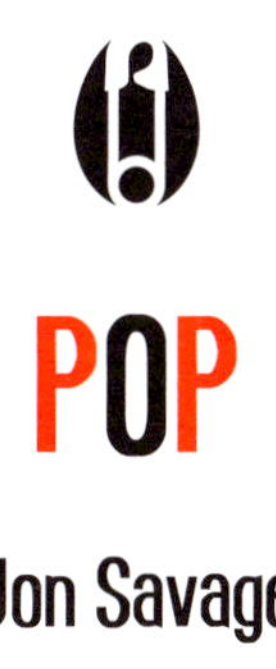

POP

Jon Savage

In Gavin Turk's *Pop*, the artist is cast in waxwork as Sid Vicious via Warhol's *Elvis*. While Warhol sourced a still from the 1960 film *Flaming Star* for his silk-screened multiples, Turk reproduces Sid's most iconic moment — the filmed performance of *My Way*, where the junk-sodden singer — in a destroyed white dinner jacket — shoots the audience in a climactic spasm of disgust.

both sources are High Pop. Warhol's images in their various forms — doubled, tripled, colour, black and white — are prime examples of Pop Art, while Sid Vicious' punk de/construction of the narcissistic nightclub standard was a Top Ten hit for the Sex Pistols in summer 1978. But they uncover a level of violence and hostility in pop culture that only the bravest seek to explore.

Before the style went national, London punk was a British version of Andy Warhol's high Sixties Factory. Many of the musicians and fans were Velvet Underground obsessives who had followed Lou Reed through 1970's hits like *Walk On The Wild Side* into his later, more self-destructive "Rock'n Roll Animal" incarnation — pure punk with his plastic clothes, dark shades, and A-head jaw-line.

There was the same self-reinvention into cartoon pseudonyms — Siouxsie Sioux, Soo Catwoman, Johnny Rotten, Sid Vicious — only these hard-etched characters were not superstars but anti-stars. Early TV footage shows the pure punk gesture: not the rolling back of the eyes or the middle finger, but the look of sheer contempt and disgust with the camera as its subject turns away.

There was the same sense of simultaneity, of young performers immersed in a complete media environment and seeking to turn it to their advantage by being faster and smarter than those who sought to capture their look, their gestures, their souls. "You wanna ruin me in the magazine," Johnny Rotten sung in his anti-media tract *I Wanna Be Me* — "you wanna cover us in margarine".

Before it was swamped by tabloid front pages and music industry money, punk sought direct engagement with the death drive implictly contained in the mass media — "now is the time to realise", Rotten exhorted, "to have real eyes". Hence all the groups with names like the Adverts and Magazine, hence songs like *EMI*, Subway Sect's *Nobody's Scared*, and the Slits' brilliant *FM*.

Both the Factory and early punk exhibited a blistering, amphetamine derived hostility. Think of Mary Woronov as Hanoi Hannah in *The Chelsea Girls* — as she assaults Ingrid

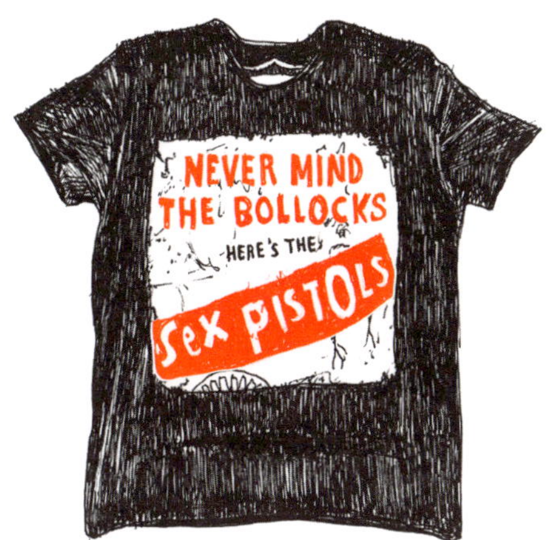

Superstar and Pepper with a non-stop "shut up shut up SHUT UP" — or Ondine at the end of the same film, turning on Rona Page with a lightning fast, unstoppable strike of violent vituperation.

SOME of this was a pose, derived from hard-faced mentors like Warhol and Malcolm McLaren. Some of it had to do with psychological and drug damage. But punk was so littered with negatives — nofuturenofeelingsnofun — that its refusals verged on the cosmic. Especially when projected into the wider culture. This was a negation that opposed the easy assumptions of everyday life.

In summer 1977, the BBC shot a special on punk in Manchester, *Brass Tracks*. Apart from valuable footage of the early Manchester scene, the programme is remarkable for the array of adults — preachers, councillors, journalists, almost every kind of adult authority figure — condemning these animals. Punk is disgusting, worthless and indicative of a sick society.

THE actual punks — Pete Shelley of Buzzcocks, Alan Deaves of the Worst, and Electric Circus amazon Denise — sit quietly while vats of shit are poured over their heads. Then they begin to argue back, quietly and reasonably, and what they say rips their opponents apart: you don't know what you're talking about; you've been programmed by the media; we're not the problem, you are.

Behind the blank façade, many early punks were highly idealistic. They believed in what they said, they were in it for the art and the self-expression, they didn't think about any idea of a career. At its best, particularly in London during 1976 and Manchester the next year, this encouraged an active atmosphere of total communication: if you've got something, bring it to the table.

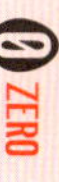

HENce the proliferation of fanzines and punk groups. Participation was the key — "I wanna destroy the passerby". Twenty years into a heavily mediated culture, many punks instinctively understood what the Situationists, and particularly Guy Debord, had defined a decade previously: that the media spectacle fostered passivity and, in fact, worked like a tranquillising drug — soma for the masses.

"Everybody's sitting round watching television", Joe Strummer howled on *London's Burning*. Many punk songs were determinedly in the world. They directly addressed the state of the nation, and what they saw was not flattering: a country obsessed by the past, in particular the Second World War, which it had not won but lost — in economic terms at least.

THe urban landscape of the late seventies was brutal. In cities like Manchester, Birmingham and London there were vast, empty spaces, often filled with rubble: bomb-sites that had never been built on, slum clearance projects stalled for lack of funds. Much punk iconography focussed on urban dereliction: soulless motor-ways, brick walls, corrugated iron.

Punk had an apocalyptic edge that came from more than amphetamine. The country had a pre-revolutionary feel, the very strong sense that something was over — the postwar Social contract — and that something new and malign was waiting in the wings. Britain's fascist party, the National Front, was making electoral gains, while Mrs Thatcher's Conservatives prepared for power.

The whole dysfunction between national image and reality was dramatised by the Sex Pistols' *God Save The Queen* in June 1977. With almost no support — certainly not from the radical left-wing — the group stood on their hind legs and laid bare the lie behind the pomp: "England's dreaming". They told a truth that no one wanted to hear, and for their pains were turned into pariahs.

Violence was endemic in Britain at that time. There were major set pieces like the Notting Hill Carnival riot in August 1976 and the Lewisham riot of August 1977 — when anti-fascist protestors tried to stop a National Front march. The Sex Pistols Jubilee boat trip was broken up by the police in a most heavy-handed manner, and then there were the much-publicised tribal punk-ted wars.

Creeping surveillance, the breakdown of law and order, the onset of fascism, the atomisation of society: it all seemed like Burroughs' *The Wild Boys* mixed with Orwell's *1984* — the year manically apotheosised by the Clash in their song 1977. And yet, in the blasted inner urban spaces — when not blocked off by serried ranks of police — there was freedom.

Occurring just before the massive regeneration programme that began in the 1980's,

the late seventies were the last time that young people could live cheaply near the city centre: whether in squats or inexpensive flats. All the Sex Pistols squatted at some point or an-other, as did members of The Clash and many other groups. The dereliction fostered the rapid city transits that spawned punk.

THE result was a brief, accelerated period when the music and media industries were forced to react to events that they could not control. When the Sex Pistols were vilified by the tabloids after the Bill Grundy show, it radicalised a micro-generation, who could see the difference between reality and its news-managed simulacrum. The adults, in this case, made monster fools of themselves.

PUNK'S problems occurred when it achieved the success that it part sought, part shunned. The whole idea of worthlessness encoded in the term made the success difficult to sustain, while the sheer level of exposure to the mass media meant that often sophisticated ideas were flattened out, turned into consumer disposables, and recuperated. Punk was fast and asymmetric, but it was soon caught.

SID'S peak performance of *My Way* occurred in spring 1978, right at the moment when punk negation was turning into self-destruction. It is a complex and problematic

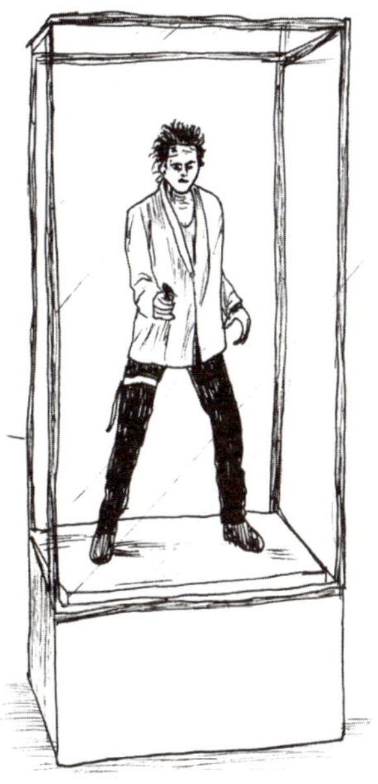

Gavin Turk Pop 1993
Waxwork in vitrine, 279 × 115 × 115 cm
Waxwork of the artist as Sid Vicious in the pose of Andy Warhol's *Elvis Presley*

clip — Sid is unwell, if not extremely stoned, but he summons up a kind of demonic energy directed at the filmmakers, at the audience —whom he shoots in the ultimate act of punk media loathing — and himself.

iN this instance, the twinning of Sid with Elvis doesn't look quite so bizarre. Both were self-made creations from problematic back-grounds who were, at various points, a kind of living litmus test for problems in the wider culture. Both were sent mad by fame and/or notoriety, and both destroyed themselves through heavy use of opiated drugs. Here is the human cost of being an icon.

ThIRty years after Sid Vicious' final overdose, punk rock is, like Gavin Turk's *Pop*, under glass. It is, apparently, in history: its bones endlessly picked over, dismembered and rearranged into lists and rankings, then finally boiled into mushy, nutrition-free gruel — all those sentimental accounts of male bonding. But it has a dark heart and a fearless spirit that is not recuperable.

It was no accident that Pop was part of a show — Saatchi's *Sensation* — that attracted exactly the kind of numbskull press attention that punk did in its heyday. Punk laid down a critique and a challenge — as did the hippies before them — that English culture wilfully refused to take up, or even recognise. What is buried and repressed always breaks out with renewed force.

pOp then is a dangerous ideal, particularly if you are trying to summon up the spirits, if not the demons of your time. Warhol suffered for telling the truth, as did all of the Sex Pistols — perhaps Sid Vicious the most. People do not want too much cultural reality, but for the true artist — or numinous performer — there is no choice but to dive deep into the collective subconscious.

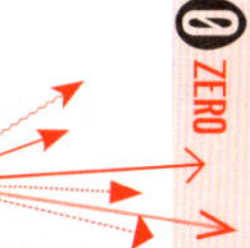
ZERO

BEFORE

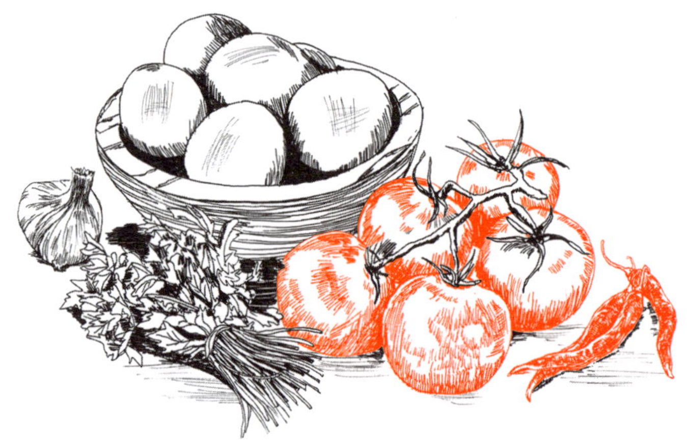

AFTER

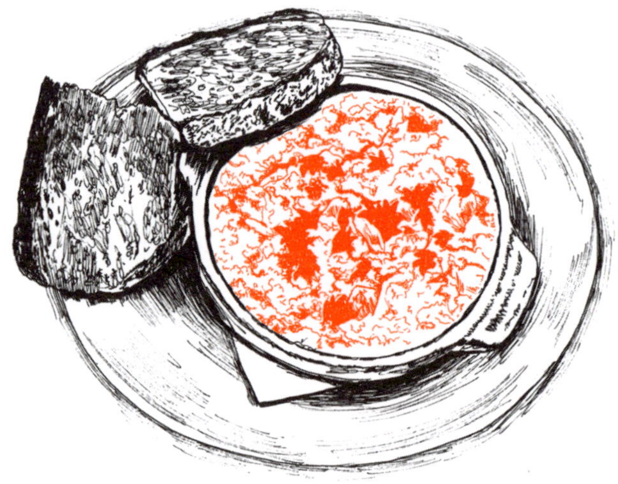

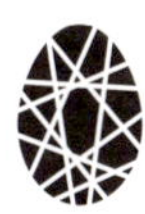

TRANSFORMATION

Michael Marriott

A recipe for Turkish Eggs

Whilst travelling up the west coast of Turkey between Izmir and Istanbul several years ago, I had this delicious meal called Menemen. *It's a traditional Turkish egg dish, which is strange, in that it contains no meat (in Turkey, even a simple vegetable soup tends to have a garnish of shredded lamb). It's also strangely coloured (like Campari and orange) because of the mixture of eggs with tomatoes. It's really quick and easy and very delicious. It can all be made in one saucepan, ideal when camping, or with limited cooking facilities; we quite often make it for lunch in our studio.*

This will make a light lunch for four people:

Big glug of olive oil	One or two cloves of garlic
Two medium long green chilli peppers	Six large tomatoes
Six eggs	Bunch of fresh coriander

Heat the olive oil in a pan, add crushed garlic and chopped chilli peppers, stew until turning soft, add chopped tomatoes, stir and leave it to simmer and reduce for a while. Once reduced, switch off the heat and break in eggs whilst stirring vigorously, so the eggs break up and are cooked by the sauce. Season with salt and pepper and a large handful of chopped coriander leaves on top. Serve it with toast (those big flat Turkish white loaves are ideal), or with pasta or couscous.

SEE ALSO:

 | 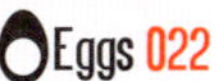 Eggs 022

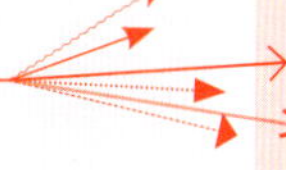

"FIRST TIME
A DICT
I THOUGHT
A POEM ABOUT
EVERY

I PICKED UP
IONARY
IT WAS

THING" Fiona Banner

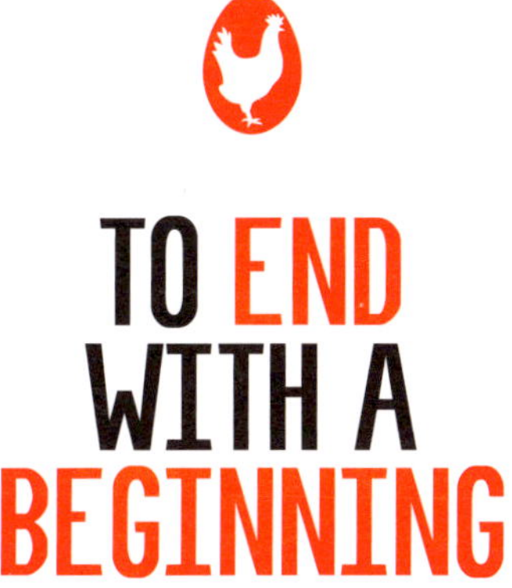

TO END WITH A BEGINNING

Rachel Newsome

Who is Gavin Turk anyway?

In a sky-lit wood-panelled room inside the Royal College of Art, mounted on an empty wall in an empty room, a blue ceramic plaque authoritatively infers the artist's passage from life to death. It reads, simply —

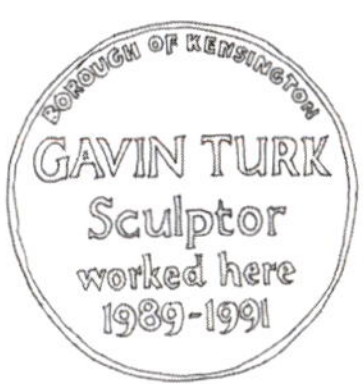

¶ *Cave* is at once an official receipt of the artist's admission into the upper echelons of public commemoration and the hushed marker of the site where once the creation of art was known to have taken place.

¶ Framed by the plaque, it is the empty space that becomes the art. Framed by death, the artist disappears; his presence is marked with one of the most powerful, mystical tools at his disposal: his absence.

¶ To extinguish yourself before your career has begun is nothing if not a punk act of self-annihilation. Even Sid Vicious, who appears in the loose hagiography of rebels and outsiders in Turk's art, managed to produce a slim body of work before his messy extinction.

¶ Turk's failed degree has become an art world legend. He is the artist who became famous for flunking — his failure was also his success. Unlike Vicious, the punk angst

that characterises so much of Turk's work is of a quieter, psycho-existential kind. If punk defined a generation born under the clouds of recession, war (Vietnam) and terrorism (the IRA), then Turk (old enough to remember, if not participate) too, begins with a blank.

¶ In Turk's dislocated universe of inconsistencies, contradictions and gaps, the guardians of the old — those pipe-smoking intellectuals proferring grandiloquent statements on beauty and truth — are melancholy characters to be mocked not mourned. Their élite art, immured in vitrines and framed in gilt, is replaced with apple cores, melons, rubbish bags and bread. The pipe-smoking intellectual is given an egg for a face and many pipes to chew on at once, while the sacred item in the vitrine is a decorator's paint roller, suggesting all art is fake necessarily because it is represented and copied in a questionable system of correspondences where symbol may or may not relate directly to fact.

❓

WHAT IS REAL?

The lingering question behind modernism as a scrapped project and the ensuing blankness left in its wake is the authority of the artist: can he be believed? Turk's art is concerned with what cannot be answered. Born from dead ends, puzzles and blind spots, twists and turns form the corridors of a psycho-metaphysical labyrinth in which there is no monster, only what Lacan called the "indestructible other". If Turk is punk, he is also zen: constructing visual koans, adding a layer of meaning with one hand, taking it with another. What is the original? What is real? Which came first, the chicken or the egg?

¶ Symbols of life, creation and originality, eggs recur again and again in Turk's work, both whole and broken and also in liquid form as mayonnaise and egg tempera.

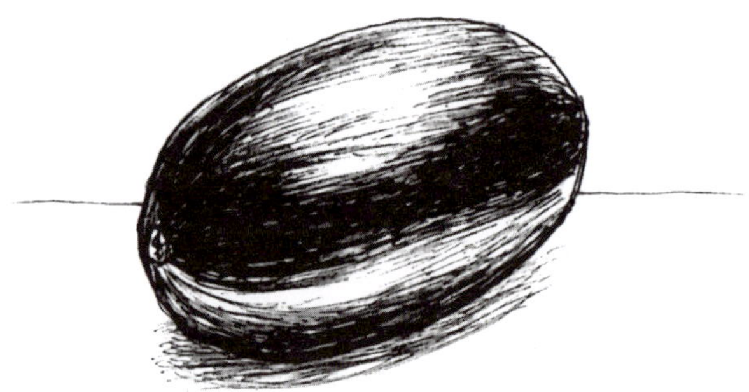

Gavin Turk Briar Melon 2003
Painted bronze, 20 × 38 × 20 cm

Transforming eggs from sacred to profane, pure to parasitical, a symbol of creation becomes something created. Giant egg cups meanwhile moonlight as porcelain fonts. Placed at church entrances, fonts are symbolic thresholds between the "dirt" of humanity and purification by water. Bearing an uncanny resemblance to toilet bowls, in Turk's work the font traverses the delicate threshold between purity and waste, highlighting how status is contingent on arbitrary values.

¶ Personally illustrating this point, Turk infamously attended the private view of the *Sensation* show dressed as a vagrant. Inhabiting various personas — not only of the tramp but other outsiders, too, Turk presents the idea of the artist as sacrificial "Other", outside of society. Far from resolving the artist's identity, Turk confuses it, presenting the identity as a fiction; he acknowledges that we frame things but are also framed by them.

¶ Derrida described this invisibility at the heart of seeing as "aporia", an impassable passage. Far from being futile, he regarded aporia as necessary to the process of making an ethical decision, even if the consequences of that decision remain unknown. And what might this unknown look like, if not the dark shadows of a primordial cave, described by Plato in his famous allegory and hinted at in Turk's work of the same name? *Cave* indicates all that is left behind of the artist is a memorial to an implied body of work and, by extension, an implied life and worth. Telling of a hidden reality that can neither be seen or known, a puzzle presents itself: what can be seen or known of Gavin Turk?

THE MACHINE

Andy Warhol didn't paint the way he did because he wanted to be a great artist or because he wanted to be famous. He assimilated an assembly line to make images recycled from popular culture in brightly coloured screenprints because, he explained, he wanted to "be a machine".

¶ By presenting the artist as an omniscient yet invisible manufacturer of infinitely reproducible copies created with minimum effort for maximum impact, Warhol's machine was a dream for the consumer boom of never-had-it-so-good shopping, celebrity and TV. Art could be for all, artists could treat the production of their work exactly the same as any other manufacturing business; not only could their art be a commodity, so could they. No longer outsiders, martyrs or suffering saints, artists became celebrities, entrepreneurs and successful brands. Artists became experts not only in aesthetics but also in advertising — especially expert in advertising themselves.

¶ Detached from the hand of God and man, devoid of mystery and emotion, the Warholian machine is a compelling symbol of the marriage between art and market economics, factory and gallery, the power of the image and money and the artist as a brand. "Pop" legitimised the recycling of ideas, creating a "licence to steal" which offered artists limitless creative freedom; in this world, everything was possible. Heralding a new utopia, Warhol's machine transformed art from the mythical and the elitist to the everyday, simultaneously elevating the superficial and banal — soup tins and cleaning products — to the status of art.

¶ Such is Warhol's influence that his dream of becoming a brand is now largely today's reality and Turk is no exception. A British artist working in a globalised market, Brand Turk no doubt sells work. Yet it is also a vehicle to question the process by which artists and their work are valued by the very same market. Unlike the instant recognisability of Brand Warhol, Brand Turk has no central identity. Contrary to appearances, what might be taken as shameless self-publicity becomes in fact the very opposite, since in commercial terms having no recognisable identity is tantamount to brand suicide.

¶ From a generation informed by postmodernism's debunking of metanarratives, fully licensed to appropriate culture's great archive of music, fashion and art, producing works based on copies of copies of copies, Brand Turk is an oxymoron. A spanner in the machine, Turk presents awkward, existential meta-art: art about art and how it is manufactured, just like salami, socks, sex, or any other product which might be bought and sold. Brand Turk is both a product of, and a response to, a mediated world constructed from the smoke and mirrors of appearances, characterised by the privileging of style over content and PR over ethics, where the real is lost to its dizzying nemesis.

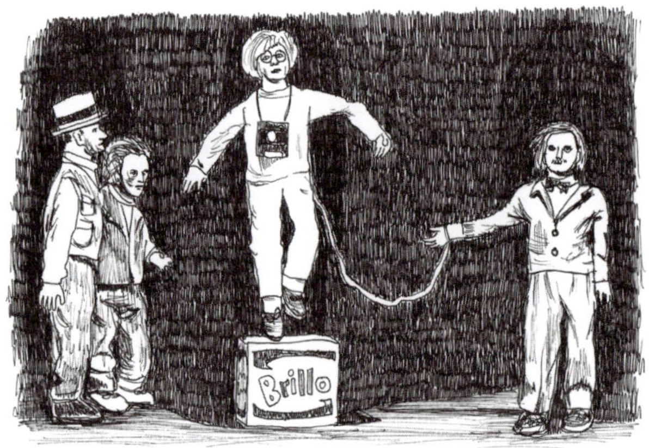

Gavin Turk   Waiting For Gavo   2005
Acrylic paint, fibreglass, clothing, hair and steel rods, dimensions variable
Puppets or art world characters parodying the characters in Samuel Beckett's play *Waiting For Godot*

¶   In Turk's collaborative work *Waiting For Gavo*, a slapstick adaptation of Samuel Beckett's play and parody of the art market, puppet caricatures of Marcel Duchamp, Joseph Beuys, Charles Saatchi and Andy Warhol, await the mysterious "Gavo". Each of the characters have a role in the real story of Turk's art career — Saatchi, the collector-svengali whose purchase of *Pop* saw Turk canonised as a Young British Artist, Duchamp, Beuys and of course Warhol as subjects for appropriation and impersonation. The enigmatic "Gavo" never appears, yet the face of each of the puppets bears an uncanny resemblance to Turk himself. Each player in this surreal art market is a puppet, their authentic selves hidden behind a construction created to engage and entertain an audience; all are performing. Turk may be the puppet master, but since the sale of his work is dependent on the arbitrary whims of the international art market, this gesture can only be viewed as ironic. *Waiting For Gavo* offers no solutions.

¶   Baudrillard for one saw little cause for hope. Equating the all-devouring nature of market economics to the final stage in a chess game where the end becomes a foregone conclusion, he described the commodification of not just art but absolutely everything as Endgame Capitalism. He says in *Paroxysms — Conversations With Philippe Petit* —

"There is no possible get-out within the logic of the system, in the sense that it has absorbed all the negativities, including the humanist, universalist resistance."

¶   A hollow, shape-shifting entity with no central core, inevitably Brand Turk becomes meaningless. Given this entropy, it is not surprising that Turk's painted bronzes of polystyrene cups, chip trays, chip forks and his signed Rich Tea biscuits with a bite taken out, all display a quiet nostalgia for a post-Empire, pre-machine working class Britain: a bit mouldy, a bit damp, a bit parochial, shabby around the edges, maybe, but certain of its identity nonetheless.

¶   And so, if Brand Turk displays a humorous uncertainty as to the precise identity of Gavin Turk the artist, then it also displays a similar quixotic confusion as to what, these days, his national identity might mean. Turk samples ideas from European and American art and incorporates them into archetypal British imagery to create mutations of Warhol's car crash multiples, restaged with white vans, and of the Union Jack and the iconography of Elvis and Che, with his own face thrown in for good measure.

¶   Plundering the dressing up box of history, Turk's "self" portraits see him trying on Joseph Beuys' felt hat, Warhol's wig and Jackson Pollock's paint-spattered boiler suit; and not just other artists but outsiders in the form of Che Guevara's beret and the bondage trousers of Sid Vicious; and not just their clothes, but their facial expressions, body language and poses, in search of answers.

¶ The result is a multi-national pile-up of references stacked one on top of the other, each layer pushing Brand Turk further towards the point of absurdity, its essential Britishness alongside its essential personal identity, obfuscated, torn apart, distressed and distorted, the whole branding exercise imploding into its surreal antithesis, a grand, excessive über brand, the last word.

¶ The last word, meanwhile, looks like artworks such as *The Fall*, a painted bronze sculpture made to represent a rotting apple core or *Stain*, a brown partial circle on paper — the remains of an overfull mug of tea. Traditional symbols of Britishness, such as apples and tea, reduced to detritus, both artworks hint at original sin and the end of innocence, signalling something far more hopeless and bleak than a spilt cup of tea.

¶ Turk portrays so many of his rebels and outsiders at the moment of their deaths. In the lifesize waxwork *The Death of Che*, Turk/Che lies lifeless on a stretcher (itself, a morbid metaphorical slippage of the frame used to stretch an artist's canvas), while in the waxwork *Death Of Marat*, Turk inhabits the corpse of the French Revolutionary. Acknowledging that even Turk's anti-brand, in the end, is still a brand, they bleakly imply the death of rebellion.

¶ So Pop has eaten itself. The gallery is a reliquary. The artist is dead. Art is just a memory. There is no meaning, nothing is real, the game has been set. There is no exit. Or…

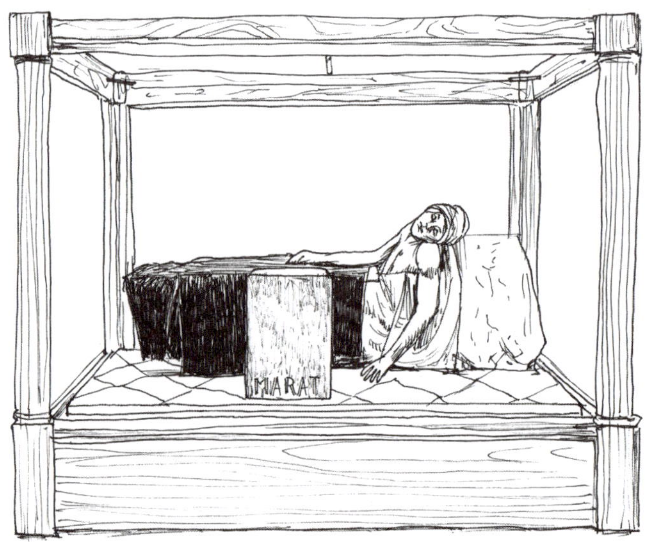

Gavin Turk Death of Marat **1998**
Waxwork in vitrine, 200 × 250 × 170 cm
The artist as Jean-Paul Marat on his death bed, based on the painting of the same name by Jacques-Louis David

0
ZERO

Such was his disillusion with the commercialisation of art that Duchamp famously swapped it for chess. As his response to capitalism's endgame, the Surrealist artist spent his last days playing an entirely different kind of game. Abstracted from the phenomenological and extracted from the gallery, chess, Duchamp claimed, was art in its purest form — the elegant geometry of moves across a board simply the visible form of a more beautiful, invisible, trace of thought.

¶ In his film *The Mechanical Turk*, Gavin Turk also engages in a game of chess. Except, typically, Turk appears in the form of a life-sized chess-playing automaton designed to look of Turkish origin. Possessing an uncanny ability to win repeatedly, as if it were a genuine chess master, the original Mechanical Turk was a late 18th century phenomenon known for performing a complex, though ultimately pointless, sequence of moves known as the knight's tour. Taking the knight across every square on the board without landing on the same one twice, the machine was almost too good to be true. It was only later revealed as an elaborate hoax, a mechanical illusion with a human operator hiding inside. Faking a fake, an elaborate double bluff, in Turk's version the artist plays both automaton and hidden master.

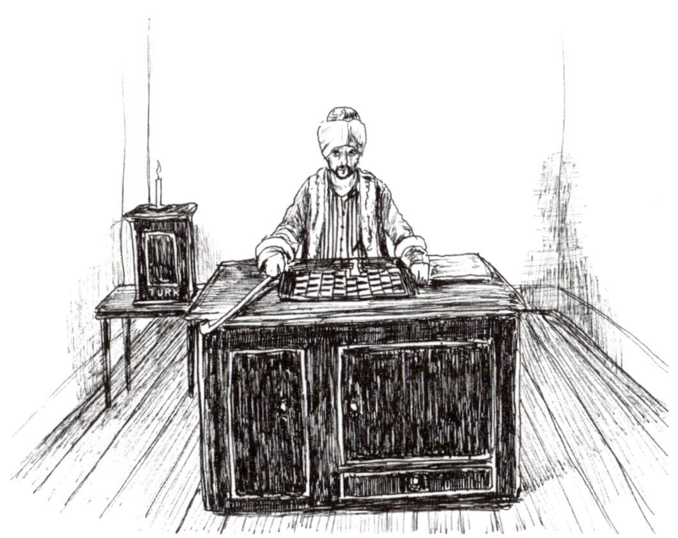

Gavin Turk **Mechanical Turk** **2006**
Film projection and cabinet with chess board
A film of the artist as Wolfgang von Kempelen's *Mechanical Turk* automaton performing the knight's tour

¶   In Turk's hands, the idea of recycling becomes Endgame Art. From overflowing landfill sites to inboxes brimming with spam, we are up to our necks in waste. It might also be said that we are up to our necks in art. Shape shifting between advertising, entertainment and consumable products, never before has art been so accessible, galleries so well visited, or artists so frequent on the celebrity circuit. Both a product of this excretion and a comment upon it, in Turk's Endgame, art becomes a black bin bag bulging with unspecified garbage or an empty beer can flattened by a tyre. It is the decayed remains of an apple, a used-up toilet roll, a piss stain, a burnt match, a dead fire, the homeless man in his sleeping bag on the street. Melancholy leftovers of the Machine, detritus and waste are beautifully presented in frames and vitrines in pristine gallery spaces, ethnographic artifacts of a lost civilisation.

¶   After the last move has been played, the fire burnt out, what is left but a void? Emptiness. Zero. At first there is darkness. And silence. Softly, at first, then becoming louder — a noise. Crying. Or is it laughing? Crying and laughing. In the face of nothing, the sound of black humour fills the void, turning nothing back into something again. Because what else is there? Why else in a pack of cards might the Joker alone have the power to trump even the Ace? In quantum physics, the Zero Point is not an empty state but constantly vibrating, flashing in and out of existence, and in art this is the moment where the vacuum is filled with paroxysms of laughter.

¶   "There is nothing that intelligent humour cannot resolve in gales of laughter," said Andre Breton, "not even the void". So Turk's art revolves almost full circle to ideas taken from modernism and its merry pranksters, the Surrealists. Next to Turk's towering *Nail* sculpture, the City of London's cathedral to consumer excrescence shrinks to a Lilliputian level of insignificance. Turk's tramp arrives, shoes stuffed with newspapers, trousers discoloured with the artist's piss, and the glamour of *Sensation*'s elitism is debased to a crude joke.

¶   But. There is no garbage, no bulging sack of waste, without manufacture. Between dying and becoming, past and present, energy and exhaustion, nothing and something, the very existence of waste suggests the presence of life. Amongst the grand projects and high ideals — the dreams of modernism gone to wrack and ruin, amid the apple cores and piss stains and burnt matches and cold ashes, in Turk's Endgame Art the disintegration of the past is a necessary process since only then can art pass through Zero to become something new. Not just recycling but something far more elemental: the eternal circle of death and creation.

¶   It was Derrida who pointed out that as the meaning of artworks degrade over time, all art becomes like a ruin. Yet it is the crack appearing in the shattered glass of their frames that suggests both cracks in the idea of rebellion and the opening up of space for rebellion to be imagined anew. So the emptiness of nothing becomes a creative charge, a negative space but also a positive one. An end but also a beginning — the blank page and

THIS IS NOT A BOOK ABOUT GAVIN TURK

the unmarked canvas like red rags to the instinct which must alter and shape in order to express a version of reality that says something of itself and how it views the world around it. "You have to treat the nothing is if it were something," said Warhol. "Make something out of nothing." Making something out of nothing, the artist is akin to the alchemist: shit becomes gold, waste becomes art.

¶   Turk's sculptures of trash transcend their status as rubbish. Elevated to this aesthetic status, a kind of transubstantiation takes place inside a gallery as apple cores and crushed chip trays become sacred. Cast in bronze and given a *trompe l'oeil* makeover, they are apple cores but also not apple cores. Inside the four walls of a gallery, by default, they are art.

¶   Continuing this investigation into art and what it might or might not be, Turk's interactive performance piece, *En Face*, was an exercise not in the representation of waste but the manufacture of waste as the by-product of a conceptual thought. Seeking to show the traces of thought, not unlike Duchamp's chess moves, *En Face* began with a series of clay busts cast from Turk's head that were subsequently handed over to an audience to mould, sculpt and deface in any manner they chose.

¶   Containing neither a clear starting point nor a definite arrival, what remained at the end of the event, was not a finished piece of work but leftovers of the process of making art, made visible in the deformed clay busts that remained. Showing the evidence of art, without actually showing the art itself, these objects, with their hollowed out eyes and stamped upon faces and customised piercings, tattoos and hair pieces, were the detritus.

¶   Somewhere in this process, Turk was also investigating the origin and ownership of the art, such as it did or did not appear in the "final" outcome. An arch-appropriator offering up his own appropriations for appropriation by others, Turk engineered an opportunity for the audience to exchange their role as spectators for participators and so become active in the thaumaturgical creation of art.

¶   With touch at the heart of the aesthetic experience, the artist-audience were releasing something hidden not only from within the clay, but also from somewhere deep within themselves, so that the art was not so much an object as a situation. In the case of *En Face*, this was a situation created by the participation of many, located in the experience of the collective and caused by a conversation between past and future, artist and audience. It was a situation, which became a metaphorical door.

¶   A painted bronze door in a frame, disembodied from any room or building, its varnish peeling, as if it had been left to the elements, Turk's *Ajar* is only activated when the audience is able to walk through it. But what might be on the other side? Where does this door lead? *Ajar* opens onto infinite possibilities and infinite nothingness; it leads everywhere and nowhere.

¶   Similarly burdened, Turk's Endgame Art proposes neither answers nor distinctions. Instead it is guided by the essential honesty at the heart of admitting uncertainty. For Turk it is not really a question of either/or but both/and — real and fake, art and not-art, something and nothing, original and copy, beginning and end.

¶   In Turk's recreation of Alighiero e Boetti's bronze self-portrait, the figure, a conflation of Turk and Boetti, holds a water pipe above his head, intermittently spouting a lacklustre trickle of water, becoming a human fountain. At intervals, a small cloud of steam rises from the artist's head as water from the "fountain" is warmed by a heated plate and transformed into mist. Referencing both Bruce Nauman's *Self-Portrait As Fountain* (1966) and Duchamp's *Fountain* (1917) it isn't clear whether Turk's *Fountain* is spluttering to a stop or spluttering into life. Nor is it clear whether the fluid is water or piss.

¶   This dismantling of meaning returns Turk's Endgame to Derrida's aporia and the beginnings of Cave with its tale of a hidden reality that can neither be seen nor known. Disappearing in a cloud of steam, there goes Gavin Turk into the lacuna, into the beyond, into the hidden reality, behind the curtain covering the canvas and hiding the stage, like Schrödinger's cat, both dead and alive, chicken and egg, real and unreal. The puzzle remains.

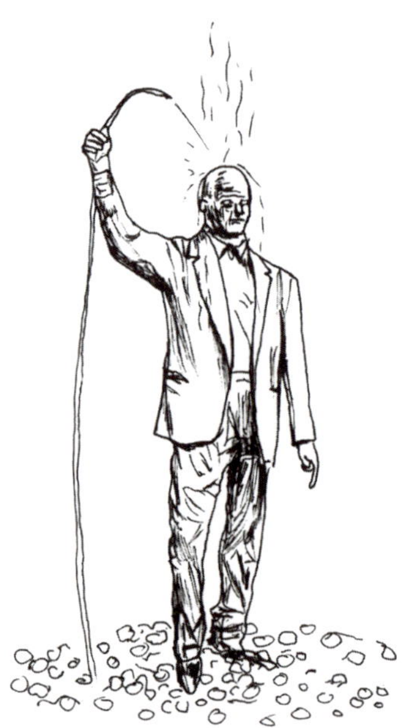

Gavin Turk Self Portrait (Fountain) **2012**
Bronze, heating element, pump, water, stones, 201 × 89 × 42 cm
Life-size bronze sculpture of the artist

Gavin Turk on Gavin Turk

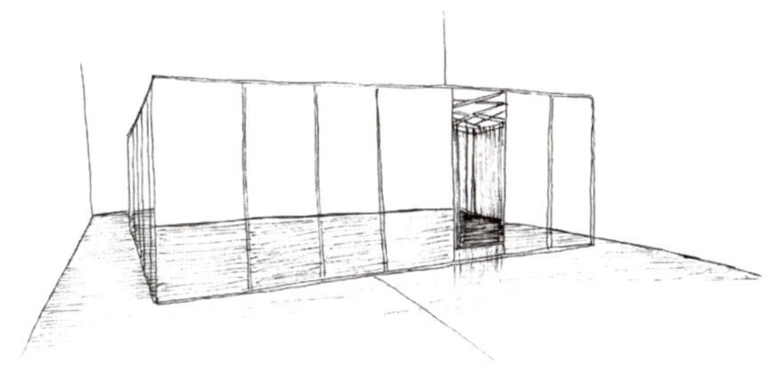

THE GOLDEN THREAD

What was the starting point for your work The Golden Thread?

The Golden Thread starts with looking at the work of de Chirico and the way he tries to introduce psychological space into two dimensional painting by using different points of perspective. He takes the viewer's point of focus to lots of different places in the same picture. What that does is give you this sense of being able to see round the back of things and that, art historically, was the precursor of Cubism.

Also, he's layering pictures of antiquity versus modernity, he's making what would be seen in contemporary terms as postmodern landscapes using classicism but then setting them against this emptiness with these strange croppings, like the two kinds of business men whispering in the background or the train moving across the landscape behind a brick wall. He creates these spaces and makes this figure Ariadne. She kind of gets abandoned and left. She's almost like a statement of a lost civilisation and Ariadne herself is the maze-breaker, she's the person who helps Theseus to work his way through the labyrinth, find the Minotaur, slay it and then find his way out again. And the Minotaur is, for me, a bit like Mr Kurtz at the end of the river. Somehow the Minotaur is a metaphor for consciousness or like eating the apple. It represents a dark sense of consciousness, of understanding, of death or maybe it's a sense of loss as well.

The Minotaur is this dark centre of something which will consume you, will eat you literally. Theseus actually manages to defy it by slaying the Minotaur, so freeing everyone of the possibility that they're going to have to deal with the dark beast in the middle of the labyrinth. I then was thinking about this notion of inside and outside – two things that are kind of only possible only through the existence of each other.

What was the thinking behind it becoming a glass and mirror maze?
The notion of inside and outside was the gallery versus the street or the institution versus the non-institution or the political power versus the opposition, we'll call it the revolutionary power. I found myself looking at Dan Graham's work – he made mirror constructions, which refer to the idea of the corporate building and the way they'd use mirrored glass as a statement of power. From the inside you can see out but from the outside you can't see in. You have the reflection of yourself on the outside. I moved towards the idea of building a frame or a construction, which could deal with the search for art with multiple focuses.

The viewers were given pictures and partial pictures of themselves, pictures partially of themselves. They saw a reconstructed version of themselves, almost as if they were the Cubist newspaper or the Cubist violin lying on the table. But they were also performing a performance and that performance was the search for art.

So I made this structure which had no true mirror. It had glass which had various mirrored films on it which gave differing degrees of transparency and reflexivity. I installed the piece first of all inside a gallery and then the piece was installed outside in a sculpture park so the audience could relate to the work in different circumstances.

What role does the audience have in this artwork?
The audience is very important in the construction of art. If you talk about a picture where part of the picture is to see the audience experiencing the art work, then I'm trying to remind people that an artist plus audience is the art work. I think it's impossible for the artist to solely make art if they're just on their own without a context. For me, art is a social construct. It's one thing that requires you to be involved within a social space.

GRAVESTONES AND THE NAME AS A READYMADE

What sparked your interest in signatures?
Spike Milligan's gravestone says, "I told you I was ill". Duchamp's says "It's always the others that die". The main thing with gravestones is you get

left with a name. It also relates to the blue plaque. A name isn't actually anything to do with the person. It's something that's constructed by the two parents. It's a given shell so it's a bit like a hermit crab inasmuch as the person occupies the name and they kind of have to make of it what they will. Generally you end up dying with the name you didn't make and that's what ends up on your gravestone. I found it funny that everyone inherits a name they've not created.

It brought me back round to the idea of my name being like a found object. It took me about a year to figure it out that actually I could use my name as something within my work. It's like a readymade. A gravestone doesn't mark the life. It marks the corpse. The blue plaque marks the place where the person was living."

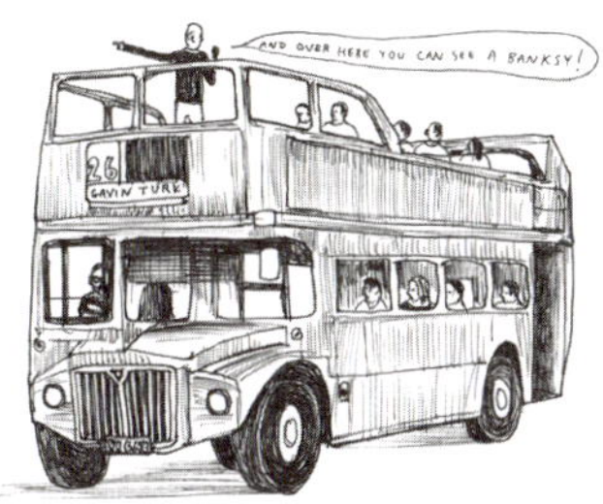

BUS TOUR

What is your abiding interest in Blue Plaques all about and how do they relate to graffiti?
I was invited to do an historic bus tour of London starting from the V&A so I found myself thinking how you could navigate historical sites in London. I've always been fascinated by blue plaques because the whole notion of remembrance seems like a really vernacular way of behaving. But then I thought about graffiti and its relationship with the blue plaque, so I organised a bus tour of both.

There's also a political motive about who gets commemorated and when and why they get plaques. The content of the plaques follow the fashions of the day. You have these sites, which remember certain people. On the whole you've never heard of these people. Apart from the blue plaque, they would vanish from a place in history. This vanishing or disappearance made it most interesting and so that seemed quite similar to the act of spraying a tag up on a wall which would keep you in the public eye or within your peer group eye for a small period of time until your tag was scrubbed over.

The fact is that lots of graffiti tags are highly coded and actually almost obfuscating. You throw up a tag on something moving – you put it on roller shutters or a train. One of the things with graffiti is the repetition. It sets up the idea of system and I think that idea seems to be the same as the blue plaques that were repeating.

On the one hand blue plaques appear on the outside of buildings, so they could be seen as a kind of defacement, or signature on a building or space. They could be seen as a signification of space in the same way that a graffiti tag might be.

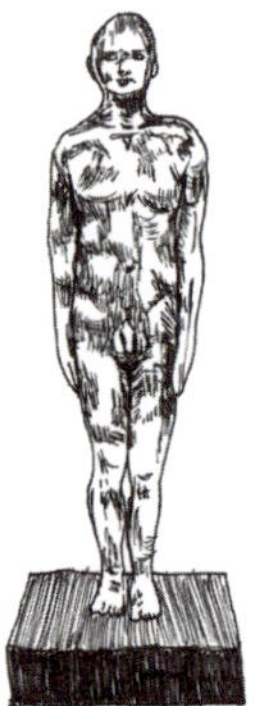

THE SPIRIT OF GAVIN TURK

What was the motivation behind your sculpture *The Spirit of Gavin Turk*?
The Spirit of Gavin Turk was a project inspired by the idea of awards and the establishment of a power structure for remembrance. What I wanted to do was to create my own award system for the artists that I felt had been the most influential to me in that year. I made a small bronze sculpture of me standing erect. I'm basically standing nude to celebrate the idea that some other artist has been able to take the soul or body of me. There's the sense that spirituality or nudity go together.

The sculpture is the tip of the iceberg. It goes on a little granite plinth and the idea was that every year someone would be awarded the prize and their name would be engraved onto the base.

In the first year it was awarded to Michael Craig Martin, who was showing with me in Berlin. Inside the private view, I had a miniature private view of my sculpture. We drank champagne and toasted to Michael's good health. I sent an email to Michael asking about the technical specs of his shelf and he said, "Oh, the shelf's made of peanut butter".

IL PORTENZA DI INFINITO

You talk about your interest in this Italian phrase. Can you say more about this?
This was a kind of parody of local knowledge where in Italian it's possible, certainly as a kid, to be superlative. You're in an economy of superlatives that get bigger and bigger, so that rather than saying something's fantastic,

you can say it was a myth. Not only can you say it was mythic, you can say that it was like ten myths. You can count and stack the amount of the myths. It was twenty myths. *Il Portenza Di Infinito* was about what if you do that childish thing of extending the myths to the power of infinity, so you say that was a *myth to the power of infinity*.

And what was the connection with pasta?
It then came up that that would be a brilliant name for pasta. If you take something which is seemingly the most extreme form of something, which is already like one of the most superlative things you could imagine and then you take it back home and you have it as the name of something as homely pasta. It's about taking something out through this thing and then bringing it back to something, which is totally local. The idea of the superlative and stacking up the myths was a local thing in itself. It was about trying to embrace the local. It was about having fun as well. We invented the name of a pasta dish at a restaurant. It would be second to last in the menus of pasta you could get – "The Myth to the Power of Infinity".

HELLO

How did your artwork *Identity Crisis* come about?
I was taking part in an exhibition in Italy that was going to use large outdoor billboard spaces as the site. The idea was for an exhibition to change and move the context of the space that the artwork operates in. I thought it was important to deal with advertising directly because art and advertising have always had this strange symbiotic relationship.

I started wondering about what I would want to advertise and began to think about the idea of celebrity. I wondered about the presentation of celebrity and also about the point when it eclipses the work – especially with artists when people become more interested in their personal life or their interior space. I thought of this *Hello* magazine idea as a way to show how society believes celebrities carry the torch.

Why *Hello* magazine and how have things changed since you made the piece?
This was 1994 and so it was at a time when *Hello* was relatively new. It was very successful. It tried to follow the Royals around and that had global interest. I'd just had a young baby and I suppose I was trying to deal with the idea of being a celebrated artist and then also trying to be a family and a parent as well.

There's that strange sense of exposing yourself or un-exposing yourself. What I ended up doing was making a hybrid cover. We did a series of photographs in the style of *Hello* magazine with a photographer friend of mine, Andy Smith. I made a kind of fake magazine where I painted the text. I then re-photographed the fake cover and put it on a slight slant as if it

had been popped down on the table at an angle in the way that you might do.

I showed that in the exhibition as an advert. It was an advert that was advertising a magazine but obviously it was also advertising that month's cover which happened to be this ecliptic moment where the artist isn't really exposing anything to do with his work, he's exposing his domestic bliss. I was trying to look at the idea that somehow celebrity can mask or stop you from being able to see the thing that you're trying to look at. Somehow the signature becomes so big that you can't actually see through it to look at the work behind it. At the time it seemed quite bizarre that an artist might be featured in a magazine like this but now it would seem perfectly normal.

NIGHT OUT

I understand you made a reflexive performance work about sponsorship and celebrity in 1993. How did this work and what was it all about?
This was a relatively early work called *A Night Out With Gavin Turk*. It took the lead from some moment where Warhol gets stuck beside a plinth in a night club and is photographed there without any explanation. In my mind I had this sense of an artist standing beside the plinth, just making an appearance instead of more specifically making an appearance to say firstly that they exist and secondly that they authorise this moment as an art moment in a Manzoni-like way, where he would sign people from the audience and they would become his art.

I was working with William Ling. We managed to get various sponsors to put some money in towards the construction of a stage in a pub in Bermondsey. I was also working with the architect Ali Rachid, who designed a partial gallery in the space like a trade fair stand with a back wall that became like a billboard-type wall with three canvases on it.

On the canvas it had the names of people who had sponsored the work. In the middle of the floor section was a white plinth. On this night, I posed in front of a camera with a roll call of people who sponsored the project coming on the stage to be photographed with me, after which they received a black and white photograph.

It felt a little bit like the Motor Show, launching a new product. I felt mildly uncomfortable. I wore a boiler suit with a British safety standard kite mark on the back. There was the sense that I was some sort of curious builder or engineer wandering around on stage with this empty plinth and occasionally other people would come up and be photographed. It had this odd feel to it because in the background was this Bermondsey pub with a pub sound track and people drinking beer. There were locals in the pub. They were quite perplexed as to what the hell was going on. It was quite profound, the whole experience. It smacked of quite a big event even though it was only a couple of hours on just one night. It felt like it could have gone on for years somehow.

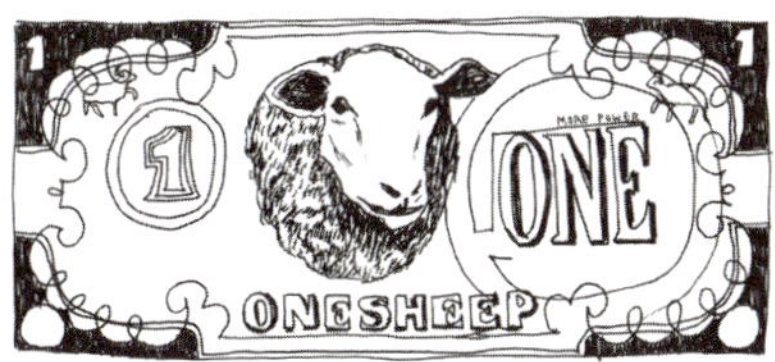

LIVE STOCK MARKET

You have pioneered art street markets and happenings – how did this start?
It was 1996 and we were living in Charlotte Road in Shoreditch. On the other side of the road there was a gallery called Factual Nonsense which had been run by a guy called Joshua Compston, only he had been found dead earlier on in the year.

Before he died, Joshua had an idea for doing street markets with stalls run by artists. He had organised three different events; one called *A Fate Worse Than Death*, which happened twice and something called *The Hanging Picnic* which must have happened in 1995. Joshua always wanted me to be involved in these projects and so I helped him curate them. And so after he died, I felt we needed to do another event.

Live Stock Market was the outcome of this. It was in honour of him but I also organised it because there's something really important about artists interfacing with the audience directly. Live Stock Market was a different kind of creative engagement somewhere between an exhibition and a fancy dress party.

We closed down Rivington Street and Charlotte Road in Shoreditch to traffic so Live Stock Market could be held there. It was five times larger than any previous events that had happened and we ended up with 80 different stalls. We made a programme with advertising space and teamed up with Frieze for publishing assistance. Artists such as Tracey Emin, Tim Noble and Sue Webster and Gary Hume had stalls as well as designer friends such as Michael Marriott and Andrew Stafford. We had our own printed money, which was called The Bull. At the end of Rivington Street, we had a truck with the sides opened out so it could be used as a stage and the experimental noise band Add N To x played.

It was around the 10th of August and the weather was a record-breaking day for good weather. We must have had thousands of visitors. The general public loved it. It was really odd, quirky and a lot of fun. We then went on to do another at the South Bank and the Liverpool Biennale called *The Articultural Show*. If it happened now, though, it would be less unexpected. I think we as country have become a lot more open to this kind of creative festival. Now you've got art events like the Art Car Boot Fair and The House Of Fairy Tales and galleries like the V&A doing evening events and new artist festivals like Hackney Wicked.

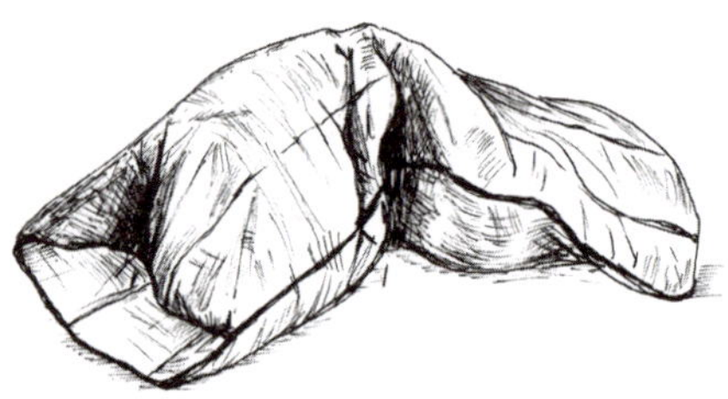

NOMAD

When you first made your sleeping bag sculpture I understand you displayed it in the street before putting it in a gallery? Why did you do this?
Because my studio was on Charing Cross Road, I was walking past people who were living on the street and sleeping in doorways on a daily basis. I was thinking about the borders – what's inclusive and what's exclusive in terms of society. I thought that in some ways there was a strange performance inside sleeping rough in a town where in the morning people are going to walk by and see you asleep. The response of the audience is to not want to be the audience because if you see someone sleeping in a doorway you have to take some sort of responsibility. Because you see them, they are there in a way they weren't before – a bit like Schrödinger's Cat.

So I made a sculpture of a rough sleeper in a sleeping bag. With the figure in the sleeping bag you'd know someone was there but you were faced with a condition rather than a person. I cast the figure in bronze and painted it to look realistically dirty. I then thought that it would be a strange thing to put in an art gallery – why would this rough sleeper be in there?

Obviously, there are examples of artists who have slept in galleries but it seemed strange and wrong to take the sculpture and put it in a sterile environment. So instead I put it in the doorway of a building that wasn't being used opposite my studio so I could see the reaction of passers-by.

People had a whole range of responses. Some people put money down. One person put a bag of nuts and seeds out for the sculpture. Then very close towards the end of the day someone realised it was a sculpture and they decided to walk on it. This horrified other passers buy who couldn't understand what was going on. I think they wanted to demonstrate to everyone they'd found out by standing on it but somehow they had broken through to a pictorial world that they didn't understand – the other world they had just broken out of was still there. They didn't realise it looked like they were jumping on a homeless person.

What was interesting was the idea of an artwork as performance where the sculpture was camouflaged and it was being something that people didn't really want to know was there. But at the same time, people are generally fascinated by the private lives of others – in this case, their bedroom on

THIS IS NOT A BOOK ABOUT GAVIN TURK

the street. So you get this curious tension between not wanting to look, feeling like you need to look and looking at a sculpture but not where it should be. It was a chance to play with the idea of inside and outside and being lucid and being opaque, overt – being dreamlike and being conscious.

THE HOUSE OF FAIRY TALES

What motivated you to set up your charity The House of Fairy Tales?
The earliest makings of The House of Fairy Tales – the children's arts charity I founded with my wife Deborah Curtis – began with Jago Eliot who wanted to use Port Eliot Estate in Cornwall to set up a Children's Arts Centre. I think we had already inspired him with children's projects because we'd set up a charity called Supernova. The idea was that we'd run a tent for a weekend where we'd do a round-the-clock festival. Tragically Jago died but we ended up not quite putting the brakes on. Instead we made something quite different as a memorial to him at Port Eliot Festival. It was the beginning of looking at how to make play and education experiences using art.

The House of Fairy Tales does a lot of things I have generally avoided dealing with in my work. Firstly it is a big collaboration. To be an artist and to work with The House of Fairy Tales is to take part in an artists' project rather than simply be the artist. I take on a totally different role. I give over a lot of my artistic licence to the bigger artist, which is all the people taking part.

Secondly, I've generally avoided narrative – and that's at the core of The House of Fairy Tales. It's a narrative project that looks at things in terms of their processes. It's not necessarily about the end, it's about the taking part. It's a more expansive approach to creativity and it's about the mechanisms of creativity. It expands and moves my exploration in art into another context.

Now we're eight years down the line and we are trying to establish a permanent venue for children in East London and an Earth Centre in Cornwall.

We are trying to encourage a better future by stimulating children's imagination. I think there's a tendency towards wanting to limit children's horizons but at The House of Fairy Tales we really value imagination and creativity. We believe that if children can stay open, they will be better equipped for solving the problems the world is going to come up against in the future.

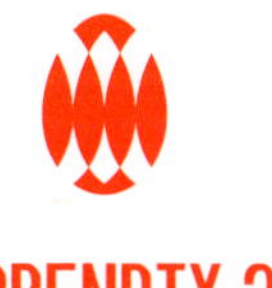

APPENDIX 2

Once More
For The First Time, Again

Joseph Kosuth

What Gavin and I share are two things, which are themselves linked. First, we share an understanding that art, philosophically, is now essentially an ontological problem, and as well (and as a result of this understanding), the necessity of a working approach to art-making that employs, in varying ways, strategies of appropriation. Even though we both come from widely different generations with decades between us, we still must face as artists (in our own way) the need for a production of new meaning which questions prior meaning, anchored, as such prior meaning is, in another historical moment and reflecting, as it does, another reality. These "postmodern" years, between the beginning of the period of my practice in the 1960s and through to the present, manifest an understanding that work must constitute a questioning process of art's ontology. And while the "why of art" is addressed, our own production of how we do that reflects our present in ways which will be seen later as special and particular to it.

The strategy of Gavin's practice, through addressing issues of identity and value, is to question the belief in and of modernism itself, toward itself, and the paintings and objects produced as a result of it. Our re-experiencing of them as we question their "authenticity" are not just the products of Gavin's activity, as a process of thinking, but they constitute a cruel and brilliant reflexivity on the belief in modernism itself, as internalised in the presumptions of many toward our culture. The present struggle of artists raging against corporate culture's agenda to have the market provide the meaning that was once the domain of artistic practice and critical reflection, has its political life within a practice such as Gavin Turk's. The challenge for all of us now is to find traction within the paradox of our own relationship with a market that both distributes information and is formative (as a society, cultural engagement is expressed in economic terms), without letting our criticality be turned into a form of currency experienced as mere decoration.

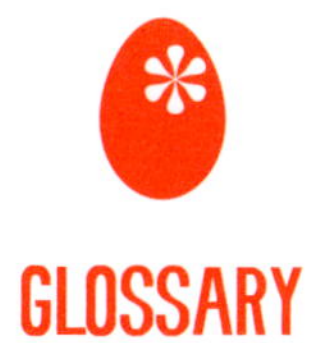

GLOSSARY

JEAN BAUDRILLARD

Philosophy's very own prophet of doom, Baudrillard saw the advanced stages of consumer capitalism coming back in the booming 80s and said no good could come of it then. Before the word recession was on anybody's lips, he predicted global meltdown was the only possible outcome of market economics. However, he did say all of this very poetically.

JOSEPH BEUYS

The art world politician Joseph Beuys famously claimed "everyone is an artist". Challenging the idea of the traditional artist in his elitist academy, Beuys' definition came from his belief in the creativity of everyday life – meaning creative thinking could be applied by lawyers, engineers, teachers and doctors.

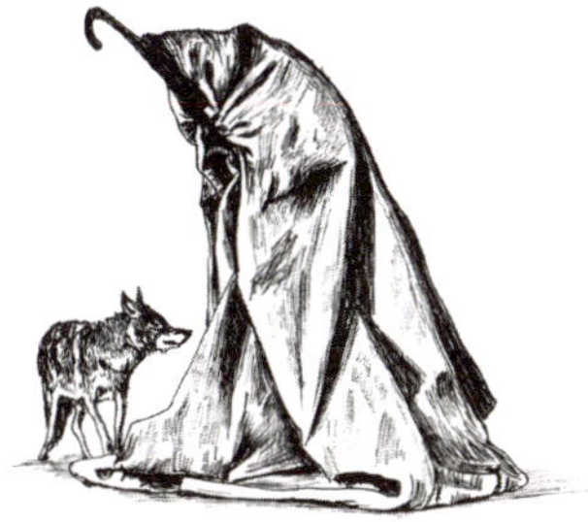

Joseph Beuys Coyote, I Like America and America Likes Me 1974
Performance featuring Beuys in felt cloak, with a cane and a coyote

---

CUBISM

Art's answer to 360 degree vision, the Cubist movement, along with its famous sons, Pablo Picasso, Paul Cezanne and George Braque was fascinated by the idea of creating images that presented people, landscapes and objects from every angle, all at once. The results were abstracted or flattened representations of the visible world which gave the impression of being created from the multiple perspective of a mysterious all-seeing eye.

MARCEL DUCHAMP

Arguably one of the most radical artists of the 20th century, Duchamp dreamt up the concept of the "readymade". Marking the birth of modern conceptual art, the readymade didn't have to be painted or sculpted because it was an object – like a toilet bowl or bicycle wheel – which already existed in everyday life. Instead, the job of the artist was to put it into a gallery, where it magically became an art object. A riddler and game player, Duchamp even gave up art for a while to play chess.

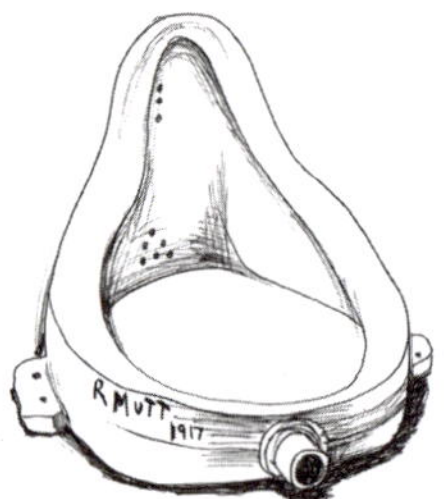

Marcel Duchamp **Fountain** **1917**
61 × 36 × 48 cm   A porcelain urinal signed "R. Mutt"

GUY DEBORD

The proto-punk leader of The Situationist Internationale, Debord's manifesto *The Society Of The Spectacle* described consumer society as a hollow theatrical event. A big influence on today's political activists, Debord wrote that traditional hierarchies and power structures could be subverted by joke-making, game playing and the creation of "situations" that activated creative thinking, which in turn could be harnessed for positive political and social change.

JACQUES DERRIDA

Derrida was a linguistic forensic scientist whose main aim was to dust away the layers of interpretation that words gather over the years to show how language is simply a system of signs to represent thoughts. Calling this process "deconstruction", he claimed that there is no such thing as pure meaning or absolute truth, only interpretation. Although, he did acknowledge the blind spot in his own proposition, which itself could be interpreted as an absolutist statement. Suffice to say, his arguments were often circular.

GESTALT

"Gestalt" means "shape" or "figure", and its theorists sought to explore how the brain organises and interprets visual material through form, context, spatial proximity and patterning. Perhaps unsurprisingly the primary concepts of Gestalt gained some supporters within the art world, in particular influencing Klee and Kandinsky a decade or so later.

YVES KLEIN

Yves Klein was fascinated by the transcendental qualities of art. Particularly, he was interested in how art could open a door onto the unknowable infinity of the void. He invented his own intense shade of blue – the symbolic colour of the cosmos – and was partial to filming himself jumping from buildings as a way to represent the idea of leaping into the void.

RENÉ MAGRITTE

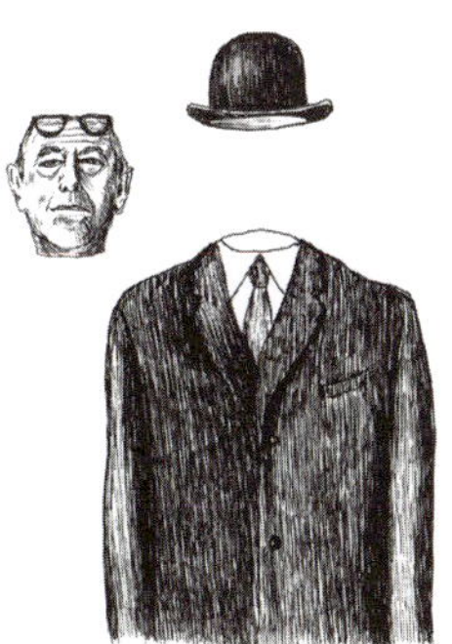

Magritte painted giant apples in small rooms, nudes with naked female bodies for faces and dove shapes "cut out" from stormy skies, all in the name of playing visual tricks with the idea of proportion and perception. Behind his work was the philosophical question – "can we really know what we see?"

PIERO MANZONI

Following in the footsteps of Duchamp, Manzoni's mission was to push the limits of what could be classified as art to its most absurd and scatological limits, epitomised by the display in a gallery of his own canned shit.

MINIMALISM

Founded on the principle that less is more, Minimalism rejected narrative, story-telling, conceptualism and metaphor in favour of a literalist Zen aesthetic of physical objects in space, as explored through Carl Andre's bricks, Dan Flavin's fluorescent light strips and Robert Morris' mirrored cubes. Most likely to provoke the claim – "A child could do this!"

MODERNISM

The revolutionary product of the Western industrial revolution, Enlightenment thinking, Romanticism and the birth of psychology, modernism set out to create a secular sanctity around art and artists, who were regarded as super human geniuses invested with the sacred job of protecting the nobility, beauty, truth and worthiness of art – for its own sake. Modernism's metaphysical twin, Surrealism privileged the sanctity not so much of art but of dreams, the unconscious and other chance states which expressed or suggested a pure reality, not necessarily visible to the naked eye. Due for a comeback.

PLATO'S CAVE

Through his allegorical tale of prisoners in a cave, who are only able to see the outside world via shadows projected onto a wall, Plato set out to demonstrate the perceptual illusion of reality (the prisoners thought the shadows were real) and that the truth can only be known by those free thinkers (such as artists) who employ philosophical reason.

POP ART!

The child of the 60s utopian ideal that art could be for all and the consumer capitalist utilitarianism that it could also be advertising, nowhere are these two uncomfortable bed partners more apparent than in the work of Andy Warhol. Fond of stealing easy-to-understand references from the media and advertising. Usually ends with an exclamation mark! Fans claim it to be a radical twentieth century art movement. Detractors say it marked the beginning of the death of art.

POSTMODERNISM

Incorporating punk, pop, feminism, gay rights and anti-racism into its narrative, while postmodernism by its very nature lacked any central ideology, it was generally about dismantling tradition, establishment hierarchies and grand meta-narratives in favour of accessibility, equality, relativity, alternative thinking and freedom of the individual. At its best, it enabled a vibrant counter-culture that questioned repressive systems and ways of thinking. At its worst, its anything goes attitude allowed a lot of very bad "ironic" art. While much of its visual imagery now seems dated, we are largely still living in a postmodern age. Just don't use the word "postmodernism".

SCHRÖDINGER'S CAT

Setting out to explore evidence that demonstrated how one subatomic particle can paradoxically be in two places at the same time, the quantum physicist Erwin Schrodinger invented a hypothetical cat who is put into a box with a radioactive substance, which at some point will decay and poison it. In this experiment, the observer wouldn't be able to see when the decay had occurred or if the cat had been killed. According to Schrodinger, at this point, the cat is both alive and dead. Schrodinger's experiment also incorporated the theory that any measurement of the cat's condition would automatically de-stabilise its in between state, so that the moment the box was opened, it would either be alive or dead but not both. At the heart of Schrodinger's Cat experiment is not only the question of indeterminacy in quantum mechanics but the question of uncertainty at the heart of reality.

THE *SENSATION* SHOW

Held by Charles Saatchi in The Royal Academy at the height of the ferment in the media and popular culture about the, then, Young British Artists, *Sensation* branded the movement as punk outsiders at the very same time it was ushering them into the hallowed halls of the academy. It also made a significant number of them a lot of money. Which seemed to be the main – if unintentional – "sensation" at the centre of all the fuss.

TROMPE L'OEIL

Meaning "cheat the eye", *trompe l'oeil* is a centuries old visual trick involving a hyper-literal painting technique, which often makes flat surfaces seem three dimensional, to achieve the appearance of reality.

EDITOR

RACHEL NEWSOME

is a writer, curator and arts academic. A former Editor of *Dazed & Confused*, Rachel writes fiction and essays and is a Lecturer in Fashion Styling & Image-Making at The University Of Salford.

ILLUSTRATOR

JIM HOLLINGWORTH

(AKA Jimp) is an artist and illustrator based in London and Cornwall. Influenced by skateboard, poster and comics art, his journalistic style spans themes of the sublime to the absurd. The instabilities and complexities of modern life are scrutinised as Jim reflects on the anatomy of the human psyche. His free imagination has produced a prolific and varied body of work over the last 10 years including live performances and murals.

CONTRIBUTORS

FIONA BANNER

is a Turner Prize-nominated artist who works with text, performance and film to explore the possibilities and limits of language. She has exhibited extensively and has had solo shows throughout the world including Tate Britain, Neuer Aachener Kunstverein, Aachen and Dundee Contemporary Arts. She has collaborated with architect David Kohn to create a nautical hotel room above the Hayward Gallery in London inspired by Joseph Conrad's journey through the Congo.

JOSIE BARNARD

is the author of five acclaimed Virago books, ranging from the novel *Poker Face*, which won the Betty Trask Award, to her work of creative non-fiction, *The Book of Friendship*, which was praised by Michele Roberts as "fascinating and discerning" (*The Observer*). Currently Senior Lecturer in Creative Writing with Journalism at Middlesex University, she has worked as an editor and as a journalist, writing for newspapers and magazines including *The Guardian*, *The Telegraph* and the *Times Literary Supplement*. She has produced many radio features and programmes for the BBC.

HARDY BLECHMAN

is the founder and head designer of Maharishi and the author of *DPM: Disruptive Pattern Material*, *An Encyclopaedia of Camouflage in Nature, Military and Culture*. In 2000, Blechman was named Streetwear Designer of the Year by the British Fashion Council. *DPM* won Best Book of 2004 in *Wallpaper*'s Design Awards and was one of the *Daily Telegraph*'s Books of the Year 2004.

MATTHEW COLLINGS

is an artist and writer. He has written many books on art, including *Blimey! From Bohemia to Britpop: The London Artworld from Francis Bacon to Damien Hirst* (1997), which was described by David Sylvester as "fearless", by Adrian Searle as "hilarious and horrible" and by *Artforum* as "the most popular contemporary art book ever." He has also written and presented multi-part TV documentaries on art, including *This Is Modern Art* (Channel 4, 1999), which received several awards, including a Bafta.

BEN CRANFIELD

is Director of the Doctoral Programme in Humanities and Cultural Studies and the MRes in Cultural Enquiry at Birkbeck, University of London. His work is concerned with ideas of the contemporary in post-war Britain, institutions, archives and curatorial form. Recent articles include *Between Consensus and Anxiety: Curating Transparency at the ICA of the 1950s*, *"Not another Museum": the search for contemporary connection* and *Students, Artists and the ICA: the revolution within?* in *Resurgence of the Sixties: The Continuing Relevance of the Cultural and Political Watershed*.

DEBORAH CURTIS

is a social entrepreneur and Director of leading children's arts and education charity The House of Fairy Tales, founded with her husband Gavin Turk. The House of Fairy Tales is an artist-led charity which draws on an extensive network of artists to create child-centred, magical parallel worlds where children learn lateral thinking and creativity through play. The House of Fairy Tales operates across a number of formats from workshops, publishing and advocacy to education packs, making learning inclusive, inventive and fun.

BETSY DE LOTBINIÈRE

was a journalist in New York, Rome, Paris and London until the day she interviewed the Mexican surrealist film maker Alejandro Jodorowsky. From that day onward, she has been a performance poet, tarot reader, curator and writer of fiction. She lives in London with her two children.

KATE DE SYLLAS

is a London-based academic and chef. She writes about matters relating to urban culture and is currently working on a cultural geography of the English seaside.

NOEL DOUGLAS

is an artist, designer, writer, educator and activist who lives and works in London. His work involves the creative use of the Graphic Arts in social and political movements and the urban environment. He is currently Senior Lecturer and Cluster Leader for the Graphic Arts course at the University of Bedfordshire and helped found Occupy Design in the UK in 2012.

PAUL FLYNN

is a Mancunian pop culture critic. He has been a feature writer for many magazines and newspapers over 15 years. He is currently Features Editor at *Man About Town*, columnist for *Grazia* and *Attitude* and Contributing Editor at *i-D* and *Love*. Previously he was *GQ Style* Features Director.

DAMIEN HIRST

is one of the most prolific and high profile artists working today. His work explores death, beauty, religion and science through installations, sculpture and painting. He has exhibited extensively throughout the world and his work is held in major public and private collections internationally. In 2012 a major retrospective of his work was staged at Tate Modern.

MICHAEL HOLDEN

is a writer working for both print and screen. He has been a columnist and contributor for the *Guardian* and other newspapers and is a contributing editor for *Esquire* in the UK. He has rewritten screenplays for major Hollywood productions and independent films, has scripts in development and optioned in the US and UK, and teaches screenwriting at The London Film Academy.

SEBASTIAN HORSLEY

– until his unexpected death in 2010 – was a writer, artist and self-confessed dandy, best known for having undergone voluntary crucifixion. Between 1998 and 2004 he ran a monthly column in the *Erotic Review* and was briefly a sex columnist for The Observer before readers complained. His autobiography, *Dandy In The Underworld* was published in 2007 and coincided with a retrospective of his work at London's Spectrum gallery.

JOSEPH KOSUTH

is an internationally renowned conceptual artist whose working practice has spanned nearly 50 years. From wall pieces and neon to major public installations, his varied artwork plays with the semiotics of ideas and language. His work has been shown with a cross section of the contemporary art world from Robert Morris to Andy Warhol and is now in major collections and museums across the globe.

HARI KUNZRU

is the author of the novels *The Impressionist*, *Transmission*, *My Revolutions* and *Gods Without Men* as well as a short story collection, *Noise*. His work has been translated into twenty languages and won him prizes including the Somerset Maugham award, the Betty Trask prize of the Society of Authors and a British Book Award. In 2003 *Granta* named him one of its twenty best young British novelists. His short stories and journalism have appeared in diverse publications including the *New York Times*, the *Guardian*, the *New Yorker*, the *Washington Post*, the *Times of India*, *Wired* and the *New Statesman*.

ALNOOR LADHA

is an activist, writer and social entrepreneur. He is the Executive Director of The Rules, a campaigning organisation fighting to address the root causes of global inequality. He is a Founding Partner of Purpose, an incubator for new types of social movements, and a board member of Greenpeace International, USA. He is based in New York City.

DARIAN LEADER

is a psychoanalyst working in London and a founder member of the Centre for Freudian Analysis and Research. He is President of The College of Psychoanalysts (UK) and Visiting Professor at the School of Human and Life Sciences, Roehampton University. He is the author of several books including: *Introducing Lacan*, *Why do women write more letters than they post?*, *Freud's Footnotes*, *Stealing the Mona Lisa: What Art Stops Us From Seeing*, *Why do people get ill?* (with David Corfield), *The New Black: Mourning, Melancholia and Depression* and *What is Madness?* His most recent book, *Strictly Bipolar*, was published by Hamish Hamilton in 2013.

TONY MARCUS

currently writes for the magazines *10* and *10+*. For many years he wrote
for the magazines *i-D* and *Mixmag*. He has contributed chapters to a couple
of books and has twice won the Jasmine Literary Award for his writing on
perfume.

MICHAEL MARRIOTT

was born in London in 1963. As a child, he quickly developed an interest
in things and how they are made before studying at the London College of
Furniture and the RCA. His practice has covered design, curation, writing
and art as well as teaching and lecturing, mostly on Design Products at
the RCA, but also at many other colleges across Britain and in many other
countries.

MATT MASON

currently serves as Vice President of Marketing at BitTorrent. Mason is also
the bestselling author of *The Pirate's Dilemma*, the first book in history to
hit the number one spot on Amazon's economics/free enterprise and the rap
bestseller list at the same time. He began his career as a pirate radio and
club DJ in London, going on to become founding Editor in Chief of *RWD*, which
grew into one of the largest music magazines in the UK. Mason has written and
produced TV series, screenplays, comic strips, apps, records, and global
advertising campaigns. His journalism has appeared in the *Guardian*, the
Independent, *VICE*, and other publications in more than 20 countries. He
lives in San Francisco.

NEIL MULHOLLAND

works collaboratively, using avatars that have interpretive flexibility.
Currently he is developing workshop models of artistic learning in
participatory settings as Shift/Work, and working as half of the
Confraternity of Neoflagellants, lay people dedicated to the investigation
and ascetic application of neo-medievalism. Recent publications include
Shift Happens JAR 3, *thN Lng folk 2go*, a neo-medieval book co-authored with
Norman Hogg, and *Bang the Whole Gang in Glam: The Performance of Style*. Neil
is Professor of Contemporary Art Practice & Theory at the University of
Edinburgh and Director of the MFA, Edinburgh College of Art.

CHARLIE PORTER

writes a daily blog and is the men's fashion critic of the *Financial Times*.
He has previously worked at *Fantastic Man*, *GQ*, the *Guardian* and the *Times*,
and has written for titles such as *i-D*, British *Vogue* and the *The Face*.

MARTINE ROULEAU

is a freelance curator. She has contributed to Tate Modern's programming and is currently contributing to the development of *Materials for the Construction of Meaning*, a learning resource and programme stemming from the *Dissent&Dialogue* gallery-based critical discussion sessions. She has also contributed original events for the Institute of Contemporary Arts, such as the series of performative talks on familiar object and habits *The Philosophy of the Overlooked*, and *N.A.N Road Show: The Seeds of Change*, a peer-led workshop for young artists pertaining to the art market in collaboration with a.n. The Artists Network. She also lectures in Art Education at the Arts Management and Policy MA programme of Birkbeck College.

JON SAVAGE

is an author and film-maker who lives in Anglesey, North Wales. His books include *England's Dreaming: The Sex Pistols* and *Punk Rock and Teenage: the Creation of Youth 1975-1945*. He is also the writer of the award winning documentaries *The Brian Epstein Story* and *Joy Division*. The film version of *Teenage*, directed by Matt Wolf, premiered at the April 2013 Tribeca Film Festival.

MARK STEPHENS CBE

is a British lawyer specialising in media law, intellectual property rights, and human rights with the firm HowardKennedyFsi. Stephens is also a broadcaster, mediator, and writer as well as the Chairman of The Contemporary Art Society, and DACS (Design and Artists Copyright Society). He is on the advisory board of the Programme in Comparative Media Law and Policy at Oxford University, and the Board of Governors at the University of East London.

RICHARD STRANGE

is a writer, musician, composer, nightclub host, curator, actor and adventurer. He founded the hugely influential mixed-media Cabaret Futura in 1980, and has subsequently worked as an actor, appearing extensively on stage, in films and on television. His numerous movie appearances include *Batman* by Tim Burton, *Mona Lisa* by Neil Jordan and *Mr Lonely* by Harmony Korine. He has worked with award-winning dance theatre company Protein Dance, Marianne Faithfull and the award winning sound artist/sculptor Haroon Mirza. His memoir *Strange – Punks and Drunks and Flicks and Kicks* was published by Andre Deutsch in 2005. He has recently finished filming *Theatre of Dreams* with Brian Cox and Toby Stephens. He has curated shows for Tate, The Glasgow International Festival of Live Art and Camp Bestival, as well as The Hong Kong Design Institute.

AMBER TRENTHAM

currently lives in London and works as a screenwriter, focusing on feature films. Previously Amber has written essays for various publications, taught screenwriting courses, edited scripts and consulted on story in a freelance capacity. She has orchestrated the screenwriting festivals at the Arts in Marrakech festival.

JESSICA VOORSANGER

explores the concept of celebrity within popular culture through obsession, fans and media representation. She received her BFA from the Rhode Island School of Design and her MA in Fine Art from Goldsmiths' College, London. She has shown extensively including: *Mystery Train*, *Art on the Underground*, The ICA, London; *Eastenders*, Whitechapel Art Gallery, London; *The Woody Allen Show*, Gallery-33 FON, Berlin; *I Think I Love You*, Collective Gallery, Edinburgh; *The Retrieval Series: Bob Geldof*, Modern Culture, New York; *Baby Shower*, Camden Art Centre, London as well as showing in many group shows in the UK and internationally.

OSSIAN WARD

is Head of Content at Lisson Gallery and a writer on contemporary art. Until 2013, he was the chief art critic and Visual Arts Editor for *Time Out* London for over six years and previously contributed to magazines such as *Art in America*, *Art + Auction*, *World of Interiors*, *Esquire*, the *New Statesman* and *Wallpaper*, as well as newspapers including the *Evening Standard*, the *Guardian*, the *Observer*, the *Times* and the *Independent on Sunday*. Formerly editor of *ArtReview* and the V&A magazine, he has also worked at *The Art Newspaper* and edited a biennial publication, *The Artists' Yearbook*, for Thames & Hudson from 2005-10. He has written catalogue essays for artists including Haroon Mirza, Sam Taylor-Wood and Robin Rhode and contributed to Taschen's *Art Now* series, as well as *The Art of Tomorrow*, published by Distanz.

DIXE WILLS

is the author of a hatful of genre-bending books including *The Z-Z of Great Britain*, *Places to Hide in England, Scotland and Wales*, and *Tiny Islands*. He is also a freelance journalist writing mainly travel pieces for *The Guardian* and has contributed to a raft of worthy magazines such as *Green Futures*, *Trail* and *When Saturday Comes*. He lives in East London.